WATCHING OVER ME:

A World War II Story of Survival and a Quest for Peace

by
Rachel Marie Hartman

Lucille Wessel,
May the Lord
watch over you!
Elfi Lee
2017

WATCHING OVER ME
By Rachel Marie Hartman

ISBN 10: 0983100942
ISBN 13: 978-0-9831009-4-2

One Body Press
info@onebodypress.org

Table of Contents

Dedication

I dedicate this book to the memory of my parents Kaethe and Walter Gartzke — especially my mother, who with her gentle prodding encouraged me to sit down and tell my story — to my loving husband Noel of more than 56 years, to my children Monica, Carmen and Timothy, to my grandchildren Justin, Garrett, MacKenzie, Shelby, Lauren, Benjamin, Daniel, Trevor, and Erin, to my great grandchildren Aubrey, Haiden, Colton, Ashlyn, Emerson, and Vincent and to any future generations that may read my life story.
- From Elfi Lee

Acknowledgments

Putting together a book is no small task, and was only made possible through the help of a long list of individuals who freely gave their time and effort to contribute to the project.

A special thank you is due to Noel Lee, who for years encouraged Elfi to tell her story, as well as her daughter Monica, who helped document memories of Kaethe Gartzke's (Mutti's) life. We're grateful to her daughter Carmen and son Timothy for their continual encouragement throughout the years.

And thank you to Todd Uebele for his guidance in bringing this book to print, and the others at One Body Press for their help in the project.

A warm appreciation is due to Chuck Sambuchino and Jenni Burke for their help with the fine-tuning and preparation process of the book proposal.

We're filled with gratitude toward Paul Hartman, who read the manuscript and provided invaluable input regarding the material and presentation. A special thanks goes to Carol Hartman for helping with the proofreading of the manuscript.

None of this would have been possible if it weren't for Michael Hartman, who not only helped instigate the project but also served as a visionary and offered incomparable support during the process.

Thank you to Heidi von Yost, Ingeborg Eckert and her family, and other friends and relatives who eagerly shared their stories, memories and pictures.

We also extend gratitude to those in historical sites in Germany and Poland, including Lukasz Bielecki in Poland, Piotr Tarnawski at the Stargard Musuem, Gunnar Wulf at the Bunkermuseum Hamburg (Air Raid Shelter Museum in Hamburg), Dr. Olaf Matthes at the Stiftung Historische Museen Hamburg (The Hamburg History Museum), and Dr. Mandred von Essen together with Dr. von Xylander at the Stadtmuseum Norderstedt (City Museum of Norderstedt).

A special thank you goes out to the Pilskie Muzeum Wojskowe (Pila Museum) in Pila, Poland, the BallinStadt Emigration Museum in Hamburg, Germany, and other places and individuals who helped make the past come alive once again.

And finally, thank you to the United States of America for the opportunities it provided in particular for an immigrant girl and her family.

Preface

I first crossed paths with Elfi in 2010. We met through my husband Mike, who had traveled through Lincoln, Nebraska, on a mission trip. He had given a presentation at St. Mark Lutheran Church on mission efforts in Mexico, which is where we were living, and stayed in Elfi's home during his time there.

Elfi shared some of her story, which begins in Germany during the years around World War II, with me and I was immediately captivated. Elfi's memories of her mother, in particular, caught my attention, as she devoted her life to raising her children in the best way she could. She worked hard and taught them about God's redeeming love and protection from early on. Even when their lives ventured through steep trials, she kept the focus on the Lord and his promise to use everything for the good of those who love him.

As you read of Elfi's upbringing in Germany, her immigration to the United States, her mother's commitment to keep God as the center of their daily life, and upbeat humor in tough situations, I believe you'll be inspired to implement the same attitude in your own situation. I hope you'll be encouraged, as I have, to trust that God's guiding hand works all of life's circumstances out for our eternal good.

- Rachel Hartman

Prologue

On Saturday, November 22nd, 1997, in the midst of a bustling holiday season, two customers walked into Sears department store in Lincoln, Nebraska. Tears ran down the cheeks of one of them, a woman in her 40s with light skin and tousled brown hair. A tall black man in worn clothing walked beside her. Speaking in soft undertones to the woman, he guided her through the store until they reached the women's clothing department.

The man grabbed a black dress from a rack and held it up for the woman to see.

The week before, a fire had struck an apartment complex in Omaha, Nebraska. The blaze, while devastating to the building, hit one family particularly hard. All of their possessions turned to ash in the fire, but that was not enough to upset them compared to their other loss. One child died in the blaze. Another child was seriously injured.

The injured child had been severely burned, and was sent to the Saint Elizabeth Regional Burn and Wound Center in Lincoln. Located about 60 miles from Omaha, the facility was known throughout the region for its strong track record in helping burn patients recover. It was also located close to Sears department store.

So that woman in her 40s at Sears that Saturday, was the mom of the burn patient. She was staying in Lincoln to be near the child. Having lost her clothing in the fire, she set out to find something new and suitable to wear. She was looking for an outfit, but not just random items to fill her depleted wardrobe. The woman needed a dress to wear to the funeral of the child she had lost in the fire.

Elfi Lee was working as a sales associate in the women's department that day. At 57 years old, she had been a Sears' employee for the past 26 years. Elfi first started in the receiving department, where she helped with the receiving of Sears' goods and supplies. After moving on to several other areas, including the catalogue department and customer service, she tried out the sales floor. With a keen sense for style and a helpful attitude, her position as a sales associate in the women's department seemed a perfect fit.

Now Elfi, with short, smooth blonde curls framing a pleasant face, watched the two approaching customers. She smiled warmly—a habit she had developed years before—at the woman and man.

Her smile faded as they drew closer. Spotting the tears and distraught face, Elfi quickly found a place where the woman could sit down. Then she pulled up a chair next to her, and asked if she could do anything to help.

The mother relayed her devastating story to Elfi. She told of the fire, the child's death, the other child burned and in rehab, and the loss of the family's material possessions. She said that she needed an outfit for the funeral.

Elfi listened to it all. "I thought every customer was special and it was like she was a friend already. She opened up her heart and situation to me," Elfi recalled later on.

Upon hearing the story, Elfi promised to help. She gathered suitable attire for the occasion. She found the perfect dress for the woman to wear. She even picked out matching shoes and a coat to go with the dress.

When the mother in mourning had everything she needed, Elfi excused herself momentarily. She said she had to go to her personal locker in the back to fetch something. She returned a few minutes later. Then the mother, her companion, and Elfi made their way to the cash register in the women's department.

Elfi scanned each of the items. When she finished, she didn't tell the mother the final cost or ask for payment. Elfi swiped her own Sears card through the register and signed her name to the receipt.

As Elfi handed the clothing to the mother and her friend, she noticed the astounded look on their faces. Moments later, the couple left the department and Elfi resumed her work. She smiled at the next holiday customers, and started helping them.

When the couple was out of Elfi's sight, instead of leaving the store, they sought out the store manager. When they found her, they relayed what had just happened. Tears filled the eyes of the mother's friend as he told what Elfi did. He explained that Elfi "not only provided great customer service, but comforted my friend in a time of need." For a family that had lost everything in the fire, the gesture was especially touching. The man added that he wanted everyone to know about the sales associate in Lincoln with a "heart of gold."

Later in the day the manager approached Elfi. When the manager shared the customer's comment, Elfi didn't accept any compliments. "At one time, my family and I were in need and received help from many sources," she explained. "I just wanted to give back to a family in need. I didn't do it for recognition."

Watching Over Me

As reflected on many years later by Elfi and reinforced with collections from her mother, Mutti, and other relatives

CHAPTER ONE: LEAVING HOME

"Abide with Thy protection
Among us, Lord, our Strength,
Lest world and Satan fell us
And overcome at length."
—Joshua Stegmann, 1628[1]

Outside of the window, a blanket of snow covered our property. Mutti and I were inside, in one of the upstairs bedrooms of our farmhouse, where it was warm. I stood in my baby brother's crib, watching my mother scramble around the room. At four years old, I was too old for a crib. From inside it, however, I couldn't get in the way while Mutti packed, or worse, have her lose sight of me. She was too preoccupied to have to worry about finding children like me—who had a tendency to wander off while exploring the farm.

My baby brother Rainer sat in the crib next to me, quietly observing. Mutti bustled around, grabbing dresses and pulling sweaters out of the closet. A potato sack lay on the floor, half-filled with items she had dug out of the closet and placed inside its burlap walls.

The makeshift luggage and scurrying about could mean only one thing: we were leaving, and very soon.

"Mutti, where are we going?" I asked in German. She didn't answer immediately. Instead, she came over to where I stood, a dress of mine on her arm. In a rush, she fumbled the garment over my head and arms—right over the dress I was already wearing.

Before I could ask about the extra clothing, she tugged a sweater over the dresses I had on. Then she pulled a pair of pants over the tights covering my legs. A heavy blue dress followed. It had a round collar, soft fabric, and small ties at the neck. It was my favorite dress. Mutti often put it on me, but not over other clothes. She topped off the mass with my winter coat.

When she finished, she stopped momentarily and brushed back a strand of brown hair that had fallen loose from her bun. Tilting her head ever so slightly, she looked me over. Her hands fell lightly on my arms. I wore so many layers I could barely feel her touch.

"Remember how I told you the enemy is coming?" she asked.

I nodded. She had told me the enemy was coming many times.

"They're almost here, and they want to capture us and hurt us. We have to get away," she explained.

"Is Opa coming?"

Mutti shook her head. "No, your grandfather is staying on the farm."

"But they will hurt him!"

"It is his decision." Mutti dropped her hands from my arms and shrugged. "Right now we need to finish packing so we can catch a train." At this, as if the words reminded her of the task at hand, she turned and went back to gathering items.

A train ride! Was she serious? Ever since our last disastrous experience with a train, Mutti had hated those rolling beasts. A set of railroad tracks ran close to our farmhouse, and trains chugged past often, on their way to and from the station two miles away. Whenever she heard a train whistle and the clack, clack, clickety-clack of the cars rolling down the track, Mutti shook with fear.

Right now she wasn't shaking, though. She rummaged through clothes in the closet, searching for something. She must be serious about going on a train, I decided, for Mutti didn't lie. Never one to mince words, she always spoke plainly to me—and to everyone else, for that matter.

Standing stiffly in all of the outfits, I peered out a window near the crib and gazed at our property below. Shades of gray signaled the near end of the short day. It had snowed earlier, but now all was still. The cows and horses were in the barn with the other animals, where they had to stay to keep warm. They didn't know the enemy was coming. Perhaps Opa wanted to stay to protect them and keep them safe.

"Will we be okay?" I asked, now thinking of the train.

Mutti nodded and patted my head. "God will be with us. He will protect us."

She pulled Papa's wedding suit, a fashionable two-piece set consisting of black pants and a black jacket, off a rusty metal hanger. She took it off the hanger, and then nodded at the garment, as if asserting she had found what she had been looking for. I watched in amazement as Mutti put the pants on under her dress.

Before this, Mutti only wore dresses. She never donned pants, and she most certainly never wore Papa's clothes. But Papa was gone, and there was no other person in our household who could wear them. After pulling on the pants, Mutti put a dress on over the one she was already wearing. Then she added another dress. On top of that, she put on Papa's wedding jacket.

What a strange sight we were, all bundled up in layers as if to be silly! But I knew Mutti wasn't playing around. Mutti didn't play games these days. She was too worried about the enemy. Ever since Papa left to fight in the war a month before, Mutti knew danger lurked in the distance. For weeks she warned me the enemy was coming.

Mutti, when talking to me, always used the word *enemy* to describe the terrible people who wanted to hurt us. But I saw the same gleam appear in her eye when she said the word *Russen*, the German word for "Russians," while speaking to other people. And she told these same people she had even seen a *russische soldat*, or "Russian soldier." I had too.

It happened the previous summer, in 1944, not long after the horrendous train ride. Back home by then, safe and sound, Mutti said it was too dangerous to travel. Heading east could result in a confrontation with the enemy.

Our home was nestled on an acreage in rural Germany, two miles outside the city of Schneidemühl. Even though we were close to town, daily life for us was quiet.

Our farmhouse stood two stories tall. It was made of red brick, with white trimming and also a sun porch in front of it. The porch had windows on three sides and overlooked the surrounding countryside. From it, we took in views of fields flowing with green waves during the summer. As the weather warmed each year, vegetables flooded our gardens. Mutti spent many days picking beans and digging potatoes, and then preserving the abundance to help it last through the winter. Yellow and red tulips sprouted up, as did lovely, delicate white lilies that I admired for hours, and often picked.

Between our home and the barn on the property loomed a large tall tree. A rope swing dangled from one of the tree's thick branches. I spent many long afternoons on that swing, pumping my legs and moving effortlessly through the air, back and forth and back and forth, planning out the next adventure in my mind.

One particular afternoon toward the end of summer in 1944, as I was playing in the yard, I heard Mutti's voice.

"Elfi, come here!" she yelled. Her tone was stern.

I turned toward the sound of her voice and spotted her standing on the porch.

While I always obeyed Mutti, there was something in her voice that day that made my legs race to her as fast as they could. When I reached the porch, I slowed to a stop and then stood next to her. Heart pounding, I glanced up at Mutti's face. She was no longer looking at me; instead, her eyes focused on something in the distance. I followed her gaze, and then saw what she was so interested in. It came from the forest.

A large, sprawling wooded area surrounded our property on three sides. Filled with slender white birch trees and plenty of greenery, the forest bloomed to life in summer. Mutti and I often walked through it, baskets dangling from our hands, searching for blueberries, raspberries, boysenberries and mushrooms that grew there. Low mountains rose behind the forest. The landscape provided a lovely backdrop for our small farm.

Mutti stared in the direction of the forest, at a figure emerging from the trees. She wiped her hands on the apron she wore over her dress.

Together we watched a man, clad in an olive green uniform, walk toward our property. He wore a military hat that matched the color of his uniform. He carried a rifle in his arms. He occasionally looked to his left and right, as if trying to pinpoint his location. As he drew closer to the house, Mutti bristled.

Up until that point, we hadn't seen soldiers from any other army outside of our own German troops. Adolf Hitler, the ruler of the Nazi party and Germany's dictator, had started a war that had been raging in Europe and elsewhere for years by then. Thus far, by God's mercy, our little corner of Germany had been spared from the fighting. Where we lived, there had been *fliegeralarm*, or air raid warnings, and occasional bombings, but no actual combat.

Now we laid eyes for the first time on an enemy soldier. I didn't have to ask Mutti about him; I knew from her furrowed brow that he was what she referred to when she spoke of the enemy. Within moments, the man reached the spot that marked the beginning of our property. Looking straight at Mutti, he lowered his rifle. Then his hands gently released it. The gun hung close to him from a strap he wore across his shoulder. Still staring at us, he drew one of his hands toward his mouth. Then he stretched it out slightly and drew it to his mouth once more, as if scooping something from his hand into his mouth. After a few more motions like this, he dropped his hand and resumed walking toward us.

"He's hungry," Mutti said. "He must want something to eat."

The soldier kept coming, and soon reached the front porch. With a steady hand, Mutti motioned for him to follow her into the house. I stayed by her side as she led him to the kitchen. There was always something cooking on the stove in our home, and that afternoon, a large pot of stew bubbled on a burner. Its hearty scent filled the kitchen.

The soldier sat at the table and waited. Mutti quickly dished up a bowl of soup and some bread and set it before him. Wordlessly, he dug in.

He gulped down the meal. We watched in silence.

Even though our area of Germany had not faced an actual battle, uneasiness had been stirring around us since the beginning of 1944. The German army invaded Russia three years earlier, with the hope of taking over its oil supplies and industrial factories. Resources ran short in Germany, and Hitler knew the country needed what Russia had if it was going to survive.

But Hitler's plan to control Russia failed. The Russian army stopped the German advance at Stalingrad, a communications and manufacturing center in the south of Russia. After a tremendously bloody battle, the tides of war shifted. Now the Russians became the ones on the attack. Germany, in turn, retreated. As the German army withdrew toward the west, Russia followed, retaking first its own country and then moving into areas previously controlled by Germany. Now the Russians were coming into Germany itself.

Alarmingly, Russia's army was headed in a direction which, if followed, would lead straight to our house. What would happen to us? What would become of our farm if the Russians took over? I didn't know, but I had seen the intense, dark look in Mutti's eyes and the furrow in her brow when she spoke of it with others. Surely it wouldn't be good.

In August 1944, the Russian army was still east of us. Yet this soldier who had come out of the forest, clad with uniform and rifle, was undoubtedly Russian. He must have been separated—either through battle or by his own choice—from his unit. Somehow he wandered to our little spot along the forest's edge.

Mutti, in her cooking apron, and I stood off to the side in the kitchen, close to the stove while he ate.

Our family shared the farmhouse with Papa's parents, and also his brother, sister-in-law, and their daughter. While some of them were surely around that day, in my mind the only ones who existed during that meal were Mutti, the soldier, and me. Chilled with fear from not only the gun, but also Mutti's tense stance, I clung to her side as the enemy dished one spoonful after another into his mouth.

After what seemed like an eternity, the soldier finished the stew. Then, without warning, he stood up. He headed out the same door he had entered. Mutti and I remained rooted to our places in the kitchen.

A few moments later, as if to check that he was really leaving, Mutti stepped cautiously in the direction he had moved. I followed, wondering where he would go. When we reached the porch, we paused and stood in the same spot where we had first seen him come toward us. We watched his figure retreat toward the woods, heading to the same place where he had first emerged.

Just as he reached the edge of our property, before entering the forest, the man paused. Steadily, deliberately, as if to avoid startling anything in sight, he turned toward us. Our eyes met, and for several long moments, we held each other's gaze. Then, slowly, his mouth turned up at the corners. He smiled at us.

It was unbelievable: a Russian soldier, the horrible enemy, wearing an enemy uniform, carrying a gun, offered us a grin. Not only that, but he continued grinning at us as the seconds ticked by.

Suddenly, as if our eyes had been clouded over but now saw clearly, we were not German and he was not Russian. We did not belong to countries that hated each other, that wanted to capture and hurt each other. We were, simply, three human beings, sharing an afternoon, a prolonged moment of reflection, enlaced in a special camaraderie that comes merely from belonging to God's group of created beings. We understood one another; we accepted each other.

The Russian soldier held his smile. Mutti and I returned it.

He raised his hand, waving good-bye. We did the same. Then he lowered his hand, turned, and disappeared into the woods.

Five months later, on a cold afternoon in January 1945, as I followed Mutti from room to room and watched her pack, I knew today would be different. We would not be serving meals to enemy soldiers as they sauntered into the kitchen, and then waving them off with kind faces and smiles.

From listening to Mutti during the last few weeks, I knew that this time, an entire army of enemy troops approached. Everyone talked about it. Mutti and our relatives spoke of the enemy who wanted to hurt us, and to hurt us terribly. They spoke of other things I didn't understand. From watching Mutti's face as they talked, however, I knew they were even worse than the things I did understand. If the Russians did in our city and farm what they had been doing in other cities and farms they had taken over, our only hope would be to be die quickly, said those she talked with. That is, if we didn't get out in time.

I followed Mutti down the stairs to the living room. She took our family Bible from its place on a small table and placed it in a potato sack. Then she grabbed a stack of songbooks and a baptismal gown and added them. She brought down a feather bed from the upstairs bedroom and packed that too. The feather bed consisted of a thick blanket stuffed with goose feathers; lying under it, I always stayed snug and warm during long, frosty nights.

I was too young to be in school, but I understood we had to leave our home. Where would we go? I didn't know. And Mutti didn't seem to know either. In spite of the heavy clothing I wore, shivers ran up and down my arms and legs. My hands trembled. Terror, not cold, consumed me.

Fear gripped me the same way the night Papa left. He was drafted for the German army just before Christmas in December 1944. After he left, Mutti did all she could to learn news about the war. To get updates, each morning, after milking the cow and finishing her chores on the farm, she biked into Schneidemühl.

Every day, for the next month, I watched from the front porch as Mutti pedaled down the dirt road leading to town. She never took me along, as I didn't know how to ride a bike yet.

Even though I stayed on the farm while Mutti was in town, I wasn't alone. Opa and Oma, Papa's parents, lived in the farmhouse with us. They owned the place, and Opa helped with the animals in the barn. Oma looked after me and my two younger brothers when Mutti wasn't with us.

Aunt Lydia lived there, too, with her daughter Ruthchen, who was five years older than me. Aunt Lydia was married to my *Onkel*, or Uncle, Willie, who was Papa's brother. The two of them ran a restaurant that was attached to the farmhouse. At least they did, until Uncle Willie left. Called to fight for the Nazi army, he headed out and we hadn't heard any news from him in a long time.

From my perch on the porch, I always watched Mutti's figure retreat in the distance. After a while, she followed a bend in the road, and her bike and profile disappeared from view.

I often accompanied Mutti in the wagon pulled by our two horses to go into town, and knew the route well. When she was out of sight, I thought of her biking further along the road, until she reached the bridge that spread over the Kuddow River, a sleepy waterway that lay between our home and the town of Schneidemühl.

As a toddler, I spent long summer afternoons by the Kuddow, a wide, calm river that was so peaceful it seemed the water drifted, rather than raced, along its God-given path. Papa worked as a blacksmith, but on his days off, when the weather was warm, he often took me to the river for a swim. I perched on his back while his strong arms cut through the water. Together we glided across the river, and when we reached the other side, we turned around and came back to the shore where we had started from. Lap after lap we swam, and I clapped my hands with glee.

Papa was a solid swimmer and fine athlete, and I loved nothing more than to cruise across the river with him. Mutti, clad in a plain dress and with her hair pulled neatly back into a bun, watched us both from the shore. She didn't know how to swim, but she always came along. Apparently, observing the two of us swim together was just as much fun for her as swimming itself.

But now Papa was gone, and no one spoke of anything fun like swimming anymore.

On the days Mutti biked into town to learn more about the war, she always went first to the Nazi office in town. The Nazi government controlled the entire city. No one came or went without them knowing about it.

At the office, each day Mutti asked the official sitting behind a desk, "Is there any news of the war?"

The officer always shook his head no.

"Any way to tell how close the Russians are?"

"We aren't granting permission to leave, if that's what you're asking."

Every day, when she came home, she shared her news with us. Yes, she asked and no, we didn't have permission to leave.

By this time, in early 1945, Germany was sinking—fast. The country was no longer conquering territory; instead, it was getting invaded from all sides. In the east, the Russian army advanced, penetrating further into Germany every day. Troops from the United States, Britain, and France closed in from the west.

Schneidemühl had an important railroad station, connecting the capital of Berlin with the city of Bromberg, a business center with a large inland port, in the east. For this reason, Hitler named Schneidemühl, along with other major cities in Germany, a *festung*, meaning "stronghold." This meant the place was to resist enemy advances at all costs. Everyone needed to fight and face the bitter end, to die for Hitler and his regime.

Surely Hitler wanted soldiers to defend Schneidemühl. But what about the rest of us? Would we, together with the other women and children of the town, be able to leave? That's what Mutti wanted to know. She had heard of Nazi authorities setting up evacuation plans for citizens living in areas further east of us. These plans helped women and children escape from the advancing Russian Army. In most cases, the plans didn't get carried out in time. Other times, the officials simply ordered everyone to stay. They caught anyone who tried to leave and executed that person as punishment.

Like Mutti, many others in Schneidemühl wanted to get out. But they knew that doing so, without permission, would have only one result: death.

That is, up until today. Today had been different, right from the start. Early that morning, Mutti woke to a *boom, boom, boom* in the distance. It was the sound of artillery firing.

Mutti knew what it meant. The enemy was preparing to advance into Schneidemühl. It was so close we could hear it coming. If we couldn't get out today, we would be trapped on the farm when they came.

That morning, when Mutti arrived at the Nazi office, she found a much different scene than the one she usually encountered. Officials bustled around, issuing orders.

"What's going on? Can we leave?" Mutti asked.

"Today everyone leaves," an officer replied. "Be at the train station before dark."

"Will there be trains for everyone?" Mutti asked.

The officer shrugged his shoulders.

Mutti ran out of the office and raced home.

She arrived back at our acreage around one o'clock in the afternoon.

"We can leave today!" she shouted at Opa and me in the kitchen. "But we must leave quickly—everyone else wants to get out too."

"Will you take the wagon?" asked Opa.

"No, the officer said to go to the train station. But I don't know if there will be room for everyone, so we must hurry."

Mutti started to leave the kitchen. Just as she reached the doorway, she turned back to Opa.

"You will not come then?"

"No, I already told you months ago—I will stay with the animals."

Mutti nodded and took another step.

"But I will take you to the train station," Opa called after her.

Even if we took a train out of town, we might not find a place to stay.

Mutti had already seen this happen. In the evening of December 19, 1944, when Papa left for the war, he went to town to catch a train scheduled to depart that night. Mutti went with him. She accompanied him to the train station, watched him board, and waved good-bye as the train carried him away.

After seeing him off, Mutti headed home. On her way, she spotted a woman sitting on the ground. The woman slumped in front of a building close to the railroad tracks. Two children sat next to her. In her arms, she cradled a small bundle. In the dim of the evening, Mutti couldn't make out what was inside the bundle.

Never one to be shy, Mutti walked up to her. "What do you have there?" she asked, pointing to the package.

"A baby," said the woman.

"How old is it?" Mutti continued.

"Ten days."

"Why are you out here in the cold?"

"There's no room." The woman motioned with her head to the building behind her. It was a sort of inn, set up to take in travelers searching for lodging.

When she heard this, Mutti marched into the building. Once inside, she confronted the workers. "There's a woman with a baby on her lap right by the tracks. She needs to come in!" Mutti insisted.

When Mutti spoke like that, people listened. Upon her scolding, several people scurried out the door. They quickly gathered the woman and her children, and took them inside. As soon as Mutti was confident they were being cared for, she came home.

Back at the house the next day, Mutti explained the woman's plight to us. She had come with her children from further east, and was on the run, trying to escape from the advancing Russians. Mutti had been furious over the lack of help the woman and her children were initially given.

Now it was four o'clock in the afternoon and snowing. Mutti had arrived three hours ago from her trip to town, and was nearly finished packing. She put the last things into the sacks, including a small baptismal outfit, and lined them up by the back door. There were three potato sacks in all. Mutti laid her purse by the sacks.

After that, she called for Wilfried and picked up Rainer from his crib, my younger brothers, to dress them. At nearly two years old and six months— their ages, respectively—they looked as lumpy and uncomfortable as I felt when she finished putting outfits on them. Then she placed all of us by the sacks and purse at the door.

While Mutti had packed up the last things, Opa went to the barn. Because of the recent snow, new flakes covered the ground and road. To travel through this weather, Opa hitched the sleigh to the two horses. Then he brought the whole apparatus to the door of the farmhouse. Mutti, my younger brothers, and I piled in the sleigh. Oma, Aunt Lydia, and my cousin Ruthchen, who was nine years old, joined us. Opa loaded up our meager luggage, and then added the baby carriage to the sleigh.

The temperature had dropped, and the wind whipped our faces. We huddled together and hunkered down beneath a thick blanket in the sleigh.

Opa nudged the horses. The animals moved abruptly, jolting the sleigh. Then they straightened out their pace, and we started gliding smoothly. We headed toward the train station. We had to get there, and fast, to be able to board a train. What would happen if we didn't get to the station in time? What if all the trains were full already?

Large snowflakes fell as we pulled away from home. I tried to block images of the enemy taking us away from my mind, and buried my head in Mutti's shoulder.

CHAPTER TWO: THE TRAIN

"Lord Jesus, who dost love me,
Oh, spread Thy wings above me
And shield me from alarm!
Though evil would assail me,
Thy mercy will not fail me:
I rest in Thy protecting arm."
—Paul Gerhardt, 1648[2]

I opened my eyes as the sleigh crossed the river. A snowflake immediately stung one of my eyes. I wiped it off, and then watched other tiny flakes flurrying around. They flew through the air, getting tossed this way and that in the wind. Some landed on my cheeks. Racing to town, away from home and on the run, I felt more frightened than ever before in my life.

The sound of artillery guns firing in the distance resonated in my ears. The Russians weren't far away now. I peered into the closing afternoon, afraid the enemy would spring from the shadows at any moment.

Inside the sleigh, no one spoke. A heavy tension hung in the air, stemming from the uncertainty we all felt deep in our bones. Mutti sat quietly next to me, holding baby Rainer in her arms.

From my spot next to Mutti, I peered at the back of Opa. He sat ahead of us, in the front seat of the sleigh, bundled in a heavy winter coat and hat. He held the reins for the horses with a steady gloved hand, despite the wind and sound of artillery. At just 5 feet, 6 inches in height, and built slim like Papa, he was not a large man. Sitting upright in the sleigh, however, with his shoulders straight and chin steady, he emitted a sense of calm. His unruffled presence soothed the horses. They plodded forward, despite the booming of the nearby guns and the snow swirling around the sleigh. We continued at a quick pace toward town.

Once we crossed the bridge and entered Schneidemühl, street lamps lined the boulevard. Their glow shed light on the scene unfolding before us.

People scurried everywhere. Just hours after Nazi officials granted Schneidemühl's citizens permission to evacuate, everyone seemed to have a sole purpose in mind: getting away, and fast. Now the residents poured out of their homes, holding bundles and tugging children behind them. Like us, they needed to get on a train before it was too late.

* * *

Before the war crept into our area, I had often gone to Schneidemühl with Mutti. While there, we watched people moving from one shop to another with bags of purchases, or coming out of a bakery carrying a loaf of bread, or simply moving through the streets on their way to visit an acquaintance or relative. The atmosphere back then had been quiet and steady. Passersby strolled along, stopping on occasion for polite greetings and bits of chit chat.

On Sundays, when the weather permitted, we went to worship in the center of town. We always attended an immense Lutheran church, complete with high walls, two steeples reaching toward the heavens, and thick front doors. Inside, from my seat on the pew, I studied the ornate decorations and vast ceiling of the church.

I loved Mutti's singing. She knew all the hymns by heart, and intoned them with a beautiful voice. When she sang, she sounded like an opera singer. Her lovely tones wafted through the whole church, ebbing and flowing within its walls and filling the place with a sense of peace. Without Mutti, the church seemed cold and dark. With her and her voice, there was always warmth and light.

* * *

Mutti sat quietly as we moved through the streets. She studied the shops, restaurants, and bakeries we passed. They were all closed up, abandoned, forgotten.

She leaned forward and called to Opa.

"We must hurry!"

He nodded in reply and urged the horses on.

We turned down a street leading to the train station. As we moved along, more citizens joined our procession. Some of those trying to get out of Schneidemühl traveled in sleighs like us. Others walked, their arms laden with heavy bundles. Some pulled a handcart. These small two-wheeled carts brimmed with bulging burlap sacks, baskets tied up with twine, and blankets

16

wrapped hastily around treasured belongings. Slouched grandparents, too ill to walk, rode on top of the packages. The vehicles, and people, trudged through the snow.

Our horses fell in step with the mass movement through town. Other travelers surrounded us, and our pace slowed.

I stared at the people in the streets. Terror filled their faces. The other mothers looked more upset than Mutti, whose mouth stretched in a straight, grim line. More notable, however, was the determined look in her eyes. Just by glancing at her, I felt certain she was not going to let anything get in her way. No matter what it took, she was going to get all of us to the train station.

Mutti's poise was amazing, considering where we were headed. For many of those fleeing that day, the idea of getting on a train meant refuge and safety. For Mutti and me, this was not the case. The last train trip we took involved a frightful escape. It had happened the year before.

* * *

In the spring of 1944, one of Mutti's seven younger brothers, Kurt, got engaged. The wedding was set for April 1st, and would be held in Marienwerder, about 120 miles northeast of Schneidemühl.

The city of Marienwerder was in the western corner of *OstPreussen*, or East Prussia, and therefore closer to Russia than Schneidemühl was. Rumors circulated of an enemy invasion in that area. While the Russians had not yet taken over the region surrounding Marienwerder, it was not considered safe to travel there.

Amidst rumors of war in the east, and despite the fact that Mutti was seven months pregnant with her third child, she and Papa decided to go to the wedding. They packed bags for themselves, for my younger brother Wilfried, and for me. They brought a baby carriage along for Wilfried, who was just over a year old at the time. At three and a half, I walked on my own. Another one of Mutti's younger brothers, my Uncle Reinhold, also came with us.

We traveled a long way by train to get from Schneidemühl to the wedding in *OstPreussen*. In those days, Germany's railroad lines followed a rigid schedule. Shortly after a train pulled into a station and stopped, passengers on board who wanted to get off left the cars quickly. Those boarding got on fast. A train only stopped at a station for a few minutes, and then went on its way again. Before leaving, a conductor glanced up and down the long line of cars. Once he confirmed everyone was on safely, the train rolled down the track, away from the station and toward its next destination.

We traveled to the wedding under this system. After purchasing tickets inside the station in Schneidemühl, we went to the platform to wait. Soon the train we wanted to take entered the station, slowed down, and came to a stop.

To get inside, we climbed up a couple of steps. Mutti and I boarded together, before the others. Papa, Wilfried in the baby buggy, and Uncle Reinhold followed behind.

To get the carriage and Wilfried up and onto the train, Papa and Uncle Reinhold worked together. First Papa climbed onto the first step that led into the train car. Then he turned around and took hold of one end of the baby carriage. From the ground, Uncle Reinhold lifted the other end of the buggy. Slowly, Papa moved backwards into the train, and Uncle Reinhold inched forward. Keeping Wilfried and the carriage between them, they moved up the steps. Through teamwork, they hauled the baby carriage and Wilfried on board.

We all found a place to sit down. Then the train chugged into gear. Down the tracks we moved, leaving Schneidemühl behind and heading toward Marienwerder.

As we traveled, I looked out the window at the passing countryside. It was early spring, and Germany was just coming to life. Fields of green rolled out before us, spreading over the land as if in drifts. Small budding yellow flowers and bursts of red tulips dotted the young grass. Trees that had been bare during the winter now held white blossoms on their branches. The awakening vegetation served as a background for the cottages, farms, and villages we passed.

We journeyed east, toward the enemy soldiers of the Red Army and toward a war moving in our direction. Nevertheless, our train trip to the wedding went undisturbed. We arrived in Marienwerder in time for the wedding. Under the sun and blue sky, with everyone wearing their best suits and dresses, the occasion felt festive and happy. The war seemed far away.

The following day, Mutti, Papa, Uncle Reinhold, and I went to the station to catch a train to Schneidemühl. Papa pushed Wilfried along in the baby carriage for the return trip.

After buying tickets, we waited for the train. Once it came into view, the long line of cars slowed to a stop. We looked for a place to get on. Mutti and I boarded first and found a seat with a window looking back at the platform and train station. We sat down, and watched Papa and Uncle Reinhold start to load Wilfried and the baby carriage onto the train.

To bring the buggy on board, Papa started up the steps that led from the platform to the inside of the car. Uncle Reinhold stayed on the ground. Then, with Papa on the step and Uncle Reinhold below, the two men began lifting Wilfried and his carriage onto the train.

Just as they had Wilfried suspended in the air between them, with Papa above and Uncle Reinhold below, a low whirring noise came from the train. It was followed by a screech, and then the wheels of the cars turned ever so slightly. The train shifted forward.

Perhaps the conductor thought everyone had boarded, or maybe officials wanted to keep the trains running on schedule.

Regardless of the cause, the train kept on moving. From our place at the window inside the car, Mutti and I stared at the others in our group. Papa was still on the step of our train car clutching his end of the carriage. Uncle Reinhold was on the ground moving in par with the train. Wilfried, in his seat in the buggy, dangled between the two men.

In a flash, Papa must have realized Uncle Reinhold and Wilfried were not going to make it onto the train. Rather than stay on board himself, he jumped off the step to join the others below.

Just seconds after the train groaned to life, Papa and Uncle Reinhold were on the ground. So was the baby carriage with Wilfried in it. Mutti and I were still inside the train car.

The train picked up speed. Looking out the window, Mutti and I watched the distance spread between us and the others. The train moved away fast from the platform and station. Within minutes, Papa and the others would be out of view.

Mutti waved frantically, called for help, and pounded on the window in desperation.

Pressing my face against the window, I watched their figures shrink as we moved away.

Then, Mutti made a quick decision. Pulling me back, she tugged open the window. She lifted me up to the height of the open space she had just created. Wrapping her arms tightly around me, she pushed us both through the window. Out we flew, away from the train and into the air. Her arms continued to hold me close while we sailed toward the ground.

Moments later, we landed with a thud. Then we started rolling. On and on we rolled, bumbling over the ground together. Mutti's arms stayed around me as we bounced on the grass.

Finally, almost as suddenly as we had left the train, we stopped. The flight, impact, and rolling made everything blur around me, and I closed my eyes to drown it out. After some time, I peeked open my lids. A moment later, I realized I wasn't being squeezed by Mutti's arms any more. I sat up to look around.

As I did so, I heard screaming. It came from somewhere very close.

I turned, searching for the source of the yelling. Mutti sat next to me, clutching her stomach. The cries came from her. Hysterical, she called for Papa and Wilfried and the baby.

Moments later, Papa arrived. Uncle Reinhold, with Wilfried in his arms, followed.

Both of them looked us over in astonishment. They couldn't believe we jumped from a moving train. The most frightening part of the leap, besides the fact that I was only three years old at the time, was that Mutti was seven months pregnant.

After a quick review, we only found a few scratches. By the grace of God, and by his grace alone, Mutti and I had not been seriously hurt during the tumble from the train. Still, we didn't know what the incident had done to the baby due in two months.

Shortly after Mutti and I jumped, someone on the train noticed there was a problem. Instead of continuing to pick up speed, as trains usually did when they rolled away from a station, ours slowed and then came to a stop. The conductor walked up to us.

"Is everyone okay?" he asked.

"I think so," replied Papa. "Just shook up."

"Let me help you back on."

The conductor and Papa lifted us to our feet. Then we all boarded the train once more.

Hours later, without any further incidents, we arrived in Schneidemühl.

The whole experience unnerved Mutti. She cried for hours, even after we were back safe and sound on the farm.

On July 14, 1944, at home on the acreage, baby Rainer was born. He was healthy, and appeared to not have been hurt when Mutti leapt from the train. Still, as a constant reminder to Mutti, trains frequently passed along the railroad tracks near our property.

* * *

Now, as we rode together in the sleigh through town, I pushed myself closer to Mutti. No matter how bad things got, I hoped there would be no jumping out of train windows this time.

I went back to watching the other mothers in the street. Soon their frightened expressions were too scary to look at, so I started observing the children. Some of them gazed back at me. Most of the little ones had a wild look in their eyes. Toddlers clung to their mothers. Babies cried. Many of the kids seemed to know, like me, that something horrible was headed toward our home. We had to get away.

I didn't see any fathers walking in the streets with their children. While some Nazi officials stood on street corners, clad in brown uniforms with a red Swastika band on their arm, there were few other men in sight. Together with Papa, most of them had left town to fight in the war. Only the very young, like my brothers, and the elderly, like Opa, remained.

* * *

At age 35, Papa was young and strong, but he had no interest in battles and did not want to get involved in the Nazi party. During the early years of the war, he avoided getting drafted because of his jobs. He worked as a welder in a factory outside of Schneidemühl, and also oversaw operations on our farm. His work in both of these areas was considered important to support the community and country. For that reason, he had not been called to fight right away.

In 1944, however, Germany's army setup changed. It faced attacks from the Allied Powers, consisting of Great Britain, France, the Soviet Union, and the United States, in both the east and the west. The country plummeted toward defeat. Key resources, including fuel, war equipment and manpower ran low.

With the intention of scraping together more men for the battle lines, Hitler and the Nazi Party created another army in October 1944. This military division was called the *Volkssturm*, or "people's army." It consisted of individuals who had not yet participated in the war, including those who had previously been considered too old or too young to be involved. It also called for the participation of many who, like Papa, had not been called to fight because of their line of work.[3]

All men between the ages of 16 and 60 who were capable of bearing arms were drafted for the *Volkssturm*. This included Papa.[4]

Some of those drafted into the new army had never even shot a gun. They also had to supply their own uniforms and equipment. Some wore army clothing from World War I. Others simply took their own clothing.

At the end of 1944, just before Christmas, Papa received orders to serve in the *Volkssturm*. The next day, he boarded a train from the Schneidemühl station to go to the war. He didn't know his final destination.

We didn't know where Papa went, or if he was still alive.

* * *

Now, evening cast its shadow on us as our sleigh inched toward the train station. Still sitting straight in the front seat, Opa helped the horses maneuver through the crowd. Soon the lamps of the station came into view. Opa pulled the horses toward the entrance and slowed them to a stop in the outside hitching area.

Once the horses were still, we descended from the sleigh. The temperature had dropped even more during our ride. While temperatures of 10 degrees or more below Fahrenheit were common during winter months,

Mutti didn't usually take us outside when it was so frigid. That evening the cold numbed me.

Out of the sleigh and standing on the ground, I felt very small. Horses, wagons, carts, and sleighs filled the open area in front of the railroad station. In addition to the large animals and vehicles, families milled about. I watched them take items from their wagons and tug them toward the station. Many cried as they moved.

I cried too. The whole scene alarmed me, and I clung to Mutti.

With me at her side, Mutti oversaw the unloading of our sleigh. She, along with Opa, Aunt Lydia, Ruthchen, and Oma, pulled out the three potato sacks she packed earlier at the farmhouse. Out came the baby carriage and Mutti's purse. Then came the two suitcases the others had brought.

Mutti led the way toward the station. Her scare from the train jump the year before was nowhere to be seen on her face. She radiated an in-charge presence, and we all followed her lead.

Schneidemühl's large train station stretched out before us. In the middle of the railroad area sat a large, two-story building. A square tower jutted from each upper corner of the building. A round clock sat in the center, on top of the structure. It displayed the time, which was now approaching five o'clock in the afternoon.

On the lower level of the station, a structure protruded outward. It consisted of five arches, lined up side by side. These arches served as doorways and marked the entrance into the building from the hitching area.

Train tracks ran along both sides of the station. Benches located on either side of the station faced the tracks. Awnings stretched over these benches. In quiet times, passengers waited on the benches for their train to arrive.

No one waited on a bench at the moment. Everyone piled into one of the trains lined up on the tracks outside of the station.

Usually, as we had for the previous trip, we purchased a ticket inside the station before boarding a train. Now, to see if we needed tickets, Mutti steered us through the arches and into the building. We entered a large lobby, and then moved toward a window where tickets were sold.

Due to the evacuation, no tickets were for sale. After talking with others, Mutti learned we could just get on a train, as long as there was room. Once she knew this, Mutti led us all back outside to the cold and the waiting trains.

We walked to the loading train. Just before getting on, Mutti stopped and turned.

"Won't you come with us?" she asked Opa.

"I'm 75 years old," said Opa. "Too old to fight, and too old to flee. I'll catch up after the Russians get through and everything quiets down."

The adults clutched our meager belongings, staring at each other.

Then, without words, Mutti hugged Opa.

When it was my turn, I felt like I was saying good-bye to Opa forever.

He pulled away, and his short figure shrunk inside his heavy winter coat.

In the distance, the heavy booms of Russian artillery continued.

Opa waited on the platform while Mutti directed us to the loading car. To make sure I got on, Mutti lifted me and pushed me through the window. She lifted Wilfried too. Opa then helped her load Rainer and the baby carriage onto the train. Oma, Aunt Lydia, and Ruthchen also boarded through the door.

Inside, people filled the seats and poured into the aisles. Babies cried, toddlers whimpered, and women sobbed.

After some searching, we found each other on the train. When passengers saw Mutti carrying a baby, they helped her find a place to sit. More passengers squeezed onto the train.

To help speed the evacuation of Schneidemühl's citizens, extra trains had come from Deutsch Krone, a town located 15 miles north of our city.

Even with the additional trains, so many people attempted to flee that it was hard—impossible even—to fit everyone. By this time, the Russians lingered on the outskirts of Schneidemühl. Anyone who didn't make it on a train would have to run away on foot, or face the enemy at home.

For this reason, even though we filled the train like sardines, the conductor waited for more people to get on. Then, with its cars bursting, the train rolled down the track, its iron wheels clicking hastily, picking up speed as it went. We left the station, and then Schneidemühl fell behind us.

Mutti turned to another passenger, a woman about her age.

"Do you know where this is headed?"

The woman shook her head. "Only west, they said."

"The officials?"

"Those that call themselves the officials."

At least this time, unlike the wedding trip, as long as we were in the train, we would be safe.

Or so I thought.

Several hours after we started rolling down the track, a siren went off. It rang a long, even tone. I recognized it instantly. I had heard that shrill sound before, back on the acreage near Schneidemühl. I glanced at Mutti. From the look on her face, I knew she also identified the sound.

It was an air raid siren, signaling an approaching attack.

The siren continued to blare. The loud noise rang in my ears. The train slowed, and then came to a stop.

Bombs were headed toward us.

CHAPTER THREE: BOMB SHELTER

"Jesus lead Thou on
Till our rest is won;
And although the way be cheerless
We will follow calm and fearless.
Guide us by Thy hand
To our fatherland."
—Christian Gregor, 1778[5]

When I was three years old, before Papa left for the war, I loved being outdoors.

Some days Mutti came up to me, carrying two baskets.

"Let's go to the forest," she said.

She held out one of the baskets and I grasped it with both of my hands.

"What are we picking today?"

"Mushrooms," she might say.

Or sometimes, "Berries."

Mutti knew where to find everything. In the forest, she showed me tender boysenberries hiding. She pointed out which mushrooms were good to eat and which ones were poisonous.

While we picked, Mutti always sang. Loud and clear, her voice circled around the trees and bushes. It echoed against the greenery and came back to us. It enveloped me, and I imagined I sat in a concert hall.

After filling our baskets, we returned home and to the kitchen. If we had picked berries that day, I always sampled some of the fruit as Mutti washed it and cleaned it up. The berries tasted delicious, and Mutti let me eat until my sides filled completely.

Mutti used some of the fruit to make *torten* (rich German cakes) for dessert. She also set aside some for jams and jellies. These lasted throughout the coming year, until the two of us again went to pick a fresh crop of berries.

We lived in the eastern region of Germany, in an area known as Pomerania. Green land, full of vegetation, surrounded us. So much food abounded during the summer months that Mutti stored piles of it away in the cellar. By the end of the warm season, rows and rows of jams and jellies lined the shelves. Potatoes, onions, and other vegetables lay in stacks on the floor of the underground room. To make a meal, Mutti only needed to tour the cellar. During those first years on the farm in Germany, I never went hungry.

In winter, snow dazzled on the low mountains and hillsides in the distance, and dotted the trees in the forest. When we went into town during those cold months, after a fresh snowfall, we traveled by sleigh, gliding along as our horse pulled us through the smooth drifts down the road, over the river, and into the city.

I liked leaving home, but only for short periods. The rest of the time, I happily roamed in my own wonderland, our acreage.

And I loved the long days of summer. During those times Papa tended carefully to the crops in the gardens on our property. I went outside nearly every day to go exploring. Gundi, our big German Shepherd dog, always came with me. Together we sought out adventures on the farm.

I adored the freedom of wandering, but I also treasured my companion. Covered with black and brown shaggy fur, Gundi trotted at my side. The two of us meandered near the vegetable garden Papa loved. We ran through the open areas of the property, and dashed around the trees. Sometimes, during our romps, we came upon Papa tending to the apple, pear, or plum trees that dotted our yard.

When I got tired, I rode on Gundi's back. I positioned my hands on his shoulders and dangled my small feet over either side of him. He moved gently, and I never fell off. After resting, I walked again, or better yet, ran. Gundi mimicked my pace.

In addition to the few cows and horses on the farm, my family raised pigs. Several geese and a gander also roamed about. I scampered around them all.

For entertainment, Gundi and I often chased the geese. Whenever I ran after them, they moved as fast as they could to get away. Their little feet scurried under round bellies and their bodies swayed back and forth as they waddled to safety. They usually honked loudly in their effort to escape, and the scene always made me laugh. Gundi's tail wagged with delight over the game.

The geese scattered when I chased them. Sometimes, however, the gander joined in the game. After I pursued him for a while, he stopped, turned around, and charged me. Then I always turned and ran as fast as my legs would take me in the opposite direction. The gander feared Gundi, but not me.

One time I set out to chase the geese. As before, they fled for safety. When the gander turned to pursue me instead, I dashed away. The gander followed, and closed in on me. When he was near enough to touch me, he reached out his neck and nipped at my leg. Then he went after my hand. Both places stung, like I had been pinched. After that, I stayed near Gundi when running after the geese.

One summer day, I wandered through the yard near our red brick two-story home with white trim. The sky was clear and blue, and a slight breeze shifted the tall grass on the lawn. I wore a short summer dress, and Gundi walked at my side. The soft green blades springing up from our lawn tickled my bare feet.

The house was behind me, and ahead lay the big tree with a rope swing Papa had hung from one of its high branches. Beyond the tree, our property spread on to the barn and then out to the forest.

Mutti and Papa were nearby, but I had lost track of them. I was in my own world, ambling contentedly about our estate without a single worry. Gundi followed at my heels.

We roamed toward the barn, located about 50 meters from the house. The barn stood two stories tall, and housed many of the animals. I loved going in and looking at the horses; their large, powerful bodies moved so gracefully. I always felt a sense of awe around them.

On this particular day, however, before I reached the door of the barn, my eyes caught sight of the roof. There, on top of the barn, knelt Papa. With his shoulders bent, he looked down at something. He held a hammer in one of his hands. Intent on his work, he didn't notice me down below on the ground.

As soon as I spotted Papa, an idea struck me. I wanted to get on the roof and be at his side. It would be my next great adventure.

Inspired by my grand idea, I sprinted to the barn. I ran faster and faster, my blonde hair flapping in the wind and my dress billowing out behind me.

I scurried past the rope swing in the tree. I ran past the geese and gander, and headed to the barn.

A ladder rested against the side of the structure. I walked over to it. From the bottom rung, I looked up. The ladder ascended straight to the roof of the barn. I couldn't see Papa, but I could make out the top rungs of the ladder. High above my head, they symbolized the gateway to the roof of the barn.

Holding on to the ladder with my hands for support, I lifted a foot and placed it on the first rung. Leaving Gundi below to watch, I pulled myself up. Using my hands to stay balanced, I tried another rung, and then lifted myself up to the third one. With each step upward, I moved closer to Papa, to the roof of the two-story barn, and to the sky.

I climbed halfway up, and then three-quarters. Finally I reached the top rung of the ladder. I grasped the edge of the roof and pulled myself toward it.

Still on the ladder, I peered over the ledge. There was Papa. He was on his hands and knees, bent over, just as I had seen him from down below. And I was very high too, nearly on the top of the barn. Delighted, I teetered slightly.

Just then, Papa looked up from his work and over to the ladder. His eyes grew big when he saw me. He looked so surprised I wondered if he would shout.

But he didn't. He spoke, his tone gentle. "Hello Elfi," he started, as if he had just walked into the kitchen and greeted me over a potato pancake breakfast.

From his position on the roof, he continued chatting with me. As we talked, he slowly set down the hammer. Then, still on his hands and knees, he moved in my direction. Soon he nearly touched the ladder.

For his next move, I thought he would surely help pull me onto the roof. But he didn't. Instead, he looked past me, down toward the bottom of the ladder and the ground below. I followed his gaze.

Mutti stood at the bottom of the ladder. She must have spotted me during my ascent to the roof and come to the scene. While Papa continued talking to me, Mutti started climbing up.

When she reached me, she helped me descend. Down we went, rung after rung, until we landed on the ground below.

I hadn't made it to the roof.

Mutti hugged me tightly on the grass. Then Papa came down the ladder. When he reached me, he gave me a hug too. In their arms, all was well. I felt safe and secure.

* * *

Papa was far away now, and long miles separated me from the barn, the geese and gander, and Gundi. The new scene unfolding before me, full of commotion, movement, and a blaring siren, contrasted sharply to those carefree days of adventure on the acreage.

My head spun from the change.

A short while earlier, when the siren first sounded, the line of train cars slowed to a stop on the track. Once the train reached a standstill, everyone inside began moving. Instead of pushing to get on board, as we had done just hours before at the station in Schneidemühl, we all wanted to get out, fast. No one wished to be trapped inside when bombs started dropping from the sky.

Mutti didn't want to stay on either. As soon as our car stopped, she rose from her seat. "We have to go," she said, turning to me. "We have to get off the *waggon*."

Working her way slowly through the crowd, Mutti led us through the train car, which was called *waggon*, literally "wagon," in German. She carried baby Rainer in one arm. With the other arm, she held on to Wilfried's shoulder. She steered him in front of her. I stayed by her side, pushing myself against her to stick together.

Behind us, Oma, Aunt Lydia and Ruthchen edged their way toward the exit too. When we reached the door and stairs leading outside, Mutti and the boys went down first. Aunt Lydia helped lower me to Mutti and my brothers. Ruthchen reached the ground, then held out a hand to help Oma descend.

I looked around. Passengers poured out of the other cars. The flow of the crowd moved away from the vehicle, separating themselves from the transport that was no longer a sign of safety.

All the lights on the train and also at the stop had been turned off as a response to the air raid, so we moved amidst a heavy cape of darkness. The siren continued to blare. Some passengers cried out softly in distress.

Cold air hit my face and hands. The wailing alarm rattled in my ears.

Our train had stopped at the far edge of a number of railroad tracks. There were enough sets of tracks for several trains to pass through. The crowd moved across all of these tracks, over the rails and ties, and away from the train. We followed.

Wanting to move quickly, Mutti carried Rainer in one of her arms. With her other arm, she held Wilfried's hand. He stumbled over the large railroad ties. I grabbed his other hand, and helped him over each track.

We reached a platform of sorts. There were no buildings nearby, and no other indications that this was indeed a train station. Still, people jostled one another in their search for safety.

* * *

In 1944, the British started focusing some attacks on key transportation and communication units in Germany. They carried out heavy raids to halt communication lines and break up specific railways.[6]

At the beginning of 1945, Allied air attacks intensified. During January 1945, Britain's Royal Air Force, the RAF, dropped 30,800 tons of bombs on Germany.[7]

* * *

Everyone who had been on board the train knew that in a glimpse, we could all be gone.

On the platform, other refugees sped up. Our group slowed to a crawl. Ruthchen supported Oma's arm to help her walk forward. Wilfried's little legs moved, but not fast enough. Even Mutti advanced slowly with Rainer on her hip.

Many people passed us. We fell toward the back of the crowd.

Noticing the lag in our group, Aunt Lydia scooped up Wilfried and carried him in her arms. Mutti sped up, as she didn't have to guide an almost two-year-old anymore.

Noting that Wilfried was no longer at her side, I moved closer to Mutti. I grabbed the now-free hand of hers. I tried to go fast like her, but my legs, while longer than Wilfried's, still lagged.

If only Papa were with us, I thought. His quiet demeanor always soothed me. I despised the dark, and running away from the railroad tracks, with the loud blaring in the background, scared me. Frigid air stung my cheeks.

My slow pace caused the group to drag. Despite Aunt Lydia carrying Wilfried, we fell among the last straggling passengers of the crowd.

Still we pushed on.

Suddenly, a man appeared at my side. In the dark, I made out the outline of his uniform. I recognized him as a German soldier. I didn't know where he came from. I opened my mouth, but he spoke first.

"*Ich habe eine Frau und ein kleines Mädchen wie du,*" he said. I understood his words, which meant, "I have a wife and a little girl like you."

I looked at him. His uniform was gray, and the night darkened the features on his face. Too afraid to form words, I stared.

He looked from me to Mutti. "*Und ich weiß nicht, wo sie sind,*" he continued ("And I don't know where they are").

His presence scared me.

Mutti looked at the soldier to assess him. Then she nodded. As if he understood her approval, the soldier took my free hand in his own. At the same time, Mutti let go of my other hand.

She put both arms around Rainer. She moved faster.

The soldier picked up speed. I tried to go quickly, but my legs still couldn't keep up.

The soldier must have sensed my fatigue. After just a few steps, he picked me up. Then he sped through the crowd.

The siren rang a two-tone pitch. The double tone signaled a different warning. A single tone, which had sounded first, meant enemy planes were in the area. This double tone, in which the siren switched back and forth from a high note to a low one, creating a woo-ooh, woo-ooh sound, noted a stronger warning. It meant an attack was imminent. Bombs could fall any moment over our heads.

The soldier sprinted. Alongside us, Mutti ran too.

We reached the edge of the platform. Before us lay an opening in the ground. In it, a staircase led down. There was no building in sight, and it looked like the steps went straight into the Earth.

Down Mutti went. The soldier and I followed.

At the bottom of the steps stretched a narrow, dimly lit hallway. Doors lined its left side. As we entered this underground area, I kept my eye on Mutti. She ducked into the door closest to us. Frantic, I pointed in her direction.

The soldier carried me toward her. I heard a loud clang above us, and looked to see what it was. A trap door closed, shutting up the entrance to the underground shelter. A soldier pulled on a chain attached to the door to secure it.

We ducked through the same door Mutti had just entered. The soldier set me on my feet next to her. Then, just as quickly as he had come, he disappeared.

I clung to Mutti for dear life. Pulling one of her arms away from Rainer, she wrapped me tightly against her. "He only wanted to help," she said, her tone soft. "He didn't mean any harm."

I snuggled closer to Mutti. Instinctively I felt protected next to her.

Our whole group stood together in the room. Mutti found a spot on a bench to sit. We followed her lead. I sat on the end with Mutti to my left. To my right was the door we had just entered from the hallway. After we sat down, a soldier closed the door.

From Mutti's side, I took in our new surroundings. Long and narrow, the room of the underground shelter had a door on each end of it. Benches lined the length of the two side walls. A domed ceiling sloped over us, and a single light bulb dangled in the middle of the room. It cast a hazy glow.

A hush settled over the dusty, cement gray place. In the distance, a boom sounded. Then we heard another boom, this time closer.

More bombs fell.

* * *

The bunker, located at a rural stop between Schneidemühl and Stargard, was one of many air raid shelters located throughout the country. Hitler and the Nazi Party built them in anticipation of these attacks. Our bunker consisted of a series of rooms; the door at the far end of our room led to another area where other passengers from the train hunkered together.

* * *

For Germany, air attacks began in the summer of 1940. After the defeat of France in June that year, Hitler turned his sights to the only country remaining in Western Europe that still resisted him: Britain. Its surrender would lead to victory for Hitler in Europe.

Hitler planned an invasion of Britain, which began with an air attack. By defeating the Royal Air Force (RAF), German forces could fly freely across the English Channel.[8]

On August 24, 1940, the *Luftwaffe*, or German air force, bombed London. German bombers targeted London's docks, but due to poor navigational equipment, the explosives landed in London's financial center. Bombs also exploded on Oxford Street, the busiest shopping stretch in Europe.[9]

In response, Britain fired off its own bombers 24 hours later. They aimed for armament factories, but hit fields, woods, and residential areas.[10]

And so the air war between Britain and Germany began.

The raids continued, raging between July to October 1940.[11]

And the inaccuracies affected our acreage. One night in early September 1940, Mutti and Papa went to bed, as usual, in their upstairs room of the farmhouse outside of Schneidemühl. Soon they fell fast asleep.

During the middle of the night, Mutti, who was nine months pregnant with me at the time, woke to the sound of an explosion.

"*Hilfe* (Help me)!" she cried.

Moments later, showers of debris struck the bedroom window. Three more explosions followed.

Even though there had been no warning signs, Mutti and Papa felt certain it had been an air attack. Indeed, when they checked the property in the morning for damage, they found plenty of it. Four bombs had struck the area. One of these hit the fence surrounding the property.

Mutti wondered if the attackers had been trying to bomb the nearby factory where Papa worked. No one knew the true motive. If, however, the planes had indeed been aiming for Papa's employer, they missed the factory and instead took out our fence.

I was born two weeks later.

* * *

When I arrived, Mutti wanted to name me "Elfi," after her very best girlfriend. Since I was born at home, Papa went in to town to register the birth and my name. He notified the authorities, who were Nazi officials, of the wish to register my name as "Elfi Karin."

He had to ask for the official approval for the name. This coincided with German law, which stated a name had to be accepted by the local *Standesamt*, or "office of vital statistics," before it was registered. To meet approval, a child's name needed to reflect the gender of the child. It also could not endanger the well-being of the child.[12]

When Papa requested the name, the officials wouldn't allow the first name of "Elfi." They said it had to be "Elfrun." This could have been because "Elfi" was considered a pet name, or not a full name. It was often short for other names such as "Elfrun" or "Elfriede."

Mutti and Papa had no other options. They had to take the name "Elfrun" for me. They decided to call me "Elfi" at home.

My name conundrum was not nearly as drastic as what Jewish families faced at the time. Persecuting Jews was a central theme of Nazi ideology, and from 1933 to 1939, Jewish people felt the effects of more than 400 decrees and regulations. These laws restricted all aspects of their public and private lives.[13]

Two of these decrees specifically dealt with Jewish names. One was issued on January 5, 1938. It forbade Jews from changing their names.[14]

A second decree was implemented on August 17, 1938. This second decree included further limitations. In order to meet approval, given names had to be "official Jewish names." This included a list of 185 names for men, and 91 for women.[15]

Furthermore, Jewish men and women who at the time already had first names of non-Jewish origin had to add "Israel" and "Sara," respectively, to their given names.[16]

* * *

As a young girl, I watched air raids at night. They became frequent in our area during the last months of 1944, after we crossed paths with a Russian soldier on our property. By that time, Britain's air force sported advanced technology, including the Pathfinder Force (PFF). Established in August 1942, the PFF consisted of first-class, experienced crews.[17]

Using improved navigational equipment, the PFF traveled in front of the force of bomber planes. Once the crews reached their destination, they dropped colored parachute flares. Yellow, green, and red flares lit up the sky. The main force bombers followed the PFF, and, using the lights in the sky, aimed their bombs at targets.[18]

These flares intrigued me. I watched them, at night, from the porch on our acreage. Since their purpose was to illuminate the target, the flares didn't drop to the ground right away. Instead, they hung in the air, dotting the sky like a frozen fireworks display.

Mutti watched them with me.

"They look like a Christmas tree," I said of the lights.

"They're beautiful," Mutti replied.

After a moment, she added, "As long as you don't think of what happens next."

Bomber planes zoomed in behind the flares. Aided by the light from these floating lanterns, the pilots searched the ground and found their target. They dropped bombs on industrial areas, factories, or a railroad yard.

When the bombs dropped, the sky burst into flames. Red and orange streaked through the air, and fireballs burst in the midst of the fight. Slowly the flares disintegrated in the sky.

The night raids I witnessed from the porch had always been far away.

* * *

Now, sitting in the bunker, listening to bombs fall close by, the bleakness of war seemed much closer.

The faint light of the bunker created odd shades and shapes. Fuzzy, dark figures huddled together. Some sat on benches. Others crouched on the floor. Everyone was quiet.

I was so scared I could hardly breathe.

After more time had passed, the mood in our room of the shelter shifted slightly. A few people stirred or spoke quietly. Others sang softly. Some prayed. Many cried.

"Elfi," Mutti said quietly, wiping my wet cheeks.

"Will we be okay?" I buried my face in her shoulder.

"There is nothing to fear. God and his angels are with us. They are watching over us."

I rested my head on Mutti's arm. Rainer sat in her lap, and Wilfried nestled on her other side. She, in the middle of us, began singing:

> Breit aus die Flügel beide,
> O Jesu, meine Freude
> Und nimm dein Küchlein ein!
> Will Satan mich verschlingen,
> So laß die Englein singen:
> Dies Kind soll unverletzet sein.

> *(Lord Jesus who dost love me,*
> *Oh, spread Thy wings above me*
> *And shield me from alarm!*
> *Though evil would assail me,*
> *Thy mercy will not fail me:*
> *I rest in Thy protecting arm.)*[19]

Mutti had often sung this tune at home, during quiet evenings spent on the acreage. Now the melody and words of the familiar song helped me calm down. I clung to the voice, and to Mutti, as we waited for the raid to pass.

Huddling in the bunker, the memory of jumping out of a moving train with Mutti a year earlier passed through my mind. All at once, landing in a quiet, green field didn't sound very daunting at all.

Mutti, who had helped me climb down a two-story ladder to safety, and hung on to me while leaping from a train, still looked after me. Her singing reminded me she wasn't the only one concerned about keeping me safe. God was watching over us too. He sent a German soldier to carry me away from the dangers of the night and into the underground bunker. What's more, he sent his angels to protect us. I felt certain their wings, though unseen, hovered over me.

Mutti's song finished. The minutes ticked on.

Silence fell in the room, periodically interrupted by gasps as explosions sounded nearby.

Still we waited.

CHAPTER FOUR: DEUTSCHES ROTES KREUZ
(The German Red Cross)

"Swift to its close ebbs out life's little day;
Earth's joys grow dim; its glories pass away;
Change and decay in all around I see;
O thou who changest not, abide with me."
—Henry Francis Lyte, 1847[20]

Despite the impending circumstances and signs of war in our area, a time of wonderment marked my first years of life on the farm near Schneidemühl. A road ran parallel to our fence in front of the house. Beyond the road stretched an open meadow. A dirt path led from our house through the meadow, on to a bridge that crossed the nearby Kuddow River, and into town. The path met the road running parallel to our property, creating a crossroads of sorts.

Standing in front of the house, facing the meadow, if I glanced right, I saw the forest. On that side lay the area where Mutti and I often went together to pick berries and gather mushrooms. If I looked left, I saw more forest. The land on that side sloped upward.

Mountains lay beyond the forest, and the road that went past our house and through the forest eventually rose up into those hills. Papa, before leaving for the war, rode his bicycle along the road and up the incline, until he reached a factory nestled in the hills. He worked shifts at the factory, and often left the place when it was getting dark.

In the evenings, around the time we knew his shift ended, Mutti and I stood on the porch of our home, watching for the light from Papa's bicycle. Squinting into the dark layers of forest and mountainside, we scanned the landscape until we saw a small shining circle. We watched the prancing dot bob down the road. It drew closer until Papa pedaled up to the fence—home at last.

Papa wore rugged clothes to the factory, but at home, he changed into a nice outfit. He shined his shoes, kept up a trim haircut, and was always clean shaven. Before I was born, he had played semi-professional soccer. A leg injury from his soccer days meant he could no longer run, but he stayed in good shape and always dressed sharp.

Our home sat on an acre of land outside of Schneidemühl, and originally began as a local forest ranger's residence. Oma and Opa purchased the place before Mutti and Papa met. Together with Papa and Uncle Willie, they turned it into a welcoming home.

When Papa married Mutti in 1940, they moved in with his parents. The house easily accommodated the newlyweds, Oma and Opa, and Uncle Willie and his family.

Then Uncle Willie and his wife, Aunt Lydia, added a restaurant. They built a sun porch on the front of the house. With its windows on three sides, the porch served as a comfortable dining area, complete with a view of the picturesque area.

We lived in the back of the house, behind the restaurant and away from the road running parallel to the front of the place. An ample kitchen served both our house and the restaurant. The living room and Oma and Opa's bedroom were on the first floor, along with a side porch looking out to the forest and mountains. Bedrooms filled the upstairs, including Mutti and Papa's room, which was situated in the back of the house, near the fence where the bomb hit. More forest lay beyond the fence.

Uncle Willie and Aunt Lydia ran the restaurant. Local town residents and travelers frequented the place. Customers dined on local German cuisine: sausages, sauerkraut, tender pot roast, potatoes, breads, butter, rich jams, and dumplings.

Clientele often requested sauerbraten, literally "sour roast." This dish had to be made ahead of time to be able to serve it upon a customer's request. To prepare sauerbraten, a cut of beef or pork was first marinated in a mixture of vinegar and spices for three days. This process tenderized the meat, which was then roasted with other vegetables and served with a sweet sauce.

For dessert, Uncle Willie and Aunt Lydia offered an assortment of sweets, including *streuselkuchen* (crumb cake) and dense tortes. These were filled with fresh apples, pears, and plums from our trees during the summer, and canned fruit in the winter.

How I loved the foods from the restaurant! Mutti helped with the cooking, and occasionally made one of her favorite meals: goose blood soup. After killing a goose from the farm, she saved the blood. She added vinegar to the blood to keep it from clotting.

Then she boiled meat from the goose, along with spices, in a large stockpot filled with water. During this step, she also cleaned the intestines from the goose, wrapped them around the feet and added these to the soup.

After the meat grew tender, Mutti took it out of the broth and pulled it off the bones. Then she returned the meat to the pot, along with dried plums and dried pears. While the mixture cooked another hour, Mutti stirred flour and sour cream into the blood and vinegar mixture. She added the concoction slowly into the hot soup, along with sugar, salt, and more vinegar. Sometimes she added potato dumplings to the dish.

This dark soup resembled chocolate in color, and sported white dumplings floating in it. "It really tasted delicious," Mutti recalled years later.

Ruthchen, Aunt Lydia and Uncle Willie's daughter, often played with me as her parents waited on customers and worked in the kitchen. She was tall, with long dark hair and pretty features. Sometimes Mutti or Aunt Lydia put matching ribbons in our hair. Ruthchen's given name was "Ruth," but we called her "Ruthchen" as a sign of endearment. She was always nice to me, even though she was five years my senior.

Aunt Lydia was tall and stout, with dark hair she usually wore pulled back in a low bun. A smart, quick restaurant manager, she always laughed and smiled. I thoroughly enjoyed her presence.

Along with the regular restaurant customers, family and friends often dropped by to visit and share a meal.

One of my favorite guests, by far, was Tante Kaëthe. She was my godmother, and wore her lovely short brown hair in curls. Friendly and full of energy, she spent hours playing with me outside.

Once when she came for a visit, Tante Kaëthe brought a white rabbit. I stroked its soft fur, and admired its glowing red eyes.

I spent the next hours playing with the lovely creature outside.

After some time, Tante Kaëthe approached me and softly touched the rabbit's head.

"It's yours to keep," she said.

"For this afternoon?" I asked.

"For always – it's a gift."

"It's beautiful, thank you."

I often cradled the creature in my arms and carried it around the farm as a pet.

When we fled, I didn't say good-bye to my special rabbit.

* * *

Now, from my seat in the underground shelter, I hoped Opa was looking after the white bunny with red eyes, the house and barn, and the other animals too.

I huddled next to Mutti for hours in the bomb shelter. I listened to planes flying overhead and bombs falling.

Then, as suddenly as it had begun, it ended. Usually, after a raid, a siren rang, signaling an all clear. That night, however, no such siren sounded.

Moments after the quiet resumed, a soldier entered our room.

"You're free to return to the train. All is well," he announced.

Passengers who, hours before, dashed from the train to the underground shelter now moved, slowly, back to the train. Fortunately, the raid did not damage the train cars. Soldiers helped us and other refugees find the right car to board. We located our luggage and sat down again.

* * *

On the train, my stomach grumbled. In our rush to leave, Mutti hadn't brought much to eat. It was now gone, but I wanted more. Baby Rainer, with his blonde hair and big blue eyes, cried on Mutti's lap. He was hungry too.

On we rolled.

Eventually, day broke.

It was Friday, January 26, 1945. Still the train moved forward.

The coach creaked, but rode on. After a while, it slowed, and the brakes screeched. Then it stopped completely.

German officials came onboard.

"Welcome to Stargard," one of them said.

"Everyone can get off. You are out of reach of any danger."

Quietly, we all stepped on to the ground.

"Where are we to go?" Mutti asked another official.

"We've issued orders for everyone in the village, who can, to take in refugees. Anyone with an extra room, either inside the house or outside, must share it."

Mutti nodded, looking past the officer and toward the spattering of houses in the village.

An officer split up our group for the night. He assigned Oma, Aunt Lydia, and Ruthchen to a room on the first floor of a farmhouse. Then he took Mutti, Wilfried, Rainer, and I to a different home. As soon as we arrived, he left.

A farmer, his wife, and their 14-year-old daughter met us as at the door.

"I'll show you where you can stay," offered the farmer.

Rather than lead us inside the farmhouse, he showed us to a barn on the property. Once inside, he pointed to a ladder in the middle of the two-story structure. The ladder led up to an open hayloft.

"Our hired man usually sleeps here, but we don't have any help at the moment," the farmer explained. "It's yours to use."

Mutti merely peered at the ladder and then at the baby carriage.

The mediocre conditions and welcome were typical of most places in Germany accepting refugees at that time. Tension and fear filled households across the country, and more so as key supplies, especially food and medicine, dwindled. No one knew what the next months would bring, and to accept refugees meant taking on new risks.

Never one to sit quietly in a situation she felt was not practical for her family, Mutti pushed Rainer in the baby carriage, with Wilfried and me walking on either side of her, and headed toward the center of town. When she spotted the mayor and a Nazi officer, she went to them and said, "You come with me."

Mutti was sturdy, with broad shoulders and brown hair pulled back in a simple bun. She was the leader, not only of us children, but also of the group we were traveling with. She had grown up in a money-strapped home close to territories that Germany and Poland fought over for years. As a girl, she helped her mother raise eight boys. This upbringing gave her a no-nonsense approach to nearly all things in her adult life.

So I wasn't surprised that these tough officers paid attention when Mutti addressed them. They followed her to the farm.

She led them to our sleeping quarters in the barn at the farmer's place. Standing at the edge of the ladder, Mutti pointed to the hayloft above.

"You show me how I can bring three little children and the baby carriage up and down the ladder," she said.

The two officials looked up into the hayloft and then at the ladder. One of them took hold of the ladder and shook it slightly. Then they looked back at each other.

That night we stayed in a room on the first floor of the farmer's house.

We remained there over the weekend, and the next week too. Due to regulations in the area, the farmer had to provide food for us, even though there was little to offer.

Another weekend passed. In the evenings, the entire village went into blackout mode to deter potential air attacks. Every night, as the sun set, all lights dimmed and then vanished. The absolute darkness unsettled us. Scared by the blackness, Wilfried, Rainer and I cried a lot.

But Mutti spread out the trusty feather bed, and at night I curled up under the soft blanket. Its warmth reminded me of home. Mutti sang our favorite hymns every evening. I drifted off to sleep under her soothing words and melodic tones.

On a Monday, about 11 days after we arrived on the farm, both Wilfried and I woke up sick with a cold. Mutti walked with us to the doctor in town. The doctor prescribed medicine, but the medication we needed wasn't available in the village. Mutti had to walk to a nearby town to get it, so Oma came to watch us while Mutti was away.

It was dark when Mutti returned. She had trekked through several miles of deep snow with her boots on to get to the pharmacy, she explained. She arrived happy, though, because she found the medicine we needed. She also brought milk for Rainer.

Oma stayed over with us that night. The next morning, Mutti washed some of our clothes and Rainer's diapers and hung them out to dry. Then she went out to buy more milk for Rainer. On the way back to the farmhouse, another woman met up with her. "Have you packed?" the lady asked.

"Why?" Mutti responded.

"The Russians are coming."

"I thought we were safe here."

"Not anymore." The woman shook her head.

"So we have to go," said Mutti.

"They're saying to be by the school before twelve o'clock today."

As the woman spoke, both she and Mutti heard the telltale signs. Just like when we left Schneidemühl, artillery was firing in the distance.

* * *

Others shared our need to flee. In fact, Germans began leaving the far eastern regions of the country in the summer of 1944. Conditions turned chaotic during the winter, when miles-long lines of refugees pushed their carts through the snow as they worked their way west, trying to stay ahead of the advancing Red Army. Mutti had spotted a glimpse of this turmoil before we left Schneidemühl, when she encountered the frightened woman and her children by the train tracks the evening Papa left for the war.

* * *

In Stargard, time was essential. Back at our place, Mutti took down the wet clothing and put it in the bags. She quickly packed the rest of our belongings. Then we followed others to the school in the village and waited to be picked up. We wouldn't be able to take a train, as news reports relayed a bomb had destroyed the upcoming tracks.

Soon we found Aunt Lydia and Ruthchen at the school. They had also received word of the advancing Russians and had come to the same place to wait.

After some time, the farmer's 14-year-old daughter drove up to us, in a farm wagon with two horses attached to it.

"My parents are not coming," she explained to Mutti.

"Why not?" Mutti replied.

The girl shrugged. "They insist on staying. But I can take you on. They sent me for you."

Mutti, Wilfried, Rainer and I piled into the back of the wagon. Oma, Aunt Lydia and Ruthchen climbed in too.

A cloth roof covered the wagon, offering us a little protection from the cold.

The girl directed the horses to a highway. Other wagons and carts traveled along it too. Everyone headed west.

In addition to a covering, our wagon had thick, sturdy sides. We saw others, however, in vehicles that resembled only a hay wagon. They had no rooftop, and their sides were made of wooden slats. There were open spaces between the slats. Sometimes luggage and other belongings toppled out of these rigs. But in our wagon, we all stayed safe.

In the next village, we arrived at a dance hall. Strangers motioned for us to get off the wagon. "You can sleep here," one noted.

We went inside the dance hall and settled in a small spot on the floor.

Aunt Lydia went out with an empty bottle to get it filled with milk for Rainer. When she returned, she said there was a creamery in the village, but the workers there refused to give her milk.

Mutti listened, and then went out. She came back, sometime later, holding the bottle, now brimming with milk.

"How did you convince them to give you milk?" asked Aunt Lydia.

"I didn't," said Mutti. "First I went to the mayor and an official in town, but when I asked them for milk, they said I couldn't have any. On the way back here, I came across a girl, maybe 12 years old. I told her I needed milk and she said her family had one cow. She took the empty bottle and asked me to wait. I did, and she came back a little later with the bottle filled."

"Good, Rainer looks so poorly," said Aunt Lydia.

He did. Rainer was so small he suffered more than the rest of us from the lack of meals. Even after Mutti gave him the bottle, he looked pale and sunken.

"He hasn't had much to eat," Mutti explained to me. "He has diarrhea and there isn't anything more I can do for him tonight. It is in God's hands."

Then she pulled out a feather bed. I laid on it and soon fell asleep.

Early the next morning, we rode in the wagon to search for a train station. We traveled for hours, arriving in Pasewalk, Germany, in the afternoon.

There we sat on the platform to wait. There were no other trains in sight. We waited and waited. The hours ticked by, and nothing came.

Then, at dusk, a train rolled toward us. Unlike our group, which was headed west, this train traveled east. Young German soldiers, and even boys, looked out the window. They spotted Mutti, sitting down with two children next to her and a baby on her lap. As the train passed by, many soldiers leaned out of the window.

"*Auf Wiedersehen Mutti*," they called out, which means "Good-bye Mommy." They waved their arms in our direction.

Mutti held on to Rainer and returned the soldiers' gaze. They locked eyes until the train passed.

For the next hours, Wilfried and I waited beside Mutti, and baby Rainer rested on her lap. The baby carriage and luggage lay beside us.

As evening approached, the station turned off all lights. The city went dark too.

Then, at about 9 p.m., an air raid siren broke the calm. Its pitch rang as a single, even tone. It signaled a coming attack.

We followed other waiting passengers to a place under the railroad station. There, frightened, cold, and hungry, we pushed against Mutti.

After about two hours, the all-clear siren sounded. We went back up the stairs to the track. Again we sat and waited for the train to come, with Wilfried and me on either side of Mutti and Rainer on her lap.

No train arrived.

My fingers and toes turned numb in the low temperatures.

Another hour passed, and still no train.

Around midnight, a second alarm sounded.

Again, we trampled below. Mutti barely made it to the shelter. After finding a place for Wilfried and me to sit, and handing off Rainer to Aunt Lydia, she laid down flat on the cement.

Wilfried and I shifted in our places in order to crouch next to her.

I turned to Aunt Lydia. "What's wrong with Mutti?"

"She's just tired," Aunt Lydia explained.

Mutti closed her eyes and slept. I watched her and she stayed in the same position for a long time. Then she woke up.

And just in time. The bombs fell minutes after she revived. One explosion sounded after another. The loud bursts racked my eardrums and rattled the walls surrounding us. My heart pounded. The noise went on and on. Everyone waited, apprehensive of where the next bomb would strike.

Finally, the loud booms subsided. It grew quiet, and then, after a little while, a whistle sounded. It was the all-clear signal. The raid was over.

We went back up the steps. Everything was still in place.

At 1 a.m. that night, after six hours of waiting and two air raids, a train pulled into the station. It was a fast train, and looked different in appearance than the first train we had been on.

Even in the dark, Mutti could see the train was bursting with people and soldiers. But it was traveling west, which is what we wanted, and it stopped at the station.

Mutti walked to the open door of a car.

"I have to get in here," she explained to the officer at the doorway. "I've been laying here with three little ones since five o'clock this afternoon—I have to get in."

"You just bring them, and we'll get you in," the officer at the door assured her.

As if by the Lord's signal, three soldiers appeared and offered to help us. Each of them took a sack, and we piled into the train.

Inside we encountered a mix of civilians and soldiers filling the hallways and cars.

The cars of the train consisted of small, private cabins. A corridor ran alongside these separate rooms. Sliding doors marked the entrance to each of the cabins.

The officer who had first invited Mutti on the train nodded to us and led us to a cabin. He opened the door, and ordered the soldiers in it to leave.

They filed out of the room and we stepped inside.

The compartment was the size of a small room. Two benches lined either wall and they faced each other.

Mutti sat with Rainer on her lap on one of the benches. I studied his face. It looked so ashen I wondered if he would survive. Wilfried and I sat near Mutti and the baby. We were both sick too, though not as close to death as Rainer.

Passengers lined the other bench. One of them took in Mutti's worn, tired face. "If you fall asleep, he will fall down," she warned.

"I will not sleep," Mutti insisted.

"He looks awful," added the passenger.

"I know, he is sick, and I need to care for him."

But the trip, with its air raids and constant uncertainty, had worn us down. Before long, Mutti started to nod off.

Then, all of a sudden, whoom! Rainer slid part way down her lap.

Mutti jolted awake, grabbed Rainer, and said to those looking at her with raised eyebrows, "I watched him—he didn't fall."

Oma, Aunt Lydia, and Ruthchen had gotten on the same train as us. They didn't come into the cabin; instead, they found a place to sit in the crowded hallway. We likely received special permission to sit with Mutti in the private car because the three of us were all so young, and the officer felt sympathy when he saw Mutti traveling with little ones.

He also likely saw what bad shape Rainer was in. By this time, we had been fleeing for more than a week with hardly anything to eat. My stomach ached for food and nourishment—anything to fill it up.

Baby Rainer had a bad case of diarrhea, an illness he had suffered from once before when he was smaller, back on the acreage. This time, however, it hit him even harder. His head caved in. His sunken eyes revealed the days that had passed without him getting the right medicine, a decent meal, or enough milk.

The officer who had helped us get on the train now stopped by our cabin and looked more closely at Rainer's craterous head. Then the officer offered to bring him something. Mutti agreed, and the officer scuttled away.

Minutes later, he returned with a paper cup. He handed it to Mutti and motioned for her to give it to Rainer. I peered in. A substance that appeared similar to black coffee filled the cup.

A closer look, however, revealed it wasn't real coffee. Instead, roasted grain and water filled the cup. By this time in the war, coffee made from ground coffee beans was hard to find. But it was something, so Mutti filled Rainer's bottle with it.

"What time is it?" I asked Mutti.

"After two in the morning," she said.

My stomach hurt with hunger and my mouth was dry. I looked longingly at Rainer drinking substitute coffee in his bottle.

Then I cried. Wilfried cried too.

Mutti surely heard us, but couldn't do anything to help satisfy our hunger and thirst at that moment.

I wiped my eyes and looked around at the other children on the train. I could tell they were hungry too. Their faces were sad and scared, and their shoulders slumped at their sides. We didn't talk. We just looked at each other and understood.

Sometime later, the officer returned. In his hands, he held two pieces of *süßes Brot*, or sweet bread. He handed a slice to Wilfried and another to me. I was so happy to have a piece of bread. I ate it quickly.

Even after eating it, my stomach roared.

The train took us to Neubrandenburg, a significant city located 180 miles northwest of Schneidemühl. We arrived during the day, and the station buzzed with other trains, people, and refugees.

Mutti turned to us.

"I need to get milk for Rainer and food for you. I'm going to go look in the nearby shops. You stay here."

Wilfried and I nodded.

Others left our cabin too. Soon Oma, Aunt Lydia, and Ruthchen came in and took their place. Mutti passed Rainer to them, and left.

Together we waited, but Mutti didn't return.

Time passed, and still she didn't come back.

I began to grow desperate. I peered out the window and only saw crowds. No Mutti.

Then, after what seemed like hours, I saw her. She was in the distance, frantically eyeing each train. We could see her from the window, but the station was so full of other people, shops, tracks and trains that she didn't find our faces.

Aunt Lydia and Ruthchen waved and called to her. They pounded on the glass of the window. But Mutti kept looking at other trains, other cars, and not at ours.

Our train began to rumble to life, getting ready to leave and Mutti still wasn't with us. We watched her helplessly. She glanced at refugee after refugee peering from the windows. Her eyes filled with terror.

After an eternity, her gaze turned to our window. Our eyes locked. She ran, then sprinted toward us. With paper bags in her arms, she raced back to the train, climbed in, and pushed her way back to us.

Once there, she wrapped us in her arms. She held us for a long time.

"We'll never separate again," she said, handing out food from the bags. "If I need to get something, we'll all get off. From now on, everyone stays together."

After that, I began to lose a sense of time, unsure of when a day started and ended. The train rolled on and on, and we journeyed west, hoping for safety. Mutti, clad in big winter boots and Papa's wedding suit under her dress and coat, boldly led us on.

During the day the train occasionally stopped. When it did, we got off to look for food. Our train avoided the cities and larger towns when possible, as these areas were at a higher risk for getting bombed. In rural areas, we trekked into villages and farms nestled in the countryside. Several times our train broke down. Then we waited outside by the tracks for a new one to come and take us further on.

Sometimes when our train stopped, I watched other trains roll by. The drawn faces of refugees, women, children—some healthy, others ill—stared back at me. They headed west too.

Rainer's head caved in more each day. The infection Wilfried had caught in Stargard hadn't cleared up. In fact, it had grown worse. It was so bad that fluid ran from both of his ears.

"Will Wilfried ever get better?" I asked Mutti.

"He has an infection in each ear," she explained. "I have to get him to the doctor, but I haven't been able to find one. First we must move on."

Sometimes Mutti bought a little food; other times she begged farmers to share with us. Occasionally farmers gave her something, but many times they simply said, "No."

Despite Mutti's best efforts, we stayed hungry. Rainer's head grew more craterous and Wilfried's ears continued to leak fluid.

At one point, the train stopped and an officer told everyone to get off. We left our car, and after waiting some time, the officer returned.

"We won't be able to continue on here," he announced. "A segment of the track ahead is bombed out."

We waited with the crowd of passengers for another stretch, and then, horse-drawn carts and people on foot filed toward our group. Some of the carts were full, but others had room for a few more passengers.

Our family climbed onto a cart. Soon we were traveling along in a procession of other refugees. From the cart, I studied the travelers. Some walked and carried a basket that held their belongings. Others rode in wagons packed so high the vehicles looked like they might tip over with a little pushing. Mutti and I saw a person dangling precariously off the side of one of the wagons ahead of us. Caked blood covered the body. Up close, I peered into vacant eyes. The person was dead.

* * *

Days after our departure from Schneidemühl, on January 27, 1945, Soviet troops reached Auschwitz, the largest camp established by the Germans. It held a concentration camp, killing center, and forced-labor camps. The place was 300 miles southeast of our home in Schneidemühl.[21]

Shortly before the Soviet forces entered, Nazis killed thousands at Auschwitz. They evacuated others, and forced nearly 60,000 prisoners to march west. More than 15,000 died during the marches.[22]

When the Soviets arrived, they found more than 7,000 remaining prisoners. Of these, the majority were sick, emaciated, and dying. It is thought that at least 1.3 million people were deported to Auschwitz between 1940 and 1945. Of these, at least 1.1 million were murdered.[23]

* * *

Somewhere after Neubrandenburg, after riding on the wagon, we came to another train station. An official directed us to an area to wait for a train.

When the train approached, Mutti rubbed her forehead.

"What is that?" I asked.

"It's a cattle car," she said.

"Should we get on? Won't it be cold?" I asked, pointing to the slots in the frames of the cars. Wooden strips formed the train car walls. In between each of the strips was an open space, allowing air to come in for animals.

"Don't worry, God will take care of us." Mutti lifted me through a big sliding door in the middle of one car. Inside I landed on a floor; nothing more.

Our whole group assembled on the floor, crammed next to other bodies. Luggage and women, with children stacked on top, filled the space. Due to the open cracks, windows, and spaces, it was arctic inside.

We didn't talk, drink, eat, or sleep; we just sat, listless from the cold and misery.

The cattle train entered Ahrensburg, a northeastern suburb of Hamburg, on February 10, 1945, one day after Wilfried's second birthday. The trip lasted three weeks, but the journey felt like forever.

Wilfried's ears still ran. Rainer looked terrible.

The train stopped at the station in the city. A German official stepped into our drafty car.

"There's a Red Cross station that way," he said, pointing to the town. "They can help you there."

We got off the train and followed other passengers, trudging through a fresh blanket of snow.

Twenty minutes later, we reached a large, long building.

"Welcome," a nurse said at the door.

We ducked inside, dazed and half-frozen. Refugees swarmed the place, taking up tables and beds. Nurses scurried about, clad in blue and white pinstriped uniforms and white hats. A white band with the symbol of the Red Cross perched on their left arms. In the center of their collared necklines, they wore a circle-shaped pin. The pin had a white background and red cross on the foreground.

One of the nurses approached us and pointed to Rainer. While the baby definitely needed attention, Mutti kept him in her arms.

"I need help for him," she said, nodding toward Wilfried.

"Ah, yes, his ears—he needs to see a doctor," the nurse replied.

"Is there one here?"

"I'm afraid not. But there is a doctor in town. His office is two miles from here. I'll point out the way for you at the door."

"Very well." Mutti nodded.

Then Mutti turned to me. "You'll be safe here."

Overcome with fright at the thought of her leaving, I couldn't speak. This went against her rule to stick together. Furthermore, Mutti was my safety; she symbolized the only way of life I had known.

"The nurses will take care of you, and give you something to eat," she continued.

Before I could answer, she handed Rainer to the nurse. Then she picked up Wilfried and walked out the door.

I stood in the doorframe and watched her leave. I felt lonelier than ever before. Mutti was gone, and Wilfried too. I wondered if I would ever see them again.

CHAPTER FIVE: THE COTTAGE

"Abide with me; fast falls the eventide;
The darkness deepens; Lord with me abide.
When other helpers fail and comforts flee,
Help of the helpless, O abide with me."
—Henry Francis Lyte, 1847[24]

"Your mother will come back soon," Aunt Lydia said, patting my back. She, Oma, and Ruthchen surrounded me. The nurses were tending to Rainer.

There weren't enough beds at the Red Cross station for everyone, so I sat on the floor with the others from our group. A nurse came and washed my face and hands. Then someone gave me milk to drink. I also received *brötchen*. The small, round bread rolls had a hard, crisp crust. Inside, the rolls were rich, dense, and delicious.

Next a nurse dished up a thick stew and served it to me in a bowl.

I gobbled it down. It was the closest thing to a meal I had eaten since we left Schneidemühl.

But my stomach had been empty for too long. Even after I finished, it begged for more.

I sat, lost in my own world, for the next hours. I had already lost track of the daily rhythms of life. Now I became unaware of the minutes ticking by. My thoughts shifted from losing Papa and Opa to realizing Mutti and Wilfried were gone now too.

More tears fell down my cheeks as the world closed around me. Despair set in.

I thought of Mutti and the snow, and wondered where she was as I sat in the Red Cross station. Perhaps she was still trekking through the deep drifts, with snow falling around her. I saw her in my mind, walking away from me as she had just done several hours before. I envisioned the back of her head, ducked down into the wind. Her thick shoulders slowly blended into the snow, and then she disappeared.

On the acreage near Schneidemühl, snow outside meant big bowls of steaming *grießbrei* (cream of wheat) on the table in the warm kitchen of the farmhouse. It meant dazzling snow drifts spread out on the high hills surrounding our house, and white glittery carpets rippling over the nearby forest floor.

It meant sleigh rides into town after a fresh snowfall. Even on cold days, townspeople and shopkeepers bustled about, bundled up to protect themselves from the cold. They attended to business with red noses and cheeks.

* * *

At the beginning of the 20th century, Schneidemühl formed a key city in our region of Germany. Albatros-Flugzeugwerke, a German aircraft manufacturer, opened a plant in Schneidemühl in the early 1900s. During World War I, the factory supplied planes for the German army, producing about 100 aircraft per month.[25]

In 1919, at the end of World War I, many nearby towns transferred from German to Polish control. Schneidemühl, however, remained a part of Germany. The new border between Germany and Poland ran three miles south of Schneidemühl.

The Vienna Convention in 1924 dictated that thousands of German citizens living in Poland would be evicted. The first phase of this eviction process began on August 1, 1925. Within one week 20,000 Germans left Poland. Due to its proximity to the border, most of the evacuees landed in Schneidemühl.[26]

The influx of people caused the city's population to grow, and by the 1930s, it surpassed 40,000 people, Mutti said. In the following years, it turned into a regional center for Nazi administration.

On Sundays, we attended church in Schneidemühl. After the service, we stayed in town for the afternoon and visited with relatives. Two of Papa's sisters lived in town, and we often spent leisurely afternoons with them and their families.

Occasionally, instead of going to church in Schneidemühl, we traveled in the wagon for an hour to the village of Kensau, where Mutti's parents lived. Mutti's mother and father, whom I called Omi and Opa, ran a butcher shop in the town.

* * *

Cowering in the Red Cross station, my mind drifted back to one of my earliest, clearest memories involving Omi and Opa. When I was not yet three years old, Opa suffered from stomach cancer. On a chilly afternoon in January 1943, we received word that he died.

Mutti, who was eight months pregnant with Wilfried at the time, decided to make the trip from Schneidemühl to Kensau for the funeral. She took me along. Papa stayed behind to tend to the farm.

On the day of the funeral, it was frigid outside. Papa hitched up one of the horses from the farm to the open wagon. Mutti and I piled in and Papa bid us a safe trip. The wind slashed at our faces as we set off.

Bundled up, Mutti and I rested against each other during the ride to Kensau. Even with all the wrappings, the wind bit into my cheeks. Soon I lost feeling in them.

The horse led us to the Lutheran church in Kensau for the funeral. Mutti helped me out of the wagon. We walked toward the big building with a steeple reaching high into the sky.

I followed the steeple up, up and further up. It seemed to reach the heavens.

"I wonder if Opa can see the steeple now," I said to Mutti.

She hugged me in reply.

Inside, Mutti and I sat next to Omi. She and Opa had shared more than 35 years together as a married couple.

In pictures from her youth, Omi had had lovely hair. For the funeral, it was pulled back in a no-nonsense bun, the usual style for such occasions. She wore all black. According to the custom, she would wear black for the next year to mourn Opa's death.

The service began. During each song, Mutti's fluid voice carried through the open space inside the church. She knew the songs by heart, and they rolled out of her, filling the interior of the building and then wafting out through the cracks of the windows, a rich contrast to the winter cold. I sat close to her. The big church seemed expansive compared to my small body.

After the service, the pastor led us back into the gusty wind and up a low hill to the cemetery. I stood close to the casket. I peered at the box and knew that underneath the lid, Opa lay in silence.

At the time, my young mind knew nothing of countries, bloodshed, war, or even being hungry. All I knew was that we couldn't come to visit Opa anymore, and I was cold.

My face felt stiff from the chilly air around me. The rest of me, from my neck to my hands, legs, and toes, shivered against the relentless winter day.

Soldiers, clad in dark green uniforms with a red band on their arms, lined up near the casket. Each of them held a rifle.

All was calm, and then boom! Crack! Bang! A smattering of gun shots burst into the sky.

Together with Mutti and the others, I looked up. But there was nothing to see in the sky except a gray, overcast curtain of clouds. So we looked back at the soldiers. They lowered their guns. Then, all eyes returned to the big closed box on the ground.

At the end of the day, Mutti and I climbed back into the wagon and headed home, my toddler figure nestled in her thick arms.

On the way, it was achingly cold. And snowy. As if sweeping in to paint a majestic portrait, white caressed every nook of the landscape. When we arrived home, trails of smoke wafted from the chimney.

It was a welcome sight.

Inside, in the warm kitchen, Papa wrapped me in his arms. Mutti fretted over my cheeks.

"I think you have frostbite," she said.

"Frost—what?"

"Just a mild case, but yes, frostbite. Your cheeks got too cold."

Frostbite or not, it was so good to be home that day! Home, where my favorite playmate and companion—Papa—lived. Home, where all thoughts of cold vanished the moment Mutti fed me spoonfuls of hot soup. Home, where the fire gave off a comfortable glow and heated the rooms. No matter how chilly it got outdoors, it was always warm inside our house.

Tucked in my crib at the end of the day, the last chills left me. Opa was gone, but my world was a safe and sound place. I drifted easily off to sleep, cozy and snug inside my little bed.

My cheeks, however, kept a touch of red in them for long time.

* * *

I sat on the floor of the Red Cross station, crouched down and hugging my knees. I wondered where Omi was. She had been living in Kensau with her youngest child, my Uncle Arnold, when we had fled. I didn't know what happened to them or our other relatives.

I was still deep in thought when someone tugged my shoulder. I looked up.

"Mutti!" I cried, throwing myself at her.

Suddenly, everything felt warmer.

"I saw the doctor, and got medicine for Wilfried."

I didn't hear what else she said; I only thought of how glad I was to have Mutti back.

A nurse carrying a baby approached us. She held the infant for Mutti to see.

Mutti studied the child for a moment and then asked, "Who is that?"

"It's your baby," explained the nurse.

Mutti looked at the baby in disbelief.

"We washed and changed him," the nurse added, gently holding out the baby for Mutti to take.

Mutti stared. Then she carefully touched the garments the infant had on. "But his clothes - " she began.

"Are new and his to keep," finished the nurse, and placed the baby in Mutti's arms.

Rainer smiled and giggled. He was so clean he looked like a different baby.

The nurses had dressed him in a new green outfit, called *strampelhosen*. The knit one-piece was popular for babies to wear at the time. Similar to overalls, it had pants that fit on the legs. Buttons by the shoulders made it easy to get on and off.

Holding Rainer close to her, Mutti turned to Oma. "He looked so nice, I wondered if it was really Rainer," she said.

Then, without warning, she laughed. She laughed and laughed, hugging Rainer again and again.

Partly because of Rainer, and partly due to how happy Mutti was, we all smiled with her. I patted the baby's back. He grinned back. With his light features and rich green outfit, he nearly radiated. I hadn't seen him that good-looking since before we had left Schneidemühl. His head still dipped in, but his eyes were brighter.

Mutti gave Wilfried the medicine he needed. Then she sat and helped him eat a bowl of soup.

By the time Wilfried finished, and Mutti ate, it was evening and time to move on. We wouldn't be able to sleep at the Red Cross station. Some of the workers told us of a place where refugees could sleep that was not far away. So our group walked over to the shelter.

The nearby place consisted of an army barracks which had been turned into sleeping quarters for those on the run, like us. Upon stepping inside, we saw other families of women and children bedding down for the night.

We laid down on an open space. Bits of straw covered the wooden floor; besides that, there were no beds or bedding.

The straw would be plenty for the night. After I lay down, I overheard Oma talking to Mutti.

"While you were at the doctor's office, a nurse came by and told me all the refugees that have been passing through, have gone on to Hamburg," Oma began.

"Not Hamburg," Mutti replied.

"I'm afraid so. And it's still getting bombed, according to the nurses."

"What about here in Ahrensburg? We are just outside of Hamburg."

I peeked up my head and saw Mutti motion to a man who looked like a worker in the barracks.

"Do we need to go somewhere in case of an air raid?" she asked. "I hear they have been bombing Hamburg."

"Nah," he responded. "This is a suburb of Hamburg. If the sirens go off, don't be too scared—we've only had one bomb fall here so far."

He shrugged and bid us good night. Then walked out the door.

The sirens sounded.

We stayed in the barracks. Other families, weary from the war and their travels, stayed too. After a while, quiet fell. The sirens stopped and no bombs fell near us.

Just as I was about to close my eyes for the night, I remembered some of the thoughts that had run through my mind earlier that day, at the Red Cross station.

I crawled over to Mutti quietly, so as not to disturb my brothers.

"What happened to Omi and Uncle Arnold?" I asked.

Mutti had had eight brothers. One of them, Karl, died of pneumonia when he was 11 years old. That left seven brothers in the family. At the start of the Second World War, they were all young men or teenagers living at home. During the following years six of them were called to fight in the war. The one remaining at home, Arnold, was 15 years old at the beginning of 1945. He and Omi were the only ones left in the family in Kensau.

I wondered if Omi and Uncle Arnold were still alive.

Mutti looked at me for a while before answering.

"I don't know," she said finally.

After another pause, she added, "Before things got so bad, we were going to leave the area with them. But then the war came between us, and we each had to flee separately. It all happened so fast, you see."

"Will we ever see them again?" I asked.

Mutti smoothed my hair. "God will take care of them, just as he has taken care of us."

So none of us knew where Mutti's mother and brother were. And there would be no way of knowing in the near future what happened to them.

As I drifted off to sleep, Mutti's singing lingered in my ears:

So nimm denn meine Hände
Und führe mich
Bis an mein selig Ende
Und ewiglich!
Ich mag allein nicht gehen,
Nicht einen Schritt;
Wo du wirst geh'n und stehen,
Da nimm mich mit.

Take Thou my hand,
and lead me o'er life's rough way,
with Heav'nly Manna feed me
from day to day.
Alone my footsteps falter
and straggle wide,
Lord who my life canst alter
be Thou my guide.[27]

The next day was Sunday, February 11, 1945. We took an electric train from Ahrensburg into Hamburg. Other passengers on the train told Mutti the same news Oma had heard the previous day: Air raids regularly targeted Hamburg.

When we entered Hamburg, piles of rubble greeted us. Stark, bombed out buildings stood above the heap of fallen beams, flooring, furniture, and broken bricks.

* * *

Situated on the Elbe River, just under 60 miles from the North Sea, Hamburg was Germany's second largest city, after Berlin. It was also one of the busiest seaports in Europe, and Germany's most important industrial center. It produced warships and U-boats, Germany's war submarines. Oil refineries dotted the area, making it a prime target for the Allies during the war.

In the summer of 1943, in an attack coined Operation Gomorrah, British and American bombers carried out their first joint raid in the war. They targeted Hamburg, and in a tag-team style, with the British flying by night and the Americans in the day, pummeled the place. The bombing started on the night of July 24th, and continued until August 2nd.[28]

On the first night of the bombing, the Allies used "Window," a technique that consisted of dropping paper-backed aluminum foil strips out of the planes to confuse the German radar systems. This resulted in fewer casualties for the Allies, as the Germans found it difficult to track and shoot down the approaching bombers.[29]

Two daytime attacks followed. Then, on the night of July 28, 1943, in just one hour and 12 minutes, British bombers dropped 2,326 tons of bombs on Hamburg. The weather in the area had been hot and humid for days, and a strong wind blew, which fanned the flames. The heat and wind created a fire which swept through the city.[30]

Winds with speeds of greater than 150 miles per hour swept through the fire. These hurricane-level gusts at the center of the storm literally fanned the flames. The heat and drafts caused a burning tornado of fire, standing 1,500 feet high.[31] The term *Feuersturm*, or "firestorm," was used to describe the blaze.

Major-General Kehrl, the Civil Defense chief of Hamburg, reported, "The scenes of terror which took place in the firestorm area are indescribable. Children were torn away from their parents' hands by the force of the hurricane and whirled into the fire. People who thought they had escaped fell down, overcome by the devouring heat, and died in an instant. Refugees had to make their way over the dead and dying. The sick and infirm had to be left behind by the rescuers as they themselves were in danger of burning."[32]

The morning after the terrible night of bombing, the wind subsided and firefighters set up a perimeter. Teenager Traute Koch, 15, recalled the damage: "I carried my little sister and also helped my mother climb over the ruins. Suddenly, I saw tailors' dummies lying around. I said, 'Mummy, no tailors lived here and yet, so many dummies lying around.'" Traute's mother told her not to look too closely. The dummies were corpses.[33]

That same day, Major-General Kehrl ordered all non-essential civilians to leave Hamburg. An estimated one million people fled the city. Another bombing raid took place on July 30th. The final one was on August 2nd.[34]

When Operation Gomorrah ended, half the city was leveled. Between 40,000 and 50,000 people had died. Ten square miles of the city were left in rubble, and more than one million Hamburg residents were homeless.[35]

The Allies continued to bomb Hamburg during the following years. The damage from the later attacks, however, paled in comparison to that of the Gomorrah operation.

* * *

For refugees like us, from the East, there were few other places to go. Still, Hamburg was considered to be better than the alternative: certain misery and probable death from the advancing Red Army.

The day Mutti, the others, and I arrived in Hamburg, all was still. No sirens sounded, and not a single bomb fell. In the midst of a ghastly landscape, full of debris from destroyed buildings and charred neighborhoods, we rode in silence through the seaport city.

Similar to the other villages we had journeyed through, Hamburg had a system to accommodate incoming refugees. In the city, officials gave Mutti an address in Harksheide, a northern suburb. They directed us to a different train to get there.

Off we went. Oma, Aunt Lydia, and Ruthchen split off to go to a different place as directed by the city officials.

We arrived at the address, and found a large home. Mutti knocked and no one answered.

She tried the doorbell with no luck. She even attempted to turn the knob, but it was locked. In fact, the whole place looked deserted.

It started to rain. Falling as a mist, the tiny drops permeated through our layers of clothing.

We stood cold, wet, and lonely on the street. I looked up at Mutti and saw tears, in addition to raindrops, cascade down her cheeks.

Mutti rarely shed even half a tear, and the change startled me. Perhaps the journey wore her out, or she was simply cold. Whatever the reasoning, her distraught face made her easily recognizable to those passing by as someone in need.

Not much time had passed when a man, driving past with a horse and wagon, spotted our sorry crew. He slowed down and pulled alongside us,

"Are you looking for shelter?" he asked.

"Yes, we're from the east, and they directed us here," Mutti explained, pointing to the empty-looking place where no one answered.

"You can come with me," the man offered. "I have a small home. It's so small my family isn't required to take in refugees. But you're welcome."

We went with him, and for two nights we slept on the living room floor of his house. The place was not well heated, and I shivered at night.

In the new place, Rainer took a turn for the worse. His cleaning up from the Red Cross seemed to wear off. His head caved even more and his eyes dulled.

One morning, Mutti pulled out the baptismal gown from our luggage. She put it on Rainer.

"Mutti, what are you doing?" I asked.

"If he dies, I want him dressed this way," she replied.

"Didn't he already get baptized?"

"Yes, but I want him to go heaven like this, if it is the Lord's will."

Two nights later, officials assigned us to a new place. It consisted of a double room divided by French doors. We stayed in an area on one side of the doors; the family that owned the place lived in the other area. With this setup, each family had one section to stay in, and the set of French doors helped separate the two spots.

* * *

During our first night in the new place, on February 13, 1945, the Allies bombed the city of Dresden, about 235 miles southeast of Hamburg. The air raids by heavy bombers of the RAF and the United States Army Air Forces continued until February 15, 1945. During the attacks, planes dropped more than 3,400 tons of explosives.

The city's population had increased before the raid, as many refugees fleeing from the advancing Russians landed in Dresden. The actual death toll remained unknown, but was estimated to be between 35,000 and 135,000 people. A resulting firestorm raged through Dresden, destroying more than eight square miles of the city.[36]

While the Dresden attack was devastating, it was far away from us. The Lord's protecting hand once again shielded us from harm and danger.

* * *

During our time in one room of the place with the French doors, Mutti looked for food, and searched for help for Rainer. She found a bit of food, but nothing for Rainer.

One day, Oma came over to watch us. Mutti wanted to look for wood to burn in the woodstove. She borrowed a hand wagon from a neighbor and set off.

When she returned, the cart was full of sticks and branches.

"Where did you get all of this?" I asked as she emptied the wagon.

"There's a forest near here," she explained. Then she put some of the bits of wood in the stove to warm our area.

When we had been in the place with the French doors for about two weeks, the people there complained the space was too small for all of us to share. So Mutti went to see about getting a different room.

This time, officials assigned us to a tiny garden house, also located north of Hamburg in Harksheide. The morning we headed there, a kind man offered to take us in his wagon. When we reached the correct street, he let us out of the cart and his horse pulled away.

We walked until we reached the edge of town. There, across the street from a dirt field, sat our next makeshift home: a small cottage. It was located along a row of small houses.

There was a fence around the cottage, and a gate that opened to a stone walkway. The path led past trees and to the residence. The place was set back from the street. Large scruffy bushes partially hid the cottage from view.

I wrapped my fingers around the rungs of the tall fence and peered in. I saw a front door, a little roof that covered the place and stuck out over the entryway, and a window.

But we couldn't get in. A large padlock held the gate shut.

"Hello? Hello? Anyone home?" called Mutti. She wrapped on the fence.

No one came.

I looked up at the big, looming gate. It was so massive, and the padlock so large, that I thought it must be guarding gold inside.

We remained outside. A gray blanket of sky covered us. With nowhere to turn, and no one in sight, we sat down on the dirt road to wait.

The frigid air ate into my bones. I huddled together with Mutti and my brothers for warmth in front of the gate.

This part of the Hamburg area seemed mostly intact. As I peeked out from our pile, I didn't see heaps of rubble strewn on the road and sidewalk like I had observed in sections closer to the center.

As the minutes ticked on, I felt more and more miserable. I was cold, hungry, and had no idea what was coming next. The road remained empty of people passing by. I worried Mutti might cry again.

But she didn't. She was back to her usual self, directing us through each step of our journey. Perhaps she thought someone would come by that could help, or maybe she wanted some time to think of what to do next.

Before she could make any moves, however, Rainer started to cry. She pulled out a bottle for him.

As we sat, my whole face began to sting. Ever since the trip to Opa's funeral, my cheeks had chilled more easily and stayed red longer. Now they burned.

Rainer refused the bottle. The milk was too chilled to drink. He kept crying in Mutti's arms.

Late in the afternoon, a girl of about 10 years old approached us. She stopped several feet away from Mutti and studied our mussed, filthy clothes. Then she watched Mutti, with Rainer on her lap, try once more to have him drink from the cold bottle.

After several minutes, the girl turned and walked away. She disappeared inside a house next to the cottage. Minutes later, she came back.

"My mother says to come in," she said, motioning to the home she had just exited.

She led us to the house neighboring the cottage. It was a nice, brick place with a basement. When we entered, a motherly-looking woman met us.

"I'm Mrs. Jühls, now hand me the bottle and won't you sit down," she said, smiling. She heated the bottle and gave us some bread. The warmth of the home, the food, and the woman's kindness helped me thaw.

Mrs. Jühls had dark brown hair pulled into a bun, and bore the harsh features of someone who had gone through difficult times.

"Two sons of mine are in the war," she began. "My husband was in the war too."

Then she paused. "But he died in 1944, in September."

The girl put her hand on the woman's shoulder.

"And this is my daughter, Hilde," Mrs. Jühls said. "She is still with me."

Hilde had blondish hair and pigtails, like me.

Since we couldn't get into the cottage, Mrs. Jühls insisted we stay with her. She led us to her basement, and showed us beds there.

Thankful to be out of the cold, and relieved to have someone reach out and welcome us in, we rested on the beds.

Mrs. Jühls said she would contact the man who owned the cottage.

After two days, he came and unlocked the place for us.

The owner of the cottage explained that he had a restaurant in Hamburg, and did not use his Harksheide place as a day-to-day residence. It was more of a getaway for him, and thus was rustic and very basic. Due to the government's regulations, he was required to lend it to refugees.

The cottage consisted of one single room. To the left of the front door was a bed. A kitchenette was straight back from the entrance. To the right, in a more open area, lay a second bed and also a table and chairs set.

Water dripped onto the second bed. I followed the drops up and saw a long crack in the ceiling. Icicles hung along the crack and dangled over the bed.

A small, three-burner wood stove sat in the kitchenette area. A pipe ran from the stove to the ceiling, serving as a vent. There was a tiny pile of wood outside on the porch where we had entered. Mutti filled the stove with wood and started a fire to warm us up.

We stayed in the cottage for a day, and then a week. Another week passed and still we remained there.

A path led from the cottage to a low fence that separated our yard from the Jühls's property. Whenever an air raid siren sounded, we ran out of the cottage, down the path, and over the fence. Then we crossed the driveway and went to a door in the back of the house. This door led to the basement of the Jühls's home.

Mrs. Jühls never locked the door. She kept it open for us, so we could come and go as needed. When we arrived in the basement, Mrs. Jühls and Hilde were always already there, waiting. We crouched with them and endured the raids.

As before, I stayed under Mutti's arms to feel protected. She sang hymns as the bombs fell.

The home of Mrs. Jühls lay south of the cottage. If we were to walk past her home, we would head in the direction of Hamburg. To the north lay more of the town of Harksheide and beyond that, the countryside.

The fence separating our property from that of the Jühls's was made of a thin wire. After many crossings, the wire drooped. The trampled slouch in it made it easier for us to hop across during an air raid and come back when it was over.

Whenever we crossed, Mutti carried Rainer in her arms. Wilfried ran alongside her, and I stayed in front of them, leading the way. Rainer and Wilfried usually cried during the trek; sometimes I had tears too.

In the basement, if a bomb hit anywhere close to the Jühls's home, we would have very little protection. Still, being a little lower in the ground and hidden from objects that might be blowing around in the blast made us feel more secure.

And sometimes we crossed the fence for other reasons. Mrs. Jühls let us wash in her basement. Since the cottage didn't have any place to bathe, we occasionally went over there to get cleaned up.

Unlike some of the other hosts we had stayed with during our flight from Schneidemühl, Mrs. Jühls was never cross. She always showed us warm hospitality and I felt welcome in her home.

Bombs fell frequently. We crouched for hours in the basement next door, quietly waiting to see if the moments spent there would be our last. As always, Mutti sang on: "Angels spread thy wings upon us…"

Whenever the all-clear signal sounded, we headed out of the basement and – always at a much slower pace – back to our residence.

Shortly after we moved into the cottage, Mrs. Jühls lent Mutti her hand wagon. She offered to watch Wilfried, Rainer, and me while Mutti gathered wood. Mutti set off, pulling the wagon behind her.

When she returned, the wagon brimmed with sticks and small bits of wood.

"Where did you get these?" I asked, helping carry pieces to the stove.

"I walked to the end of our street," she explained. "After several blocks, it slopes down and I came to a meadow."

"Like the one by our farm?"

"Yes, but this one has more trees. And behind it, there is a small wooded part. I collected these sticks there. It's not far, I'll take you some time."

Our new neighbor and friend Mrs. Jühls often gave us food to eat. But even with her help and kindness, my stomach ached. It always wanted more.

* * *

A rationing system was in place in Harksheide when we arrived in the spring of 1945. Everyone got little booklets through the program. Pages of stamps filled the inside of these books. The stamps represented food and other supplies, like butter, lard, bread, sugar, and clothes. Sugar and clothes were the hardest of these to find and thus, the most valuable.

While the stamps contained the promise of food and goods, things did not always work out that way. Not everything on the stamps was available. Many times the butcher had no meat, the creamery had no milk, or the bakery had no bread. Food was scarce for everyone, and we lived from one day to the next, on a constant hunt for more to eat.

While at the beginning of the war Germans had consumed a healthy average of 2,570 calories a day, by 1945 this had fallen to slightly more than 1,400 calories a day.

"Hunger knocks on every door," wrote one German housewife in February 1945. "New ration cards are to last for five weeks instead of four, and no one knows if they will be issued at all. We count out potatoes every day, five small ones each, and bread is becoming more scarce. We are growing thinner and thinner, colder and colder and more and more ravenous."[37]

* * *

Sometimes Mutti found *kartoffeln*, or potatoes. To make them stretch, she chopped the potatoes, cooked them, and then served the dish as a soup, keeping the broth with the potatoes.

For meal times, we usually sat at the table in the cottage to eat. But the activity of eating was far from fulfilling, and sometimes, when I finished and was still hungry, I felt angry.

One day Mutti made potato soup. After she had chopped and cooked the potatoes, she distributed the meal to us. When she served me a bowl of soup, I looked down at it, discouraged. My bowl wasn't even half full.

The more I looked, the scanter the bowl's fillings appeared. I couldn't hold back anymore.

"*Mutti du hast so viel und ich habe nichts*," I told her, meaning "you have so much and I don't have anything." I was convinced my portions were so small because Mutti was purposely holding some of the food back.

Mutti tried to explain. "You have the potatoes and I have just the liquid," she pointed out.

I inspected her bowl, then grabbed her spoon and stirred it through the bowl's contents, searching for chunks of potatoes.

But Mutti was right. Her bowl only held watered down broth. While I thought I had been short-changed, Mutti had actually given me a larger portion of potatoes. I hung my head in shame.

Sometimes we dined on small bowls of porridge or cream of wheat.

While other food items dwindled, turnips didn't. In our area of Hamburg, the turnips Mutti found were round—almost like a small apple—with leaves. Deep red and white markings traced the outside. The inside was pure white.

To prepare the turnips, Mutti peeled them. Then she cut off the stalks attached to them, quartered them, and cooked the pieces.

Turnips turned into a mainstay in our diet. We ate turnips so often that Mutti started to think of creative ways to prepare them with our thin resources. Sometimes she made a soup with turnips, cooking them and serving the soft chunks in broth, as she did with potatoes. Other times she boiled the turnips, and then mashed them up. If she had a little milk, seasoning, or sugar, she added that too. We even ate them raw, like apples.

Serving turnips at the dinner table was not something that had always been done in Germany. In fact, prior to World War I, Germans used turnips only for animal feed. When food shortages hit during the First World War, the root vegetable was introduced as food to fill people's stomachs.

Turnips appeared at the dinner table scene again during World War II. Many people found the taste of them to be bitter—appalling, even. For me, though, they filled my stomach and helped it not hurt so much.

In March 1945, as Easter approached, the Hamburg area continued to get hit with bombs. When Good Friday came, on March 30, 1945, we heard the sirens go off yet again. Soon a series of deep blasts resonated in the distance.

I ran out of the cottage and jumped over the fence. Mutti and my brothers followed close behind. We arrived in Mrs. Jühls's basement with no time to spare.

As I sat there, in the dark of the underground room, next to Mutti, I cried softly. Mrs. Jühls and Hilde sat next to us.

Mutti turned to Mrs. Jühls. "Who is it this time?"

"Probably the Americans. They always bomb in the day; the British prefer the night skies."

"How can the Americans bomb on Good Friday?" I asked. "We didn't do anything against them!"

"I don't know why," Mutti answered. She squeezed my shoulder. "We will be okay. The angels are with us. Look how they have watched over us so far, and they will not stop now. God is always looking after us, you'll see."

The raid ended and we returned home, unharmed.

When Easter week ended, so did our stays in Mrs. Jühls's basement during air raids. At that point, Mutti decided to stay in the cottage, rather than going over to the neighbor's house for every bomb threat. There were bomb shelters in the city of Hamburg, but none were close enough to run to for safety from the cottage. In reality, our makeshift home provided about the same amount of protection as Mrs. Jühls's basement.

In a way, it was more comfortable to stay in the cottage. Mutti remained confident that God was in charge. During quiet nights, Mutti, Wilfried, and I slept in the two beds, and Rainer slept in the baby carriage. If a siren went off, we all grouped on one bed with Mutti. She always kept her clothes on throughout the night, in case we had to dash out of the cottage. Then, with us in her lap and next to her, she told us Bible stories and prayed with us.

One time when the sirens blared and planes buzzed overhead, Mutti went out of the cottage and on to the porch. I trotted at her heels.

I followed her gaze into the night sky. The planes flew right over the city. The whole sky over Hamburg was lit up like a Christmas tree. It was the most beautiful and terrifying scene all at once.

Shortly after, we ducked inside.

How far we were from food, and the farm, and life as we had known it.

Despite my bouts of anger about food, I looked to Mutti for security. I trusted her words that God knew where we were and had a plan for us.

We grew closer as a family, forging a solid bond under God's ultimate protection, even as my stomach grew hungrier.

CHAPTER SIX: PEACETIME

"Take Thou my heart and hide it in folds of grace.
Though pain or woe betide it to know Thy face
Draw, Lord, of Thy good pleasure Thy child to Thee,
And grant me faith's full measure though naught I see."
—Julie Katharina von Hausmann, 1862[38]

At the cottage in Harksheide, a routine of survival began. Each day the challenge of finding food consumed Mutti. She took her rations book with stamps from the government and went to the nearby shops to see if they had supplies. She also walked outside of town, to farms, and begged for vegetables.

She found enough to improve Rainer's condition, but he remained weak. Oma, Aunt Lydia, and Ruthchen lived close to the cottage, and we saw them on occasion. For the most part, however, we faced the air raids and food shortages on our own.

With Mutti busy scrounging for meals and caring for Rainer, Wilfried and I entertained ourselves. We played in the dirt road by our home, and explored the nearby fields. Our area in Harksheide didn't bear the same signs of all-out destruction as much of Hamburg. In fact, when the sirens didn't blast, the streets were quiet and—compared to the leaky cottage—inviting.

One day Wilfried and I ventured into the dirt field on the other side of the street from the cottage. Wilfried ran ahead of me. I watched his back as he raced into the field. Suddenly he came to a fast stop, and then jumped up and down. He pointed at something beyond where I could see.

"Elfi, come look!" he called.

I ran up to him, and followed his waving hand.

A large sunken area lay before us. It was fascinating—full of scrap metal and dipping down deep into the ground. Holding Wilfried's hand, I helped him totter down a slope of dirt.

The sunken pit stretched on and on. The lower floor of it was uneven. After a few steps, a sharp pain struck one of my legs. I looked down; my leg had scraped against a sharp metal object. Blood trickled out.

Eager to continue exploring, I ignored the blood running from the cut and led on. Wilfried and I came across more pieces of metal. Many of them were small, jagged bits, and stood out against the rock and soil. Other pieces were round and sturdy, almost like a ball. Still others were large and looming. I looked at these malformed and twisted objects, but didn't touch them.

I tried to help Wilfried avoid the metal, but soon the scrap cut his legs too. Curious, we went further in, losing track of time.

When we finally returned to the cottage and Mutti that day, she took a long look at each of us.

"Where were you?" she asked finally.

I glanced at my legs. I had forgotten about the scrapes during our adventure, but now in the calm of home, I looked at the dried blood dotting my limbs and Wilfried's too.

"We found a pit full of metal," I explained.

"That's not a pit; that's a bomb crater," Mutti replied.

"But I didn't see any bombs fall there."

"No, a bomb landed there and formed the pit before we arrived. Mrs. Jühls told me about it."

And before I could ask more questions, Mutti set about cleaning our soiled hands and tending to our wounds.

For Wilfried and me, the bomb crater turned into a sort of war-time playground. After our initial visit, we frequently headed back to search the pit. We meandered through the broken metal pieces carefully. And if a siren sounded, we ran up the crater's sides and scurried home.

Somehow during that time, spring started peeking through. It chased away the dripping icicles in the cottage and brought a bit of warmth to dry out the winter damp. Amidst the gray rubble, a scattering of yellow tulips bloomed. Small flowers sprung up among the metal in the bomb crater. The linden trees, great and tall, on our street began to fill out with buds. Specks of vibrant green dotted their expansive branches.

As the flowers bloomed, and the leaves on the trees grew, my spirits lifted. God had kept us safe and given us spring too.

Even so, the air raids continued. The risk that our cottage could turn into a crater in an instant remained. And yet, Mutti focused on each day as it came, on getting things to eat, and keeping us all alive.

We lived as little dots on a map in Germany. How our own particular journey would end—and if we would survive the war—we didn't know. I could see in Mutti's eyes that she didn't have the answers. Yet she faced the realities of war with quiet courage, and only occasionally confided in me. When she did speak of the danger, it was to say she was grateful Wilfried and Rainer would probably not remember the horrific situations we were going through—that is, if we lived to tell about them.

* * *

Between bombs falling and armies advancing, many citizens in our area, and other parts of Germany, despaired. For some, the war became a heavy, hopeless veil. It smothered any vision they may have had, at one point, for a brighter future. The weight overwhelmed them; the destruction penetrated their inner core.

Suicides in Germany came in three waves during 1945. The first surge began in January of that year in the eastern territories of Germany. These self-murders coincided with the arrival of the Russian army in some places. In others, suicides took place when citizens knew the Red Army was approaching.

In early 1945, a mass suicide occurred in Schönlanke, a village less than 15 miles from Schneidemühl. As the Red Army took over the area, around 500 citizens killed themselves. A female clerk of the city council claimed, "Out of fear of these animals from the east, many Schönlankers ended their lives. Whole families were wiped out in this way…"[39]

On February 5, 1945, a 71-year-old pensioner named Otto V. was found gassed to death in his apartment in Fuhlsbüttel, a suburb of Hamburg. His lodger informed the police that Otto V. had believed "the Russians would come here," in which case "he did not want to live." The criminal police added, "Supposedly, V. could not adjust himself to the situation, since he was afraid of the Russians conquering [Hamburg]."[40]

Franz Karl H., from Zorndorf, located in the middle of the country, explained what happened to his daughter when the Russians invaded their village on February 12, 1945: "As a result of the events taking place then, our daughter E. became so mentally exhausted that she killed her two daughters, aged one and a half and five years, and then drowned herself."[41]

The second wave of suicides happened in April and May 1945. During this sweep, many Nazi officials took their lives. Furthermore, authorities in some places handed out cyanide pills to the local population. Pharmacies stocked poison for those who wanted it. Other citizens opted for razors.

Terror shook the area when the Russians arrived in Neubrandenburg. This was one of the cities we had stopped at on our trek from Schneidemühl to Hamburg. The Red Army burned nearly 80 percent of the section known as the old town to the ground. During that time, about 600 people committed suicide.[42]

The fear of the advancing Russians was enough to break the willpower of many.

So was hunger. A diet severely lacking in calories made it difficult for individuals to think straight.

Yet taking our own lives, or giving up, was out of the question for Mutti. Rather than reaching for pills or poison, Mutti clung to the Bible she had brought from Schneidemühl. During the day, when there was a spare moment, she read passages from the book to us.

"The Lord watches over you," she read from Psalm 121. "The Lord will keep you from all harm—he will watch over your life."

Another time she opened to Romans and read, "In all things God works for the good of those who love him."

"God will take care of our family," she said, closing the Bible. "We left the acreage for a reason. Even though we don't know why, God does."

And she left the logic, as well as the future, to Him.

* * *

Our living setup continued on for the next weeks, with Mutti going to the creamery to look for milk, the bakery for bread, and the farmers for vegetables, and me thinking of how hungry I was. Once in a while we had milk or bread, but not often. Our diet consisted mostly of potatoes and turnips. Mutti prepared simple meals with what she found.

Food consumed my thoughts day and night. In our area, things were particularly rough. Hamburg's influx of refugees, coupled with a shortage of farms nearby, made sustenance notably scarce.

As April wore on, we went with Mutti to see Mrs. Jühls and listen to the news on the radio at her home. All reports indicated Germany was plummeting.

The Russian army continued to advance into the country from the east, and the Americans, British, and French moved in from the west. By the end of the month, the Red Army had surrounded Berlin. Soon the capital of Germany was cut off from the rest of the country.

During the spring of 1945, Adolf Hitler spent his days in an underground bunker in Berlin. Sensing the reality of defeat, he took his own life on April 30, 1945.[43]

Three days later, on May 3, 1945, Hamburg surrendered.

The city fell to the hands of the British after very little fighting.

In reality, the years of air raids had already defeated Hamburg.

Several days after Hamburg fell to the British, Mutti dropped the two boys off with Mrs. Jühls. Then she and I walked down the road.

Mutti didn't tell me what we were going to do, and I didn't ask. Together, we walked for some time. When we reached a train leading to the heart of Hamburg, we got on.

Perhaps Mutti wanted to observe the city, to take in any changes now that it had surrendered, and see what our new reality was. If that was the case, she wasn't alone. Other people were out and about too. Many looked around in silence, keeping their thoughts to themselves. The mass had sorrowful eyes.

We walked down the sidewalk of a large, main road. Caved-in buildings lined the streets. They swallowed any noise coming from the footsteps of those moving about. We moved through a city of tombs.

As we neared an intersection, a loud rumbling overtook the hushed atmosphere of the city. Soon the whirring grew, and a crunching followed.

I grabbed Mutti and cried, "Bombs!"

"It can't be," she replied. "Hamburg has surrendered."

Still, we stopped in our tracks on the sidewalk.

Before long, we saw the source of the loud noise. A tank appeared down the road from us. More followed. Soon a line of tanks rolled down the street, moving directly toward us.

I stayed next to Mutti, rooted to the sidewalk and scared sick. Mutti remained calm, her mouth in a straight line and shoulders stiff. We stood in silence, waiting.

Other people stopped their activities as well. They stayed on the sidewalks, forming a line as if taking in a local parade.

The tanks drew closer. Soldiers, clothed in green army uniforms, sat on top of the immense machines. I had never seen the type of uniform they wore before.

Suddenly one of the tanks was right at my side. Two soldiers perched on top of the vehicle. I craned my neck to see them.

"Mutti, these are not German soldiers."

"No, they are British."

Another tank rolled past. This time, the soldiers on top smiled and waved.

I continued to stare, wondering what their intentions were.

This went on for some time. Tanks rolled by and we watched. Mutti placed her hand on my shoulder.

After the first set of tanks passed, another line of tanks approached. The soldiers on these tanks appeared to be throwing things. I cowered into Mutti.

Glancing out, I spotted onlookers picking up the items that fell. Smiles began popping up along the dreary street.

"What are they throwing?" I asked Mutti.

She didn't answer right away. But when a tank rolled by, and a soldier tossed an object that landed near Mutti's feet, the answer was evident. "Chocolate bars," she said, and scooped up the treat.

Another tank came our way. One of the soldiers on it leaned in my direction. He held out his hand and gently lobbed a chocolate bar right at me.

I stretched out my arms and caught it in both hands.

I drew my clasped hands to my chest. Then I opened them.

There, wrapped in a lovely dark wrapper, was a beautiful Hershey's chocolate.

Suddenly, things were starting to look better.

I looked up, and the soldier grinned and waved. I smiled and waved back with one hand. In the other hand, I gripped the chocolate.

More tanks rolled by, all carrying British soldiers. None of them seemed angry or mean at all.

Mutti remained reserved as they passed us. I, on the other hand, saw their coming as a big relief. All at once, a sensation I hadn't felt in ages—perhaps peace—wafted in the air. The soldiers were so friendly. Surely those who tossed out chocolate bars would know where to get more food.

I ate my chocolate, but Mutti saved her candy bar for Wilfried. I walked home with a lighter step. Even Mutti seemed pleased when we relayed to Mrs. Jühls how we saw tanks pass through Hamburg.

One week after Hitler committed suicide, and days after Hamburg fell to the Allies, Germany surrendered.

The ending of the war on May 7, 1945, triggered the final wave of suicides. Rather than face the consequences headed their way, Nazi officials killed themselves. Others in Germany, unable or unwilling to face the Allies taking over their areas, also took their own lives.

The surrender of Germany brought a significant change to Harksheide. No planes buzzed over the cottage. The sirens no longer wailed during the day, or in the middle of the night. Bombs didn't burst and light up the evening sky like a Christmas tree, and I no longer spent hours waiting, leaning on Mutti, listening for the all-clear siren to ring out.

The stillness woke me up at night. It also gave me, and Mutti, time to think about Papa.

In the months since Papa left for the war, we hadn't heard a single word from him. Not one letter or message. Now that the fighting was over, we wondered what had happened—or would happen—to him.

We also hadn't received word from Mutti's brothers. Six of her seven brothers had fought in the war. And we didn't know what happened to Omi and Mutti's youngest brother, Arnold.

Uncle Willie, Ruthchen's father, was also missing. He left before Papa to serve in the war. And we had no idea what had become of Opa, who had taken us to the train station in Schneidemühl and then returned to the acreage to look after the animals and wait for the Russians.

At the cottage, besides the missing people, I wondered many things. What would become of us? Where would we go, and how would Papa, if he were still alive, find us? What about the others? What had happened to our home and farm back in Schneidemühl? A thousand questions hung in the air.

The day Germany surrendered, and the days and weeks that followed, came and went. Besides getting used to the peace and quiet enveloping Harksheide, we carried on as before. Mutti kept searching for food during the day and taking care of us.

Coinciding with the war's ending in Germany, the Allies divided the country into four sections. Different powers controlled each of the zones. Hamburg, along with the northwestern section of the country, fell under the British zone. The French oversaw the southwest region. The Americans occupied the southeastern section of Germany, and Russia took over northeastern Germany.

Hamburg and other cities lay in ruin. Farmland had been lost during the war, and farms ran short of workers. Furthermore, Britain faced its own food shortages at home. There was no quick solution to help the food insufficiencies in our area.

So under the new setup, food rations continued.

Ration cards only provided limited amounts of food. Since she had a certain number of stamps for bread and milk for our family, Mutti often looked for ways to get more. One of the strategies she used for this was to exchange her coffee stamps with others. Mutti loved coffee, but she placed more value on having something to eat on the table for us children, so she traded her coffee stamps for bread or milk stamps.

May turned to June. We kept living day to day. There was still no sign of Papa.

Oma, Aunt Lydia, and Ruthchen had, like us, made it through the war. When we saw them, the adults pondered the circumstances of the rest of the family. Where were they? Were we the only ones left? There was no way to know. The conversation always ended with placing the next events in God's hands.

Sunday, June 17, 1945, began as the days before.

But in the evening, there was a knock on the door.

I followed Mutti to the door.

She opened it, and stood face to face with Omi, Mutti's mother.

Scarcely able to speak, we swept her inside and helped her sit down. I sat next to her.

The last time I had laid eyes on Omi, her short silver hair had been nicely styled in waves. Now it was tousled every which way. Deep lines cut into her skin under her eyes.

Omi smiled. She looked at me, Rainer, Wilfried and Mutti. Then she asked the question that was on everyone's mind.

"Where are my boys?"

I looked from Omi to Mutti and back again. Mutti shifted her gaze from her mother to the door and back.

"I don't know," she said at last. "I don't know where anybody is. How did you find us?"

"Through the Red Cross, bring me something to drink and I will tell you all about it."

We listened closely as she recounted her own tale of fleeing from the Russians.

By January 1945, Omi and her youngest son Arnold were the only ones left at their place in Kensau, Germany.

When they heard the Russians were coming, Omi knew there wasn't much time. She also feared if Nazi officials saw Uncle Arnold, who was 15 years old, they would force him to join the army.

So Omi did the only thing she could think of—she dressed her son in girls' clothing. She hoped the disguise would protect him from the front lines.

The two of them fled in a wagon pulled by their horse, traveling south and west. The route took them to the Harz Mountains, an area of high hills and dark forests. One of Omi's relatives, a farmer, lived there.

The Harz Mountains form the highest mountain range in Germany. Located south of Hamburg, in the middle of the country, the peaks stretch out 68 miles from east to west, and 22 miles from north to south. The tallest peak, Brocken, rises 3,743 feet above sea level.[44]

While the mountain peaks are not overly tall, they stand out above the surrounding terrain. On the northern edge of the mountain range, the land elevation is 787 feet above sea level. Along the southern perimeter, the land measures 886 feet above sea level.[45]

Omi and Arnold fled through this area, until they reached the relative's farm. They stayed there, tucked away in the mountains, until the war ended.

The route Omi and Uncle Arnold had taken led them through an area south of the path we had traveled on during our own flight. For this reason, we hadn't seen each other, even though we both had fled from our homes around the same time.

Of course, during the trip Omi and Uncle Arnold remained above ground. Little did they know that underground, near the southern section of the mountain range, stretched a concentration camp. Situated north of the town of Nordhausen, the workers produced rockets for Germany. The camp, known as Dora-Mittelbau, held more than 60,000 slave laborers between 1943 and 1945. Many were tortured, emaciated, and left to die. In all, some 20,000 died at the camp during the war.[46]

Oblivious to this, after finding shelter, Omi revealed that Uncle Arnold was indeed her son, and not a girl traveling with her. Uncle Arnold began to help on the farm. When the war ended, he continued working on the farm. Omi, for her part, came in search of us. With the help of the Red Cross, she found our address.

What a thrill to have Omi with us! Mutti and Omi chattered away, catching up on all that had happened since we fled from eastern Germany.

Around 10 o'clock in the evening, as Mutti fixed the beds for the night, another knock sounded at the cottage door. Omi opened the door.

Moments later she gasped.

Mutti ran to the door. I trailed at her heels.

Papa stood in the doorway, looking down at me.

Then he picked me up and gave me a long hug.

"I can't believe it," Mutti said. "Two home in one night."

That night, the cottage filled with laughter. It spilled out of Mutti and Papa and bounced off the walls. I thought they would never stop smiling.

I fell asleep to the sounds of Mutti and Papa's voices. When I woke up the next morning, they were still talking.

Later that same morning, Mrs. Jühls arrived at the cottage door. "I never heard so much laughter as I did last night," she said, beaming. "I am so happy for all of you."

Papa filled us in with the details of what had happened to him during his time as a soldier. "After I had been called to fight," he began, "I waited three weeks for a uniform. When I finally got one, I realized I was lucky. Many of the others with me in the *Volkssturm* did not receive one."

I crawled onto his lap and kept listening.

"I went with my unit to fight the Russians. Every time we faced a battle, we fled. The Red Army was too much for a unit made of working men and boys. At one point, some other soldiers and myself were in a village occupied by the Russians. We knew the Americans controlled a neighboring village, so we looked for an opportunity to get away and then hustled over to the American side. I was put in an American prison camp, and stayed there until I was transferred to one overseen by Britain. I stayed there, in an English camp, until the war ended. Once I got out, I went to the Red Cross. They helped me locate you all."

I touched the wedding band on Papa's finger.

"Look at that," he said. "When I was in the American camp, some American soldiers wanted this. I refused, and they never did ask for it again. I'm so thankful for this wedding band—and to be alive," he said, pulling me into his arms.

We hadn't gone to church during our weeks on the run in Germany. During the time we lived in Harksheide before the war ended, and even in the weeks after it was over, we didn't go anywhere to worship. Everything—from the churches themselves to the transportation systems we needed to take to get to church—had been affected by the bombs. The city was full of rubble and debris that needed to be cleaned up. This made it difficult to get to church, and some places didn't hold worship at all, as they were still recovering from the war.

Even though we didn't physically go into a church building, Mutti flamed our faith at home. She told us stories and read from the Bible. She taught us how God had rescued his people, the Israelites, from Egypt. He took them away from a place where they had to be slaves, and even made a sea open up so they could cross the water and be free.

She told us of how Jesus came to die on the cross and take away our sins. She said he was now in heaven, caring for us each and every day.

Living as refugees meant the days were hard, and often long. Just as she had sung in Schneidemühl before the war, and as she had comforted us with music during the air raids, Mutti again took up singing. I helped her with the wash and listened to her voice:

Weil ich Jesu Schäflein bin,
freu' ich mich nur immerhin
über meinen guten Hirten,
der mich wohl weiß zu bewirten,
der mich liebet, der mich kennt
und bei meinem Namen nennt.[47]

I am Jesus' little lamb,
Ever glad at heart I am;
For my Shepherd gently guides me,
Knows my need and well provides me,
Loves me every day the same,
Even calls me by my name.

Like the budding, growing linden trees standing on the street outside of the cottage, we had survived thus far. We too would mend.

CHAPTER SEVEN: OUR DAILY BREAD

"If thou but suffer God to guide thee,
and hope in him through all thy ways,
he'll give thee strength, whate'er betide thee,
and bear thee through the evil days.
Who trusts in God's unchanging love
builds on the rock that naught can move."
—Georg Neumark, 1641[48]

Papa was back, and things had changed.

There would be no more river swims together. The sunny summer days on the acreage, filled with animals and discovery while Papa worked, were in the past.

But in Harksheide, when I showed up at his knee, Papa always carved out time for me. I told him all about our train rides. I detailed how awful Wilfried's sick ears looked, and Rainer's odd-looking, sunken head. I raved about our new play area in the nearby bomb crater.

Papa listened to it all. In fact, Papa's quiet demeanor balanced well with Mutti and Omi's ongoing chatter. Mutti had been thrilled since the two arrived, and talked at length about food and family. The cottage felt full with their presence. A sort of happiness, running deeper than the delight the chocolate bar from the British had brought, spread through our home.

Yet it was a subdued joy. We still didn't know the fate of many of our other relatives. They could have been dead for months already, or alive in a place unknown to us. We had no way of finding out. The only option available—as before—was to wait.

In addition to lending me his ear and gentle spirit, Papa tackled jobs around the cottage. One of his first tasks was to gather burning material for Mutti. To do so, he looked for *torf*, or peat. Made of partly decomposed plant material, and found in wet areas such as bogs, it could be cut from the ground. When formed into pieces and dried, the peat turned into logs for fuel.

Glashütte, a neighboring village of Harksheide, had a history of peat harvesting. For years, peat had been cultivated in that area, and then sold as fuel to bakeries or other places in Hamburg.[49]

Papa set out early in the mornings to harvest peat. He cut, and cut, and cut through the soil. He lifted the pieces out, and when they'd dried, they resembled logs of dirt. He stacked these outside of the cottage. Mutti burned the logs in the stove when she cooked.

Mutti's meals increased to coincide with our larger family. Omi stayed with us in the cottage. With the new arrangement, Mutti cooked for three adults and three children every day.

Furthermore, our little cottage opened its doors to more visitors. One week after Papa came, another relative arrived. This time it was Uncle Kurt. He was the uncle who had gotten married in the city of Marienwerder in East Prussia during the war. Our trip to his wedding had included the fateful incident of Mutti and me jumping from the train on our way home.

Uncle Kurt showed up on the step by the front door, just as Omi and Papa had. His wife Elfriede and their baby girl, Ingeborg, were with him.

Mutti and Omi rushed them in. Commotion swirled in the cottage as the new family of three entered. Mutti, Papa, myself, Wilfried, Rainer, Omi, Uncle Kurt, Aunt Elfriede and Ingeborg filled the small room. I stood against a back wall to make space for the others.

Uncle Kurt's eyes and face drooped slightly; I thought he looked much more tired than the last time I had seen him, at his wedding. That took place in April 1944, and Germany had greatly changed. He seemed less happy now.

Although weary, Uncle Kurt and Aunt Elfriede looked relieved. They, too, had survived the war. So had their baby girl.

"Tell us everything," Mutti said.

Uncle Kurt explained that before the Second World War started, he worked as a policeman. When the war started, he was drafted, and ended up in eastern Germany. When he learned the area he was in was going to be turned over to the Russians, he grabbed a horse and wagon and took off. He fled west, like so many before.

Along the way, he left the horse and wagon behind. But he met up with Aunt Elfriede and their baby Ingeborg, and then found us through the Red Cross.

Their family of three, plus our family of five, and Omi, made for a total of nine people squeezed into the one-room cottage.

When Mrs. Jühls, our lovely neighbor and friend, heard of the arrangement, she offered her basement to Uncle Kurt and his family. They agreed, and Uncle Kurt, Aunt Elfriede and their baby Ingeborg slept in the Jühls' home at night, and spent the days with us at the cottage. They also looked for a place to house their family.

* * *

Many others had poured into Hamburg during the war. After the war, new arrangements were made for Germany. These changes caused a further influx of citizens to western Germany and the Hamburg area.

In all, there were three waves of refugees. Mutti, Oma, Aunt Lydia, Ruthchen, Wilfried, Rainer, and I were among those in the first wave. This included the Germans who fled and were evacuated from towns facing the advancing Red Army. The movement started in the middle of 1944, and lasted through early 1945.

The second wave of refugees was marked by more disarray and disorder than the first. It consisted of Germans who fled after the death of Hitler and Germany's surrender in May 1945. Like Uncle Kurt and Papa, many ran to escape from the areas occupied by the Soviet Union once the war was over.

The third, and final, phase occurred under government orders, and followed a post-war agreement reached by the Allies. After Germany surrendered, leaders from the Soviet Union, the United Kingdom, and the United States met in Potsdam, a suburb of Berlin. Those in attendance included President Harry S. Truman from the United States, General Secretary Joseph Stalin from the Soviet Union, Winston Churchill, and Clement Attlee, who was elected prime minister during the conference. The event, known as the Potsdam Conference, lasted from July 17 to August 2, 1945.[50]

One of the most important items on the agenda during those days of meetings involved Germany. The Allies needed to decide what to do with

Germany, both in terms of reparation and also establishing peace. At Potsdam, it was agreed that Germany was to be completely disarmed.[51]

Furthermore, the Allies addressed the ongoing war in the Pacific. While the war was over in Europe, it hadn't come to a conclusion in the Pacific. To bring it to an end, they called on Japan to surrender.

In addition, leaders at the Potsdam Conference established new borders for Germany. The country needed to return territory it had taken over to other nations. This included land east of the Oder and Neisse Rivers, which was given to Poland.

The border changes affected Schneidemühl. The city and its surrounding region were turned over to Poland. Coinciding with this shift, Schneidemühl took on the name Pila.

The new map of central Europe left many Germans living in areas no longer ruled by their country. To accommodate this, the Potsdam Agreement, which was developed during the conference, called for Germans living in territories that now belonged to other countries to return to Germany. It approved orderly and humane expulsions of Germans from Poland, Czechoslovakia, and Hungary.[52]

German citizens were also expelled from Denmark and Romania. Had we remained on the acreage, and somehow lived through the Red Army takeover of our region, we too would have had to leave.

While those at the Potsdam Conference called for orderly expulsions, some nations used the mandates as an opportunity to carry out revenge for the suffering they faced during the previous years. They blamed German citizens for the war, and sent them to prison camps and forced labor camps. Many died from the poor conditions of trains and camps.

From 1944 to 1948, at least 12 million Germans were expelled from Eastern Europe and resettled in Germany.[53]

Many refugees landed in Hamburg and its surrounding suburbs. This area formed part of Schleswig-Holstein, a northern state overseen by the occupying British forces. The population of Schleswig-Holstein increased from 1.6 million in 1939 to 2.6 million people in 1946. Most of the new habitants came from Pomerania and East Prussia.[54]

Some incomers lived outside of the cities, and bunked with farm families. Others settled in hut-like barracks at refugee camps.[55] Makeshift housing units sprang up around Hamburg to accommodate the new families.

Between the war's end in May 1945 and October 1945, Hamburg repaired 100,000 dwellings, created 10,000 new dwellings, and constructed 2,000 temporary units. Some military barracks were converted to civilian housing.[56]

Nissen huts dotted the area. Called *nissenhütten* in Germany, they were named after Peter Norman Nissen, the man who designed them. Nissen, a Canadian engineer and officer in the British Army, developed a structure in 1916 that could be set up quickly and efficiently. After World War II ended, these huts were used as emergency quarters for Germans who had been bombed out of their homes, and also for refugees. They were particularly prominent in the British occupation zone. Nissen huts had semi-circular roofs, and resembled halves of oversized tin cylinders laid on their side. Many didn't have insulation.[57]

During World War II, Germany had started *Behelfsheim*, a program to provide temporary housing for citizens who lost their homes during air raids. Because of the eventual collapse throughout the country, the program never took off. After the war, the British continued the program's initiatives. They put Konstanty Gutschow, a German official who had been involved in building directives, in charge of the planning and building of Hamburg.[58]

* * *

By God's mercy, just one week after they arrived on our doorstep, Uncle Kurt and his family found a different place to live. After they left, we waited for other relatives to find us.

Papa also found a job. Since he had worked as a blacksmith in Schneidemühl, and labor was in high demand, he picked up work quickly. Using his skills, he joined others taking the first steps to rebuild Hamburg.

In 1945, approximately 75 percent of the built-up areas in Hamburg were destroyed. It was noted that if the city's rubble were to be loaded into normal freight railroad cars, the train would reach around the earth. As it was, there were roughly 20 cubic meters of debris per inhabitant of the city.[59]

Papa helped remove the debris, fix what could be repaired, and—little by little—reshape the city. The work was grueling, and the pay, minimal. Papa's earnings weren't enough to buy the food we needed, even if it had not been in short supply.

The city needed to be constructed, and the food problem had to be solved. As more mouths arrived in the area, the amount of food allotted to each person dwindled.

At the time, rations for an adult in Hamburg amounted to 1,295 calories a day. This included three slices of bread, four carrots, five potatoes, 10 sugar cubes, and one package of cream cheese-like spread. It also meant 1.3 ounces of meat, 1 ½ tablespoons of butter, 1.3 ounces of cheese, 1 tablespoon of flour, and ¾ tablespoon of substitute coffee.[60]

Even with this rigid schedule, rations were not always available.

We remained hungry.

As before, Mutti employed her resourceful and frugal nature to help us. We lived near the edge of town, and there were farms just a short walk from our home. Mutti sought them out.

Some days she went from farm to farm, asking for anything that could be spared. At every place she stopped, Mutti explained she had three little children to feed. Sometimes the farmers gave her a few extra potatoes, carrots, or vegetables. Other times, they had nothing to share.

In Harksheide, I focused on the next meal. Life depended on surviving from day to day, and I didn't think about much else. My community consisted of Mutti, Papa, Omi, and my brothers. Our cottage, the street, and the bombed out crater were my stomping grounds.

On August 6, 1945, Americans dropped the world's first atomic bomb on the city of Hiroshima, Japan; upon impact, 90 percent of the city disappeared and 80,000 people died. Three days later, on August 9, 1945, Americans dropped another atomic bomb on Nagasaki, wiping out an estimated 40,000 people. Six days later, on August 15, Japan announced its surrender.[61]

I watched Mutti's face twist in horror as she listened to the news of the bombs with Mrs. Jühls and her radio.

As significant and life-changing as those events were for millions, I only knew of our daily routine at the cottage, my trouble sleeping with an aching stomach, and my dreams of food.

In August 1945, record temperatures scorched the streets of Hamburg. The blazing sun bleached the city's ruins. At night, a crisp breeze blew in from the Baltic, bringing a touch of relief.[62]

After a terribly hot summer, the rains of autumn came. Unaware that this change was coming, Mutti left the stacks of peat outside where they had been all summer. During the first hard downfall, the rain drenched the stack of dried peat Papa had so carefully gathered. When Mutti tried burning one of the damp peat logs, the cottage filled with dense smoke.

The rains marked a change of season, of cooler weather on the horizon. With a stack of wet peat logs, Mutti searched for other options for fuel and heat. One day in September 1945, she and Papa trekked to the nearby forest behind the meadow at the end of our road. In the woods, they cut down a tree. Hoisting it on their shoulders, they set out to haul the timber home.

As they moved toward the edge of the forest, however, a forester approached them. He faced them, blocking their path, and pointed to the log.

"You can't take that," he said.

Mutti didn't budge.

"You can't—we have limits I need to enforce," he continued.

Despite the weight of the tree on her shoulders, Mutti straightened, bristling. "I need this tree," she began.

"We are limiting the trees that are cut down—we need to restore the forests just as much as the cities," explained the ranger.

No one moved.

"I need this tree," repeated Mutti. "I saved my three children through the war, through the bombings and our flight and kept them from starving to death. I can't allow them to freeze to death now after all we've been through. I need this tree to keep them warm, to feed them, and keep them safe."

After that, the forester said no more. He held his ground, but Mutti and Papa maneuvered around him, with the tree still on their shoulders.

At home, Papa chopped the wood, and then covered the fresh logs well to keep them dry. We had firewood for cooking and heating again.

The next morning, when I woke up, Mutti was talking to Papa and Omi. I strained my ears to hear what she said.

"It was the most vivid dream," she said. "I'm sure I saw Herbert."

One of Mutti's younger brothers, my Uncle Herbert, had been drafted to be an anti-aircraft gunner. He had left home in the winter of 1944, six days before Christmas, as a scrawny 16-year-old. He was assigned to a place near Auschwitz.

"In my dream, Herbert was standing right in front of me," Mutti continued. "He had a cap on his head, and a little jacket on to keep warm. He had a small bundle on his back."

Omi wiped her eyes. "Saying good-bye to Herbert was one of the hardest things I ever had to do. Just a boy! 16 years old, and gone to the war," she said.

"But the dream seemed so real," Mutti said.

Omi nodded. "Yes, we mustn't lose hope."

"In time we will know," said Papa. He pulled on his coat. "I must leave for work. We can discuss this more in the evening."

Papa patted my head and then left, closing the cottage door behind him.

The room turned quiet, with everyone lost in our own thoughts.

Bits of sunlight streamed into the cottage.

A few minutes later, the door opened and Papa reappeared.

"Guess who I brought?!" he announced.

He shuffled to the side, making room for his guest to enter. When he did, we all gasped.

Uncle Herbert stood before us. He wore a cap on his head, a small jacket, and a little bundle on his back.

Papa turned to Mutti. "I hadn't even walked a block when I saw the image from your dream, exactly as you described it," he said.

It was September 12, 1945.

Mutti and Omi hugged Uncle Herbert. For the rest of the day, Mutti was overcome with emotion. So was Omi. Indeed, there was great reason to rejoice in the cottage. Another family member had arrived, another soul had made it through the war alive.

And not only was Herbert home; he had returned somewhat incredibly. He explained to us that he remained at his assignment near Auschwitz until February 1945. He then moved with the anti-aircraft batteries to Berlin for the final defense of the city against the Red Army. While there, he collected data for anti-aircraft gunners. The bombing was heavy and nearly continuous at the time.

Then Uncle Herbert caught cholera, and was admitted to a hospital in Berlin in April. He was there when the city fell.

On April 26, Soviet officers entered the hospital where Uncle Herbert was recovering. They told the patients, including Uncle Herbert, that they were prisoners. They also told everyone to not look out the windows. One German sergeant disobeyed orders, and looked out the window. The guards swiftly shot him between the eyes.

On May 12, 1945, while we were carrying on in the cottage in Harksheide, the Soviets marched Uncle Herbert and 300 others who were well enough to walk to a prison camp 50 miles east of Berlin. At the camp, which held more than 40,000 prisoners of war, Uncle Herbert had his 17th birthday. He was released in August 1945.

At the time, he weighed only 70 pounds. He had nothing to his name except for the clothes on his back.

He went to a relative's house in the Harz Mountains, to the same place Omi and Uncle Arnold had gone during their escape. When he arrived, he met up with Uncle Arnold, who related that Omi had moved on to the Hamburg area.

The relative's place in the Harz Mountains was in a region that the Soviets controlled. Uncle Herbert wanted to go on to Hamburg, but it was dangerous to do so. At that time, the Soviet zone was guarded well and difficult to escape from. This was different than when Omi had journeyed through the area, as it had not yet been under such tight Soviet control.

Even so, Uncle Herbert wanted to get away and decided to take a risk. He left the farm and reached the border between the Soviet zone and the British zone. There he encountered a fence made of barbed wire, machine gun towers, and roving patrols guarding the Soviet side.

"It was 200 yards to the fence over open ground," recalled Uncle Herbert. "On my first try, I saw the patrol when I was part way to the wire. I hit the ground and crawled backwards into the tree line. When they had passed, I tried again. That was the fastest 200 yards I've ever run in my life."

But it wasn't over.

"When I reached the wire and crawled under, the strangest thing happened. I saw a man running towards me. The horrible thought struck me that I had gotten turned around and was still on the east side. I was prepared to surrender again to the Russians. It turned out that this fellow was trying to get into East Germany. I told him how to get under the wire and wished him luck. Then I took off west as fast as I could go."

Uncle Herbert's appearance marked a series of arrivals in our little cottage. Two more of Mutti's brothers, my Uncle Gottfriedt and Uncle Reinhold, found us in Harksheide. They had also been in the war, and located us when it ended. We rejoiced and gave thanks with the appearance of each one.

By then, Mutti's brothers Kurt, Herbert, Gottfriedt, and Reinhold had made it to the Harksheide area. And we knew where another brother, Arnold, was. He had stayed with our relative in the Harz Mountains after fleeing with Omi from their home in Kensau, Germany.

That left two of Mutti's brothers unaccounted for: Hans and Lothar. By the end of 1945, they still hadn't found us. They also hadn't sent any word, and we didn't know what had happened to them or where they were located.

On Papa's side, we had heard nothing from his brother Uncle Willie. He had another brother, my Uncle Erich, who had fought in the war and was missing also. In addition he had two brothers-in-law we had heard no news from. We also had received no news from his father, my Opa, who had stayed on the farm to watch the animals when we fled from Schneidemühl.

* * *

In addition to trying to find relatives through the Red Cross, many individuals left notes around the Hamburg area. The messages, scribbled on hastily set up boards on the inner walls of train stations, addressed loved ones. They begged relatives to find them in new locations. Many included photos as well. As the months passed, the weather caused the ink to fade and the pictures to curl. Still the notices clung to the boards, their authors refusing to give up the hope of a happy ending.

And while the reuniting with family often brought beautiful moments, the ultimate result was not always sheer happiness. Even in Mutti's family there was evidence of this. One family member in particular was quite bitter about how the war had ended. This was my Uncle Gottfriedt.

Gottfriedt was the second child, falling in line after Mutti, in their family. As the oldest brother, he had signed up to fight in the German army at the beginning of the war. Of all of the relatives, he was the only one to take this type of initiative. The rest waited until they were drafted and had to leave.

In the army, Gottfriedt became a paratrooper. He spent the remaining years of the war jumping out of planes. He was a German soldier to the very core, completely indoctrinated with the Nazi way of thinking. He desperately wanted the country to win the war.

This, of course, didn't happen. And when the smoke cleared, the white flags were raised, and Germany officially surrendered, it was unfathomable to him. He couldn't believe the country lost the war.

Shortly after coming to Harksheide and staying with us, Uncle Gottfriedt moved to a different place in our area. He often showed up at our gate, crossed over the low entryway, and entered the cottage. He talked about his frustrations with the outcome of the war, and his lost efforts in Germany's fruitless fight. He pored over what could have been done differently, how everything ended, the unfairness of it all. We listened to him for long hours.

His words were new and foreign to me. In our family, Gottfriedt was alone in his thinking. Mutti and Papa never spoke like he did.

Rather than dwell on the past, my parents focused on the present need to live.

I did too. I didn't understand how Uncle Gottfriedt could talk so much about things in the past when I thought about little more than my next meal. Each week, I thought my stomach rumbled more than the week before.

In September, I turned five years old. Around that time, Mutti asked me to help with chores. I started walking with her to pick up the rations we were allotted.

In our area, everything we needed for survival was located fairly close to our cottage. This was a blessing, because we had no horse and wagon or other way to get around. When we ventured outside, it was on our feet. We walked everywhere.

The places we usually trod were toward the north, away from Hamburg and in the opposite direction of Mrs. Jühls's home. If we walked a couple of blocks north, the street went down a hill. At the bottom of the descent there was a bakery, a creamery, and other shops that distributed rationed goods. The meadow and forest were beyond these locales.

Mutti and I left about 5 o'clock in the morning for our rations. We got to the shops before they opened, and stood in line with others. Supplies always ran out fast, so Mutti tried to be amongst the first customers of the day in order to get our appointed amount of goods. When the doors opened, and it was our turn, we got our share—if the items were still available.

The bread we received through the rationing program came as dark, oblong loaves. They were heavy and usually contained substitute ingredients. But it was food, and I found it delicious. I was always glad if we got some before bread ran out for the day. The hardest part about picking up bread was waiting until we got home to eat it.

To get milk, we walked with a liter-sized tin can and ration stamps to the nearby creamery. If the creamery had milk that day, the workers poured some into our tin. The milk always had a blue tinge to it. This was because fat, at the time, was in such high demand that most of it was taken from the milk before it was distributed.

I carried the can to the creamery and Mutti carried it once it was filled with milk. On the way home, I often stared at the blue-tinted liquid. Mutti held the tin carefully so nothing spilled out. Even without the fat, I considered the milk a treat.

A black market was also near our home. Black markets had popped up throughout parts of Germany during the war, and continued on after as well. Those ready to trade or buy brought their suitcases full of bicycle tires, lightbulbs, and fruit to the street.

Mutti didn't buy anything at the black market. It was not only illegal; it was expensive.

On the black market, prices soared during and after the war. A pound of butter went for 200 to 250 marks, a jar of Nescafé instant coffee was 130 marks, and a pound of coffee beans was 400 marks.[63]

Papa made just 50 marks a week.

Families without money sometimes traded their treasures and family heirlooms at the black market. They turned in gold, lovely jewelry and watches, and walked away with a bit of food to eat during the next days. A camera could be traded for a pound of butter. Silver spoons might be exchanged for sewing thread.[64]

We didn't have any family heirlooms or valuable possessions to trade. Our most important belonging was the family Bible, and Mutti would never have given that up. Instead, she kept doing what she had started during the end of the war: giving away her ration cards that were valid for substitute coffee, known as *ersatzkaffee*. In return, she received more bread and butter rations.

A trend of unique recycling spread through the area, as those with inventive minds repurposed the war debris from around the city. Strainers made from steel helmets appeared in homes. The broken spike of a bicycle wheel could be turned into a hand needle. Half of a defused hand grenade casing served well as an egg cup, a small container to hold a boiled egg upright while it is eaten.[65]

A stick grenade, a type of German grenade with a long wooden handle, could be turned into a potato masher. Airplane parts were formed into room furnaces. Gas mask filters also worked as cooking ladles.[66]

The repurposing didn't end there. Materials for wedding dresses were difficult to find in post-war Hamburg, and the little bit of cloth that was available was outrageously expensive. Instead of looking for new material, brides turned to parachutes. With some sewing, the material from parachutes made lovely wedding dresses for those walking down the aisle.[67]

September turned to October, and the winds of fall arrived. Omi turned 60 years old on the third of the month. That same day, she received a room as a refugee. She moved out of the cottage and in to the room, which was close to our place. Soon some of my uncles, Mutti's brothers, joined her there.

Even with one less person to feed, Mutti's hunts for food continued. She grew desperate as supplies dwindled further, and reached out to anyone she could, including the farmers nearby. To get to the farms and fields, she walked north on the dirt road our cottage was on, called Glashütter Weg, and past the buildings where rations were distributed. Beyond these, the dirt road came to an end, and intersected with a street that ran perpendicular to it. She turned right on this road and walked down it. It led out of town, up to slightly higher ground, and then on to the fields and farms.

One particular day, Mutti went out to ask for vegetables and came across a farmer harvesting potatoes.

She walked up to him. There was a whole bucket of potatoes at his feet, and some strewn on the ground next to him.

"Do you have anything to spare?" she asked.

"No," he replied, without looking up.

"Please, I have three hungry kids."

"I don't have anything."

Mutti thanked him and walked away. Later, when it was dark, she went back to the same field. The potatoes were still there, just as she had seen them earlier that day, but the farmer was nowhere in sight. Thinking of her famished kids, and not wanting to see them suffer more, Mutti took some of the potatoes.

When she showed them to us, Mutti told us she asked God for forgiveness for taking the potatoes that didn't belong to her.

Her actions mirrored others in our area. Refugees and citizens alike fought to stay alive. Sometimes their actions were bold. Out of 816 cases of burglary reported in Hamburg in October 1945, 540 involved food stores.[68]

Not long after Mutti took potatoes from the farmer, we learned of another way to get food. This time, the setup was legal. After the potato harvest, authorities allowed residents to go through the fields. The practice was known as *stoppeln*, which means "stubble," and referred to searching harvested fields for remnants of the crops, like undiscovered potatoes or dropped heads of wheat.[69]

I found *stoppeln* to be wonderful. Imagine, free food! And for the taking! It was almost beyond my greatest wishes.

I went along with Mutti to glean a potato field. As soon as we got to the field, we began. The adults used hoes and shovels. I kneeled down and dug with my hands. Mutti gave me a bag to gather what I found. I went deep into the ground, searching for spuds that had grown further down and had been passed over during the harvest.

I found small potatoes, and then a few larger ones. I placed them in the bag. After checking another row, my stomach growled. I grabbed another potato from the ground and tried to ignore the rumbling.

It was of no use. My stomach sensed food within reach. I glanced up. Everyone else was working, intent on the task at hand. Without thinking, I put the freshly gathered potato in my mouth. The raw spud tasted delicious.

The *stoppeln* trips helped us get through the day, but overall, the living situation took a turn for the worse. In October 1945, food and water shortages, disease, poor sanitation, and ongoing electrical blackouts rattled Hamburg. During the last months of 1945, civilian deaths dramatically increased throughout the country.[70]

While we felt minor effects of these, no deadly catastrophes struck our home during those months.

Christmas came in quietly that year. It was the first Christmas since 1938 that the world had not been at war. There was peace on Earth, and we felt it in our cottage. Our clothes were old and torn by then, but it didn't matter.

On the acreage, Mutti had always put up a tree on Christmas Eve and decorated it with real candles and tinsel. We also, like many others, put out wooden shoes by the window sill during the days before Christmas. Every morning we checked our shoes to see if there were gifts in them. Small presents always appeared in the shoes on Christmas Eve.

That first Christmas in Harksheide in 1945, there were no gifts. No tree or candles graced our low, wooden home. We didn't go to church, as Mutti and Papa didn't know of any in the area that were functioning.

Still, I didn't mind. I didn't even feel sad. Many of our family members had safely arrived in Harksheide, and now lived near one another. We got together with my uncles and Omi, and Aunt Lydia, Ruthchen and Oma during the days leading up to Christmas. I always felt happy around them.

It snowed during the day on Christmas Eve that year.[71] In the evening, we sat at the table in the cottage and bowed our heads. We prayed, "*Komm Herr Jesus. Sei unser Gast und segne was Du uns bescherret hast* (Come Lord Jesus, be our guest, and bless what you have bestowed on us)."

It was good to be together, and it was good to be alive.

As night fell on Christmas Eve, Papa pulled out the Bible and opened it. We gathered round and listened as he read the Christmas story from the book of Luke to us:

"And there were shepherds living out in the fields nearby, keeping watch over their flocks at night. An angel of the Lord appeared to them, and the glory of the Lord shone around them, and they were terrified. But the angel said to them, 'Do not be afraid. I bring you good news that will cause great joy for all the people. Today in the town of David a Savior has been born to you; he is the Messiah, the Lord. This will be a sign to you: You will find a baby wrapped in cloths and lying in a manger.'"

Then Mutti started singing hymns. We joined her, and sang into the late hours of the night.

Leise rieselt der Schnee,
Still und starr liegt der See.
Weihnachtlich glänzet der Wald:
Freue Dich, Christkind kommt
bald!
In den Herzen ist's warm,
Still schweigt Kummer und Harm,
Sorge des Lebens verhallt:
Freue Dich, Christkind kommt
bald!
Bald ist Heilige Nacht,
Chor der Engel erwacht,
Horch' nur wie lieblich es schallt:
Freue Dich, Christkind kommt
bald!
(Eduard Ebel - 1895)[72]

Softly falls the snow,
Quiet and frozen lies the lake.
Christmas-like sparkles the forest:
Rejoice! The Christ Child will
soon be here.
In our hearts it's warm,
Silent are sorrow and grief,
Life's worries fade away:
Rejoice! The Christ Child will
soon be here.
Soon it's Christmas Eve,
Choir of angels awakes,
Just hear how lovely it sounds:
Rejoice! The Christ Child will
soon be here.

(translation: Hyde Flippo)

CHAPTER EIGHT: CARE PACKAGES

"I need Thy presence every passing hour.
What but Thy grace can foil the tempter's power?
Who, like Thyself, my guide and stay can be?
Through cloud and sunshine, Lord, abide with me."
—Henry Francis Lyte, 1847[73]

During the winter that spanned the final months of 1945, and continued on through the early part of 1946, the Allies didn't allow anyone outside of Germany to send food parcels to residents inside of Germany. The Allied authorities also rejected requests by the International Red Cross to bring in provisions to alleviate the suffering.[74] It was thought that by prohibiting care packages from coming in, it would be easier to keep the German standard of living close to the average of the surrounding European nations.[75]

I often sat at the table in the cottage for lunch. Before me, on a small cracked plate, lay a cooked, sliced turnip. Next to it sat a cup of substitute coffee.

While it was easy for different sides to point fingers after the war, the fact remained that in our nook in the Hamburg area, most days we were hollow with hunger. My stomach always hurt.

After Christmas, the New Year came quietly to the cottage in Harksheide. Unlike the previous January, when Mutti felt the intense pressure of the approaching enemy, January 1946 brought new challenges to the horizon. Day after day, a cold, cloud-covered blanket of sky draped over our home. The atmosphere set a grey, dismal mood for the month.

It was cold in January. Mutti burned anything she could find in the little woodstove. We lived in the layers of clothing she brought for us. I wore several dresses and a coat on top to stay warm.

Washing clothes was hard, and with our scarce resources, they simply didn't get cleaned all that often. When Mutti did wash clothes, she got out a wooden washboard with metal running down the middle of it. I helped her scrub the clothes on the washboard, and then rinse them and hang them out to dry. Mutti always sang while she washed. When it was too cold or cloudy to dry clothes outside—which was often—she hung them over a bed post, on a chair, or in other parts of the cottage.

On March 5, 1946, Winston Churchill warned that an "Iron Curtain" had descended across the center of Europe.[76]

While the powers of the United States and the Soviet Union sought to cast their influence over other countries, we battled our own fight. By March 1946, the normal daily ration of food for Germans in the British zone was only 1,014 calories.[77]

When spring began to peak in that year, it brought rain. Sometimes it misted, and other days it poured. The steady stream of showers meant that April 1946 fell upon a miserable, damp, and dirty city.[78] Soon our clothes matched the weather.

Easter came in the latter half of April. Unlike the year before, when I spent hours huddled up with Mutti listening to bombs fall, in 1946 I spent a good part of Holy Week playing outside in the mud that filled the street. Wilfried and I invented games while Mutti tended to the cooking, housekeeping, and caring for baby Rainer inside the cottage. Each day, Papa worked on rebuilding the city.

Easter Sunday arrived on April 21, 1946. Mutti found a church to attend for the occasion. It would be the first time we went to a service since our arrival in Harksheide.

To get to the place of worship, we took the train into Hamburg. After getting off, we walked for a long time.

Inside the church we sat on a bench toward the back. I studied the interior of the large place. Ornate décor filled the walls and front. When the service began, Mutti's lovely singing voice carried far.

It was a treat to go to church. It was also a big trip. We got home, hours after the service ended, exhausted.

"That was a pricey trip," I heard Papa comment to Mutti.

"And long," she added. "We won't be able to go very often."

Instead, Mutti instilled our faith and propelled it forward at home. She prayed with us, sang with us, and explained how Jesus died on the cross to save us from our sins. She was convinced everything in our immediate future would be alright, and that we would have enough food and clothing to meet our needs. God would look after us, according to his promises, she assured us.

I believed it too.

At night, she sang with us before bed:

Müde bin ich, geh' zur Ruh,'
Schließe beide Äuglein zu.
Vater, laß die Augen dein
Über meinem Bette sein.

Hab ich Unrecht heut getan!
Sieh' es, lieber Gott, nicht an!
Deine Gnad' und Jesu Blut
Macht ja allen Schaden gut.

Kranken Herzen sende Ruh,
Nasse Augen schließe zu.
Laß den Mond am Himmel stehn
Und die still Walt besehn.

(Luise Hensel, 1817)

Now the light has gone away;
Father listen while I pray,
Asking Thee to watch and keep
And to send me quiet sleep.

Jesus, Savior, wash away
All that has been wrong today.
Help me ev'ry day to be
Good and gentle, more like Thee.

Now my evening praise I give;
Thou didst die that I might live.

All my blessings come from Thee;
Oh, how good Thou art to me!

(Now the Light Has Gone Away—Frances R. Havergal, 1869)[79]

Living on very little, and trusting in God for guidance, had been a part of Mutti since the time she was little. Surely those characteristics helped her get through each day as a refugee. And yet, those measures were not the only ways God prepared her for our time in Harksheide. War, too, was familiar to her.

Mutti was from Netztal, Germany, a town about 25 miles east of Schneidemühl. Before she was born, her mother lost three babies: a boy, then a girl, and then another boy. They all passed away in their cradle, a type of death known as a crib death. It was the early 1900s, and times were tough.

Then, in 1912, Mutti was born. She escaped crib death and became the oldest surviving child. Her parents were my Omi, the grandmother who fled with Uncle Arnold to the mountains to escape the advancing Russian army, and also Opa, my grandfather who died of stomach cancer before we left our home near Schneidemühl.

In 1914, soon after World War I started, Opa, Mutti's father, left home to fight in the German army. While he was away, Mutti and Omi went to live with Omi's parents in Lindenwerder, Germany, just nine miles from Netztal.

One time during the war, when she was nearly three years old, Mutti went to visit her father. To get to the barracks where he was stationed, Mutti and Omi took a train. The ride—her first trip on a train—enchanted her.

When they arrived at the soldiers' quarters, Mutti played with another little boy while her parents visited. The two children entertained themselves near a big iron stove in the barracks. Mutti had so much fun she didn't want to leave when it was time to go home.

During his time serving in the German army during World War I, Opa periodically came home on leave. He always stayed for a day or two. The family usually did not know when he was coming, so his arrivals always came as a surprise.

Mutti's grandparents produced much of their own food. Behind their home, the family had plots of land where they grew barley, oats, and rye. A river ran along the edge of the property. As a young girl, Mutti pitched in with the work. In the garden, "we planted potatoes and turnips," she remembered.

Relatives drifted in and out of the home. They stayed for periods of time with Mutti, her mother, and grandparents before heading to faraway places, like other parts of Germany—or sometimes, even to America. Mutti's Uncle Leo and Aunt Zelma Krenz were among the relatives that headed over to America in those years, as well as her Aunt Emilia Lehman. Day-to-day life for Mutti was quiet, but the ongoing war caused a great deal of movement for many in Germany, including her relatives.

Omi, who watched three babies perish prior to Mutti, lost another one after her. Then, in 1916, she was expecting another child. The baby was due at the end of the year. That December, on the night before Christmas, the family went to a Christmas Eve service at the Lutheran church in Lindenwerder. That evening, after church, the baby was born.

The family named the infant Gottfriedt. Like Mutti, he lived. Mutti helped care for him almost immediately. While Omi worked in the kitchen, peeling potatoes, Mutti stood by the cradle. If Gottfriedt got upset, Mutti turned a handle on the cradle. This made the cradle rock, and comforted the baby so he stopped crying.

From early on, Mutti spoke her mind. When she was five years old, she went to see an uncle who owned a windmill. After the visit ended, her mother asked what she had thought of the windmill. "I didn't like it," Mutti replied. "There was a big living room, but no chairs, so I couldn't sit down."

One day, Mutti went with her mother and new baby brother to a neighbor's house. Everyone gathered in the kitchen. They sat around the ample table in the room, and together prepared filling for goose feather beds.

To make the filling, they first sliced the soft sections away from the stems. The soft feather could be used in a feather bed. Once complete, a feather bed resembled a heavy comforter. It was placed on top of a single fitted sheet on a bed, and provided enough warmth to keep a body snug throughout the night.

Mutti watched as the others with her sliced away. They chatted while they worked, and the time passed quickly.

Suddenly there was a knock at the door. Everyone looked up from their work and toward the door. Omi got up from her chair and went to the window to have a look. She peeked through the curtains and then gasped.

There, standing before her and the neighbors, was Opa. He was on leave, he explained, and would stay for a few days. "That was a big joy," Mutti recalled years later.

Opa soon left to return to the war and fight for Germany. The German empire, along with Austria-Hungary, the Ottoman Empire, and Bulgaria formed an alliance known as the Central Powers. Together these countries fought against the Allied Powers, which consisted of Britain, France, Russia, and the United States.

During the war, the Allied Powers blocked some of Germany's ports. The blockades affected both food and other basic items. Due to this move, supplies in many parts of Germany ran short, making it tough for German citizens.[80]

Mutti's family felt the impact from the shortages, but they also had their gardens and crops to help them through. Others were not as fortunate.

One Christmas during the war, Mutti received two dolls as gifts. Her eyes shone with excitement. The figures were lovely to look at, and she couldn't wait to let her imagination create names and invent stories for them.

But that didn't happen. Before she could play with the two dolls, Omi took them from her. After studying them, Omi announced, "You don't need two big dolls. We'll give one away."

"But why?" Mutti protested.

"With the war going on, some children have no dolls at all," Omi explained.

And with that, she sent one of the dolls to a nearby orphanage.

The First World War drew to a close at the end of 1918. As a result, new lines were drawn to divide the countries of Germany and Poland. The fresh boundaries brought changes for Lindenwerder, the village where Mutti's grandparents lived. Like many other towns in the area, Lindenwerder switched sides; instead of being overseen by Germany, it went under Polish control after the war.

To mark the transition, on January 17, 1919, Polish soldiers marched into the town of Lindenwerder to take over the village.

Shortly after the Polish entered, a fight broke out between the Polish troops and what Mutti referred to as the "home guard," meaning German soldiers that were in town, or back already from the war.

After a couple of days of skirmishes, the Polish army gained control. When that happened, the streets of Lindenwerder quieted down. The Polish troops hung the flag for Poland in the town, officially marking the transition.

When Opa came home from the war, at the end of January 1919, he found the town under Polish control.

Upon his return, Opa hung up his soldier's uniform. He had worked as a butcher before the war, and now that it was over, he set up a butchering business once again. He worked for farmers in the area. He also opened a shop to sell some of the meat he butchered.

Mutti started school in April 1919, the month when schools in Germany began their yearly session. At the time she was six and half years old. It was chilly during the first days of school, so her mother dressed her in a white rabbit fur cap that had a bow on it. She also wore a hand muff made of white rabbit fur to keep her hands warm.

Since Mutti's family lived in an area that had such a mix of German and Polish backgrounds, her schooling consisted of both languages. Even though German was her native language, Polish came easily to Mutti. She was gifted at languages in general, and consistently did well in school.

In the years that followed, Opa and Omi moved several times, always taking up residence in territories that at one time belonged to the German empire but shifted to Poland after World War I. The butcher business eked along, and the family grew. A son, Kurt, was born in October 1919; then Hans, in 1921; Karl in 1923; and Lothar in 1925.

Mutti went to school for seven years. In 1926, she finished eighth grade and graduated from elementary school. The following summer, she got confirmed. At the time, there wasn't a Lutheran pastor in the village where Mutti and her family lived. There was a Lutheran pastor, however, in

Lindenwerder, where her grandparents were. So Mutti went to stay with them, and took confirmation lessons for three weeks.

For confirmation classes, in the mornings, she walked a 20-minute route that took her to the church. The class studied from eight o'clock until noon. Then the students took a break for lunch, and returned at two in the afternoon to study for two or three more hours. There was a whole book of songs and Bible prayers to get through.

Learning continued to be easy for Mutti. So easy, in fact, that the pastor suggested she consider going to business school. To do so she would have to live in a different city, as there were no schools nearby. Leaving her family to attend school in an area far away was a problem for Mutti. She didn't want to live away from her parents for an extended period of time. Also, as the only girl at home, she felt responsible to care for the others.

Every so often, for a break, Mutti joined her friends in the area and headed out for a picnic with them. The group often met in a nearby forest or meadow. At these gatherings, everyone sang together. Mutti loved singing more than any other activity.

Mutti's choice to stay home turned out to be a helpful one for the family. In the following years, the household continued to expand. Mutti's brother Reinhold was born in 1927; Herbert in 1928; and Arnold in 1929.

As the United States toppled into the Great Depression in 1929, Mutti's family faced their own bout of difficult times. By 1930, Mutti had eight younger brothers. Her father's butchering business brought in little income, and the family struggled to make ends meet.

Mutti worked hard, cooking and cleaning and helping her mother care for the younger boys. She sewed pants and shirts for her brothers. She also pitched in with the butchering business.

Due to the low income, combined with so many mouths to feed under one roof, Mutti's parents sent some of the older sons to stay with relatives. Mutti's brothers often lived with extended family in nearby villages for a time, and then came home. This lightened the burden on the family. Also, the children helped out at the places they visited. Of all the brothers, Gottfriedt, the oldest son, spent the most time away from home.

Despite the daily struggles, a large part of Mutti's upbringing revolved around being a Christian. Her father served as a lector at church, and often helped with readings during the services. Mutti enjoyed singing in the church choir, and the Christmas programs were a special treat.

As a teenager, Mutti occasionally left home to stay with others for a short time, just as her brothers had. Once she went by train to her Uncle Reinhold's homestead, where she stayed and helped for two weeks. Her favorite place to be, however, was right at home with her parents and siblings, doing whatever she could for them.

Bumps in the routine of daily life were frequent. Sickness regularly struck the children. One time, there was a measles outbreak and all of the children and Mutti's father got sick. Only Omi was well, and she took care of the rest of the family while they were ill.

Mutti's younger brother Lothar was just a little lad at the time, and the sickness hit him especially hard. The measles went inside his body and he turned as white as snow. He refused to eat or drink anything, and his health deteriorated quickly.

The others recovered, but Lothar continued to worsen. When the doctor came to look at Lothar, he told Omi the child wasn't going to make it. Indeed, he looked close to death.

One day, Opa sat on a chair at the dining room table with Lothar on his lap. There were some pickles on the table, and Lothar reached for them.

Opa said, "Give him some—it won't hurt him anymore." The boy's face was full of red marks and he looked like he would die soon.

Lothar ate the pickles. The salt from them seemed to make him thirsty. He asked for a drink—something he had been refusing to do since his illness began.

That drink was a turning point for him. Soon he began to feel better. Eventually, he recovered completely.

Other times bouts of illness did not have a happy ending. In 1935, when Mutti's brother Karl was 11 years old, he walked barefoot in a freshly plowed field. The cold and wet ground seeped into him, and he caught pneumonia.

The disease struck Karl with great force. Unlike Lothar, he didn't regain his health. Instead, he steadily got worse.

The sickness ate at Karl, and the doctor reported nothing could be done. In his last days and hours, his siblings and parents sat with him. Together they sang hymns and prayed.

One day, when his time was nearly up, the whole family sat around Karl, who lay in bed. They all sang a hymn together. Then Karl closed his eyes.

In an instant, a light seemed to surround Karl's body. The family knew that upon his death, Karl was immediately taken to heaven, where he would suffer no longer. It was a peaceful, serene moment.

Karl died in 1935. At the time, the family was living in a town called Weisenhoehe. They buried the boy in the cemetery there.

No matter which village in Poland the family lived, conflicts rose between Opa and other butchers. These skirmishes often stemmed from the tension between the Polish and German people in the area. Mutti's family was German, but their presence was not appreciated by many of the Polish residents around them.

In 1938 the family was still living in Weisenhoehe, which was part of Poland at the time. There Opa ran a butcher shop. That year, another butcher shop in the area undersold Opa's shop. The other butcher marked his prices so low that Opa couldn't imitate them. The competition was too much; soon Opa went out of business.

Desperate and poor, the family received the permission needed at the time from the authorities to leave the village and head to Germany. The night before they left, Omi went to visit Karl's grave at the cemetery. Mutti stayed home with her father and brothers.

In the evening, when it got dark, Mutti was in the shop cleaning. She looked out the window and glass doors, which were both open, while she worked. Outside, she spotted a Polish father and son approaching the butcher shop. From the little light on the street, Mutti saw each of them carrying a long iron rod. Their eyes gleamed with a deadly glare.

Mutti smelled danger. The hatred in their eyes, combined with the rods in their hands, surely meant they came with the intention of doing something dangerous. Mutti also knew if a rod struck her, she could die.

There was not a moment to spare. Mutti ran to the doors of the butcher shop, which were still open. She slammed them shut as fast as she could.

"Papa!" she screamed. "Papa, come!"

Opa came running.

The attackers broke the glass in the doors and tried to beat their way in.

Opa grabbed a stick and hit one of the intruders over the arms. Mutti, realizing the skirmish was getting serious fast, scurried to an open window and jumped out.

"Help!" she yelled, jumping up and down in the street in front of the place. "Help, somebody help!"

Suddenly a couple of farmers appeared, and broke up the fight.

When it was over, they explained they were in the area when they heard Mutti call, and jumped in to help.

Others in the village who heard the commotion went to Omi, who was still at the cemetery. "You'd better get home," they warned. "They're killing your people."

Omi raced home. When she arrived, she found a shaken—but otherwise intact—household. The farmers had come just in time to help steer away the intruders.

The next day, the family left for Germany. The same farmers who had rescued them the previous evening escorted the group from their home to the German border. They crossed safely, and then settled in an area outside of Schneidemühl.

Now, after the Second World War, Mutti lived with us as *flüchtlinge*, or "refugees." In Harksheide, she hunted for ways to keep daily life going in an unfamiliar part of the country. Throughout it all, Mutti focused on caring for others.

Just as we had scavenged for potatoes after the harvest in 1945, in 1946 we continued to scour the fields. When the farmers finished cutting wheat, we went and collected what was left over. We brought whatever we gathered back to the cottage. Mutti took the kernels of wheat and roasted them in a pan on the stove. They turned a dark shade of brown when they were done roasting. Then she ground them into a powder. She used that powder to make substitute coffee. She drank this mixture and shared it with us too.

The whole process of gathering, and then eating or drinking what we picked, created an exhilarating feeling. While it was hard work to glean the fields, it also meant that as a result, the food we gathered was ours to keep.

We also foraged for barley, my favorite grain, after the harvest. Like wheat and potatoes, to gather barley we went through the fields near Harksheide after the farmers had finished their work in them. I sifted through the dirt to find remnants in the soil. At home, we rubbed the barley in our hands to make the kernel come out of the hull.

The kernels of barley were small and pearly white. I loved how they looked, and especially how they tasted. Sometimes Mutti roasted the barley kernels and then ground them into substitute coffee, just as she did for the wheat.

She also cooked barley for meals. When the pearls were wonderfully soft, Mutti put them in soups, porridges, and stews. They gave the meal a nutty, earthy flavor that filled my mouth. Barley eased my hunger pains better than the other foods we ate, and my stomach felt almost full after eating.

In the autumn of 1946, overcast skies and rain greeted most days, and the nights swarmed with thunderstorms. The booms that resounded from the thunder reminded me of the bombs we had heard drop and explode during the war. One rumble overhead, and I shook with fear at the noise.

We got together regularly with the other relatives in Harksheide. Sometimes when we visited Aunt Lydia and Ruthchen, the sky darkened and a heavy, blusterous storm rolled in. Aunt Lydia always went to the door of her place to watch. The storms fascinated her, and she gazed at the jagged lightning bolts cutting through the sky. The loud crackles of thunder never caused her to budge. Her bravery amazed me.

I so enjoyed visiting Aunt Lydia. There was familiarity in seeing her, as we had lived in the same place at one time, and fled together. I listened when she spoke of other storms she had seen. She didn't laugh as much as Mutti, but she was friendly. She always seemed so tall and strong, and I was completely comfortable in her presence.

In those days, I was skin and bones, as were most of the children around us. Since food delved into so many of my thoughts during the day, it was only natural that eating—or not eating—drifted into my dreams as well. Sometimes I dreamed there was absolutely nothing to eat. Other nights I dreamed of large, heavy portions. In those visions, I sat down to a table with piles of cheese, cakes and jams. I ate until my stomach felt absolutely full. And then, instead of getting up from the table, I helped myself to another serving.

In 1946, I regularly went with Mutti to wait in long lines for rations, as I had the year before. That year, she occasionally assigned me the task to do on my own. Early in the morning, I walked down the street to the shops, armed with the stamps I needed. Then I waited in line, got the rationed items, and headed home. Sometimes I took Wilfried, who was three years old, along on the errand.

Mutti often sent us to get bread. Wilfried and I walked a block to the nearby bakery. We handed our stamps to the baker, who then held up a long, dark-colored loaf for us to see. He handed us the loaf, and we took the precious commodity home.

One day in the fall of 1946, when we went to pick up bread, Wilfried and I got the loaf just like Mutti wanted. The bakery had lots of loaves that day, and my nose tingled at the warm aromas of grain wafting throughout the bakery. Everything smelled so wonderful I wanted to eat it all.

But I didn't.

Instead, I took the loaf the baker handed to me and started for home. Wilfried walked beside me.

Pretty soon I could no longer focus on the street, or the trees, or the other people outside. Everything grew a little blurry and faded into the background. All I could think about was that loaf of bread. By this time, I was even hungrier than when we first set out to get the loaf. The smell of freshly baked bread enchanted my nose.

We walked a few more steps. Then, without hardly thinking, one of my hands moved toward the loaf. I broke off a small chunk and popped it into my mouth.

Wilfried did the same.

Then I did it again.

And he did too.

The rationed bread was so good, it tasted better than cake to me.

I pulled more from the remaining loaf. Continuing on, Wilfried held on to one end of the loaf. I kept a hand on the other end. We both took pieces from our ends, and crushed them into our mouths. We continued taking nibbles and bits until we got home.

By the time we arrived at the cottage, all that was left was a small hunk of the previously-whole loaf. When Mutti saw it, she put her hands on her hips and her eyebrows furrowed. She was upset—the bread was supposed to feed our family of five, and Wilfried and I had nearly eaten it all.

But her anger dissipated in a few moments. Surely she understood our disobedience was caused by hunger pains. Wilfried and I weren't punished for eating so much of the bread.

Our suffering was commonplace. The Nazi regime, and the war it had ignited, had fizzled from the Earth. But the embers of destruction lingered in our area, and would remain there for years.

* * *

At the time, I had no knowledge that in 1946, the first international trial held in Nürnberg, Germany, drew to a close. The event marked the first of various trials that revealed the depth of some of the nearly incomprehensible crimes committed while the Nazi government was in power.

The Holocaust, or killing of millions of Jews and other people by the Nazi regime during World War 2, consisted of a ghastly list of crimes: murders, wrongful imprisonments, and tortures, to name a few. When it was over, the world's countries faced the challenge of seeking jutice for such acts. The International Military Tribunal held at Nürnberg, Germany, attempted to approach this challenge on a legal basis.[81]

Some involved in the Nazi regime escaped the trial. Hitler committed suicide right before the war ended. Still, many important Axis leaders fell into Allied hands, either through surrender or capture. These individuals, who became the defendants at the trial, included Nazi Party officials and high-ranking military officers. German industrialists, lawyers and doctors were also among the defendants.[82]

The Nürnberg Trial started in November 1945. During the trial, 21 defendants faced charges of crimes against peace, war crimes, crimes against humanity, and conspiracy to commit these crimes. Testimony presented at Nürnberg revealed previously unknown information such as details of what went on in Auschwitz, and the estimated six million Jewish victims.[83]

The prosecution brought out haunting evidence, including tanned human skin with tattoos on it from concentration camp victims, preserved for the wife of the Commandant of Buchenwald. The Buchenwald concentration camp was located in east-central Germany. The commandant's wife, Ilse Koch, liked to have the flesh formed into objects such as lampshades for her house. Another piece of evidence consisted of a fist-shaped shrunken head of an executed Pole, which had been used as a paperweight.[84]

One of the most powerful testimonies of the trial came from a French woman named Marie Claude Vallant-Couturier. She had been a member of the French Resistance, which had fought against the Nazi regime occupation of France, and then spent three years at Auschwitz. Vallant-Couturier described how a Nazi orchestra played happy tunes as soldiers separated those destined for slave labor from those who would be gassed. One night, she said, she was "awakened by horrible cries. The next day we learned that the Nazis had run out of gas and the children had been hurled into the furnaces alive."[85]

When the trial came to an end in October 1946, 11 defendants present at the trial were sentenced to death by hanging. Seven others received time in prison as a sentence. Three were found not guilty.[86]

One of the leading members of the Nazi Party who had been sentenced to death, Hermann Goering, committed suicide before the hanging. The rest of the defendants sentenced to death, however, were hung. On October 16, 1946, starting just after 1 a.m., the hanging of the last 10 men began. By 2:45 a.m., it was all over.[87]

And with that, the world took a step—perhaps a small one, but a step nonetheless—away from the Nazi Regime. It started to move past the horrors of the Second World War, and to think about how future crimes would be handled. Many leaders now had the experience to treat other international issues involving genocide.[88]

At a time when many Jews could not count the number of family members they had left, I was part of a whole household. Mutti, Papa, Wilfried, Rainer and I were together. We had all survived.

* * *

The rains cleared toward the end of fall in Hamburg in 1946, and the temperature cooled. Children walked about in coats made out of blankets. Turnips graced the table for lunch, and potatoes for supper. If the day had been especially tough, we ate turnips for breakfast, lunch, and supper. When each meal ended, I was still hungry.

I filled my days playing on the street, wandering in the fields, and weaving through the bomb crater near our home. I imagined and created a play world in the midst of the shrapnel. I was one soul, saved by God, walking through a place barely on the edge of recovering.

Yet Mutti had hope and continued to instill it in us as children.

"God has taken care of us, and he will keep providing for us," she told us.

And she sang:

> *Gott heil'ger Geist, du Trüster werth,*
> *Gieb' dei'm Volk ein'rlei Sinn' auf Erd'*
> *Steh bei uns in der letzten Noth*
> *G'leit uns ins Leben aus dem Tod.*
> *Martin Luther – 1541*

> *O Comforter of priceless worth,*
> *Send peace and unity on earth.*
> *Support us in our final strife,*
> *And lead us out of death to life.*
> *(Lord, Keep us Steadfast in Thy Word*
> *Translated by Catherine Winkworth, 1863)[89]*

Around that time, the ban on sending goods to Europe was lifted. An organization known as CARE, which stood for the Cooperative for American Remittances to Europe, started sending food relief to Europe. The organization was based in the United States, and thousands of Americans, including President Harry S. Truman, contributed to the effort.

The early packages sent by CARE were actually extra parcels that had originally been intended for the U.S. Army. Known as "10-in-1" food parcels, they had enough supplies in them to make one meal for 10 soldiers during the planned invasion of Japan. While prepared for this purpose, the packages were not needed for the war efforts. Instead, CARE received them at the end of the war.[90]

These first CARE packages contained one pound of beef in broth, one pound of steak and kidneys, 8 ounces of liver loaf, 8 ounces of corned beef, 12 ounces of luncheon loaf, 8 ounces of bacon, 2 pounds of margarine, one pound of lard, one pound of fruit preserves, one pound of honey, and one pound of raisins. They also had one pound of chocolate, two pounds of sugar, 8 ounces of egg powder, two pounds of whole-milk powder, and two pounds of coffee.[91]

When the "10-in-1" parcels ran out, CARE assembled its own food packages. To create these, CARE began a service that let Americans send parcels to friends and families in Europe. Americans had the option of buying a package or making one.

If they wanted to purchase one, it cost $10. For that amount, CARE guaranteed the person on the address would receive the package within four months.[92]

People who wanted to contribute toward a package could make a donation. This donation was often in the form of a dollar. The program used the money received to create boxes and send them over. During 1946, 1.9 million CARE packets were handed out in Europe.[93]

Individuals also began sending containers of supplies on their own. They put food and other items in a package, and sent it on its way.

Since before the war, Mutti had corresponded with her Aunt Emilia Lehman. Mutti had known Aunt Emilia from the time she had been a girl. Years before the Second World War, Aunt Emilia went to America. She and Mutti had kept in touch through letters before we fled from Schneidemühl.

While we were living in the cottage in Harksheide, Mutti sent her Aunt Emilia a letter to notify her of our new address.

One day, in 1946, Mutti received a letter from Aunt Emilia. In it, she confirmed she had received our new address.

The next day, a package arrived. It was the first one we had received. Emilia's name and address were written in the sender section.

"I can't believe it!" exclaimed Mutti when she peeked inside. There were food supplies in the package, as well as thread, needles, and coffee. There was even a pair of shoes for Mutti.

"It's like it was sent from heaven," Mutti said, sitting down amidst the contents and smiling. She cast an admiring gaze over everything she pulled out.

This event triggered a new component to our survival. We kept receiving care packages, and they came with wonderful goods inside. We got flour, sugar, lard, and chocolate chips—many items that were scarce or unavailable to us at that time in Harksheide.

One day, an unusual-looking bundle arrived at the cottage. The cardboard box was torn in several places, but overall still held its shape. Eager to see what it held, we opened it right away. It was a care package, but the box had been damaged during transit. Nearly everything inside had broken apart. The chocolate chips were scattered among flour that had spilled out, and the sugar bag was torn open. It was a mess.

But it didn't matter. I was so excited to see chocolate that I carefully picked the chips from the heap. The chocolate tasted sweet, and melted in my mouth.

There was also a container of lard inside. It had remained intact. We opened it up and eagerly spread it on our rationed bread. The lard clung to our stomachs wonderfully; our bodies eagerly absorbed the fat.

Another time when a care package came, Wilfried helped us open it. When he saw a container of lard, he got up and ran to the kitchen. He came back with a big spoon Mutti used for stirring soup. He opened the lard and dug the spoon in. He sat on the floor, spoon in hand, lard container on his lap, dishing up one heaping spoonful after another for himself. His cheeks flushed with contentment.

The care packages started arriving just in time. A deep freeze set in to mark the winter that began in 1946. Living conditions worsened, and that winter came to be known as the Hunger Winter.[94]

CHAPTER NINE: FINDING FRIENDS

"Rock of Ages, cleft for me,
Let me hide myself in Thee;
Let the water and the blood,
From Thy riven side which flowed,
Be of sin the double cure,
Save me from its guilt and power."
—Augustus Montague Toplady, 1763[95]

Two factors set the tone for Europe's frightful winter which began in 1946 and lasted until the spring of 1947. First, farmers faced severely high temperatures and little rain during the growing season, which led to a poor harvest in the fall of 1946. This meant less food to go around. Second, cold weather followed the bad crop. The trees' once-green leaves turned brown, shriveled, and fell to their death. Then, in November 1946, throughout Europe, the thermostat plummeted. Temperatures suddenly dropped below freezing point.[96]

By January 1947, ice covered 37 miles of the Rhine River, a main river in Germany. The frozen sections of this important channel were located in the zones occupied by the French and British. The Elbe River, another main waterway, froze completely. These rivers, which in good weather were used to transport supplies within Germany, could no longer be used to carry goods from one place to another.[97]

Many people had little protection from the cold. During the war, 25 percent of homes in Germany had been destroyed, and another 25 percent had been badly damaged. As a result, around 20 million people lived in ruins after the war.[98]

Those living in makeshift dwellings faced poor insulation and heating capabilities. In Hamburg, in 1946 and 1947, between 40,000 and 60,000 people lived in Nissen huts. These people shivered inside their homes, which consisted of corrugated steel.[99]

The walls and interiors of houses often appeared to be covered in glitter. The shine actually came from a paper-thin layer of white frost. The frost formed when people breathed, coughed, or sweated. The moisture accumulated and then froze, creating the sparkling surface.[100]

We slept in our clothes. Even with the warmth from the wood stove, I felt the icy air seep into the cottage through the cracks in the roof and around the window frames. In the morning, a thin layer of ice covered the water Mutti kept in a bucket in the kitchen.

Folks fortunate enough to live in a well-insulated home also faced struggles. This was because they couldn't find much suitable material to keep their abodes warm. There was a serious lack of coal for heating homes.[101]

Food became harder to find. In some areas of Germany, the actual rations people received fell to 1,000 calories per day, or 800 calories, or even fewer. Everyone was so desperate that looting was commonplace. In Hamburg, the police counted 9,200 thefts during January 1947.[102] Black market activities, though illegal, soared. Anyone with household goods of value looked for ways to sell them or trade them for food.

Production levels for many goods plummeted. The Allies sometimes took down factories that had not been bombed in an effort to demilitarize Germany. And the remaining facilities faced further challenges. If machinery at a plant broke down or needed to be replaced, it was next to impossible to fix the equipment or get new devices. Shortages extended to a wide variety of items, including matches, shoe polish, shoe laces, yarn, thread, razors and soap.

The season was unforgiving, especially to the young and elderly. Many died from the cold, from hunger, or from a lack of strength to fight illnesses when they struck. Fatalities caused by the cold came to be known as *Weisser Tod*, which means "White Death."[103]

For many, it was the coldest winter in living memory. About 12,000 people died when temperatures hovered around thirty degrees below.[104]

The combination of freezing temperatures, a poor transportation system, dismal housing situations, and food shortages made life extremely tough.[105]

The conditions led some citizens to take action. They protested and carried out demonstrations in the American and British zones during the first months of 1947. At these protests, the people held signs with messages such as *"Wir Wollen Kohle, Wir Wollen Brot"* (We want coal – We want bread)[106].

Breakfast for us during that time consisted of turnips. For lunch, we had turnips once more. And supper was, more often than not, turnips for the third time that day. I wondered when we would eat something else.

Due to the bleak conditions, care packages became part of our lifeline. If one showed up, we ate from the package and got a break from turnips. These wonderful packages tended to come unexpectedly, so we never knew when another one would arrive in the mail. When a new box came, we always dug in immediately. Mutti considered each one to be a special blessing from above, sent to help take care of us.

Throughout the winter, it was too cold to play outside. And while the cottage protected us from the outdoors, it was still chilly indoors. Mutti and Papa knew the place, with its icicles leaking inside, could not hold up much longer. As each month passed, conditions at the cottage further deteriorated. The roof leaked more and the place grew draftier.

Perhaps for this reason, during the first months of 1947, the government assigned us a different place to stay.

The new quarters were not far away. The cottage was on a street named Glashütter Weg. The next place was just one block away, on a street known as Grozkoppelstraße. Glashütter Weg and Grozkoppelstraße both ran east to west and were parallel to one another.

We carried our few possessions over to the new house. We hauled some of the things in the potato sacks Mutti first packed for the flight from the Russians. We walked a block and then looked over the new place.

The home on Grozkoppelstraße was a mansion compared to the small wooden house we started in. It stood two stories high, and had red brick and stucco on the outside. It also had a large front yard filled with trees and bushes. A fence and gate surrounded the property.

Mutti knocked.

A man opened the door and greeted us with a scowl.

His face had dark, lined features that looked like they had hardened with time. I practically heard him thinking, "We will follow orders, but I'm not going to give them any more than I have to."

He introduced himself as Mr. Menzer, and led us to our portion of the home. To get there, we first walked through a wide front entrance. To the left there was a closed door. Mr. Menzer opened it, and waved his hand inside. "You will stay here," he announced.

The door opened to a fairly large room. It had one window in it, about the size of a bedroom window. In the center of the room was a big bed. There was also a small table and chairs. The space would serve as the living room, dining room, and bedroom for the five of us.

We had access to one additional area of the home. This was located on the first floor near the back entrance. It consisted of a small room with a stove Mutti could use to cook our meals. Off of that room was a bathroom. There was also a door leading from the kitchen area down the stairs to the home's basement. We weren't allowed to use the basement. The rest of the house was also off limits.

We settled quickly into the bedroom. The house was much more insulated than the cottage had been. There were no icicles in the home, and our living space stayed consistently warmer than the inside of the cottage during winter.

The home's owners, Mr. and Mrs. Menzer, lived at the place with us. We didn't see them much. The space was large enough that they could live their lives mostly separate from us. When we did cross paths, they seemed aggravated. Clearly they didn't like sharing their home with refugees.

Fortunately for us, and more importantly for others with less shelter, the icy temperatures didn't stay forever. As spring started to creep into Hamburg, the weather warmed up.

Then it rained. And poured.

The heavy downpours quickly led to a new issue: flooding. Torrential flooding occurred in Britain, Germany, and many other parts of the continent. Hamburg's gutters overflowed, and its bomb craters turned to lakes filled with black polluted water.[107]

I watched the rain through the window. I touched the cool, damp glass. I wanted to go outside, but Mutti wouldn't allow it. I might catch a cold, she explained. When I tired of watching the gray drops splatter on the ground, I sat on the bed and wondered about my next meal.

Every day, my stomach gnawed, wishing for more food. It wasn't much use talking to Mutti about how hungry I was. She knew, and she steadily searched for something for us to eat. Even though it wasn't time for harvesting, she went to the nearby farmers to ask for some of their stored vegetables. Some days Mutti returned home empty handed, after a farmer refused to spare a few potatoes or turnips. When she did, I always hung my head. It meant less food on the table for the next meal.

We encountered two types of people in our lives during that time. Some, like Mrs. Jühls and our relatives in America, truly wanted to help. After we moved, we continued to visit the nearby Jühls family. Also, Mutti let our connections in the United States know of our change of address. This way, they could still send care packages to our new place.

Mr. Menzer fell into the second camp of people. Whenever he laid eyes on us, he was mean and evil-spirited. Perhaps he disliked refugees, or couldn't cope with a fallen Germany, or simply didn't want to be told what to do by the new government. Whatever the reason, he was quick to take his frustration over the situation out on us.

March 1947 turned into a dismal month. There was very little indoor lighting in our room at the Menzer house. I played inside in the dark, even during the day. Outside the sun hid behind dark clouds.

When the temperatures finally warmed up, and the rain subsided, Wilfried and I ventured outside. Soon the sun joined us, and the clear skies lifted my spirits.

There were many fruit trees in Mr. Menzer's yard. In summer, the trees blossomed with fresh produce. Pears, plums, and apples filled their branches. Berries dotted the bushes, including gooseberries and raspberries. Bunches of luscious grapes formed on vines growing along a wall. There was such a selection of fresh food it was tantalizing.

The fruit loomed in front of us. One day, while leaving the house with Mutti, I spotted a ripe pear dangling from a tree. The lush green fruit nearly called out to me. I grabbed it, and snapped it off the tree.

At that exact moment, Mr. Menzer came out of the house. He clipped toward me. He had brown hair and a slight build, but his glare was fierce. I could tell he was angry.

Pointing to the trees and the fruit hanging from the branches, he said, "You can't pick that fruit and take it."

Then he waved his hand toward the ground. Bruised and spoiled pieces of produce lay on the yard, half-covered with dirt. He continued, "You can only have what's fallen from the trees."

To keep the peace, Mutti instructed me to follow his orders. She also told Wilfried and Rainer to only pick up the fruit from the ground. From then on, we merely looked at the fruit in the trees. We never picked it.

Mr. Menzer also did not allow us to play in the yard. So Mutti led my brothers and me to places where we could run around, outside of the fence. She walked us from the house, through the yard, and past the gate. Outside of the gate, a dirt road ran past the place. We played there, on the road in front of the house.

Despite the unpleasant living situation, packages from America continued to arrive. Our relatives had received Mutti's notice about our change of address and sent boxes to the Menzer house. The packages nearly overflowed with the generous offerings. The anticipation of a package coming, along with the excitement of receiving one, became bright spots in our lives.

One day when I was playing, I met a girl named Heidi. She lived in Harksheide too. I was six years old then, and she was nearly the same age. She had blonde hair and wore it in braids down her back.

Heidi dressed in old, torn clothes, just like me. We lived on the same street, three houses away from each other, and instantly became friends. Since neither of us went to school, and both of our mothers were busy, we had many free hours to fill.

Heidi was born in Berlin in 1941. During the war, her mother took her out of Germany's capital. Together they traveled to Harksheide, where Heidi's grandparents lived. Even after the war ended, they stayed with Heidi's grandparents, whose home was just three houses away from ours.

I enjoyed having a friend so close.

Like my Papa, Heidi's father had left home during the war to fight. Unlike Papa, however, Heidi's father never returned. During the course of the war, he went missing in battle. The family heard no further news from him. And when the war ended, he never came home.

Heidi's mother worked as a seamstress, and she sewed for other people in the neighborhood. Making clothes wasn't easy at that time because of the shortages. There was barely any cloth available. The supply of clothing to the population in Germany had dwindled during the war. After the war, textiles nearly disappeared.

Heidi's mother used whatever she could, and recycled material as resourcefully as possible. She made coats out of blankets for children, and trousers from coats. She said it was not important what a person wore; what mattered was that a person had something to put on. In return for her efforts, she received a little money and food from her customers.

Even so, like me, Heidi was often hungry. Her family had friends in the area who were farmers. When Heidi and her mother visited them, she sometimes went to look at the pigs on the farm. "When I smelled the potatoes the pigs ate, I was envious," she recalled. Her stomach yearned for the food the animals had.

Heidi and I always found plenty of things to do together. We often spent time outside. I particularly loved playing marbles in the dirt road in front of our house. Shortly after we met, Heidi's mother made two dolls out of rags for us to play with. We loved those dolls dearly. We had few other toys, but that didn't bother us.

While playing outside, we frequently ran into other children. We also encountered adults, heading to and from work, or walking to pick up rations. Children paid respect to grown-ups according to the local customs. When greeting neighbors, boys took a bow and girls curtsied. Heidi and I followed the tradition. When we came across a grown up outside, we always stopped and curtsied to show good manners.

As the weather warmed, we ventured further from home. The bomb crater I loved to play in had filled with water from the flooding earlier in the year. With the sun and breeze, coupled with higher temperatures, it slowly dried out. Then Heidi and I explored the crater together. Sometimes we brought the dolls Heidi's mother sewed for us, and other times we brought jump ropes. Most of the time, though, we only took ourselves. We made up games and played them together in the crater.

Soon vegetation started growing in the crater. We slid and rolled down the grassy slopes to get to the bottom.

On occasion, Wilfried, who was now four years old, joined us. Some days, Mutti put me in charge of Rainer, who was nearly three years old. Wilfried and Rainer stayed with us while Mutti prepared meals or searched outside for food.

Everyone, including Heidi, loved Rainer. He was a sweet-looking boy with blue eyes and blonde hair. He tagged along as we played games and acted out make-believe scenarios. Wilfried became known in the area for his—quite literally—hard head. He could bang it on a fence post and not even wince. He said he didn't feel any pain, and indeed, he never acted as if he did.

With so many other kids in the neighborhood, soon Heidi and I made more friends. Two in particular, Karin and Inge, became close companions and playmates. All of us lived in the same area, and the four of us met regularly to play.

Inge had light brown hair. She was fair-skinned, like Heidi and me. Karin had a deeper skin tone and very dark hair. We all wore our hair in braids. And all of us wore ragged clothing, but it didn't matter. We had fun playing together.

There was a meadow at the end of our street. We regularly spent the morning or afternoon there. In spring, it came to life. The area filled with grass, and lovely blue cornflowers sprouted. They swayed and danced in the wind. Then red and yellow flowers sprung up, adding more color to the place. With so much of the Hamburg region bombed out, this quiet, seemingly untouched bit of nature became a bit of a haven. It was a lovely place to play, and my newfound friends and I spent many hours there.

The meadow also had some trees. One in particular, a great linden tree, towered above the others. If a thunderstorm struck while we were playing in the meadow, which happened frequently, we dashed to the safety of the big Linden. We clustered under its branches to escape from the lightning and the rain. Even though I felt safer by the tree than in the wide open parts of the meadow during storms, the thunder still terrified me.

When we fled from Schneidemühl in 1945, I wore a pair of shoes for the trip. The shoes were the only footwear I owned. During our time in Harksheide, my feet grew. To accommodate for this, Mutti cut off the top of the toe on each shoe. This allowed more room for my feet to fit. Other kids in the neighborhood faced a similar situation, and I often saw open-toed shoes on their feet too.

During the spring of 1947, Mutti noticed a bone protruding below the inside of my left ankle. It went through my ankle and then, instead of curving back toward my foot, it bulged out. A bone stuck out near the inside of my right ankle as well, but the deformity was more severe on the left side. On my left foot, in addition to the bone sticking out near the ankle, a bone protruded out of the top of the foot.

Mutti thought I may have been born with the problem. In Schneidemühl, the deformities had never bothered me. In Harksheide, however, the bones started to hurt. Walking, in particular, turned into an uncomfortable activity.

Mutti took me to a doctor in the spring of 1947. He looked at the structure of my feet, as well as the misplaced bumps from the bones.

After the examination, he sat down and looked across his desk to Mutti and me.

"Well, she has flat feet," he began. I looked down at my feet. They didn't look flat at all.

"And there are some deformities in the bone structure, especially on the left ankle."

He and Mutti continued talking, and I swung my legs back and forth under the chair.

"She'll need special shoes," the doctor said. "By wearing tall boots with laces, we can get her legs and feet in alignment."

I needed new shoes? I thought. I looked at Mutti. Her brows were wrinkled up.

"How expensive are they?" she asked.

"Usually about 50 marks."

"That's how much my husband makes in a week."

The doctor shrugged. "Yes, they are pricey, but they will help get the bones in the right places again. And she'll need to do exercises too."

Somehow, driven by a desire to help with my foot problems, Mutti and Papa managed to buy the shoes. They were dark brown and rose up high over my ankles. They fit well on my feet, and reduced the pain right away.

To do my foot exercises, I stood on the outside of both of my feet. This position pulled the ankles inward, placing them back where they belonged. I stood on the outside of my feet every day. Since I could only stand for a little while with my feet in that particular hold, the doctor told me to do a set of 10 exercises two times a day.

In April 1947, when I was six and a half years old, Mutti took me to register for first grade. The school I would attend was just a few blocks from our home.

In Germany, the school year started in April and continued on right through the summer. Some time off was given in fall so children could help with the harvests. There were other short breaks at Christmas and Easter too. Overall, the school ran year round, with vacation time interspersed with weeks of study.

After the war, schools in our area were divided into two sessions: a morning session and an afternoon one. This setup helped accommodate the large population of children living as refugees in Harksheide. I went to the morning session of classes.

For the first day of school, Mutti helped me put on my high topped shoes. I also wore knee-high socks, a dress, and a coat to stay warm. On my back I carried a *schulranzen*, or satchel. Inside the bag was a chalk pencil and slate board. I used the pencil to write on the slate. Then, to clean it, we wiped the slate with a rag. My hair hung in a fresh braid.

Before I left home that morning, Mutti gave me a *schultüte*, which was a large, cone-shaped bag. According to German tradition, the gift celebrated the beginning of a school year. It was also designed to help ease any anxiety about the first day of classes.

I looked inside my paper bag. It was full of flowers.

"Oh Mutti it's beautiful!" I exclaimed. "Did you pick these?"

"Of course, just for you," she said. I threw my arms around her.

"These flowers and God will be with you," she continued.

"I know," I replied. I gave her a kiss and headed off to school. I walked there with Heidi, who also had a special bag for the first day of school. When we arrived, I saw that many of the girls I had met on the street were in the same morning session.

I smiled broadly, with the gift in hand, until I reached the classroom. Other kids filled the room, and as I walked in, two of them were chanting, "Refugee, refugee," and pointing to a small boy.

I stood in my place, and watched the child wipe tears from his eyes. I wasn't from the area either, and tension quickly squeezed my body. Would I get treated like an outsider too?

Nothing happened the first day, but over the next weeks, my concerns about how I would be treated turned out to be fairly accurate. One of the ways our teachers dealt with *flüchtlinge*, or refugees, like me, was through harsh treatment. My instructors were quick to punish me during school, even if I felt I hadn't done anything wrong.

To issue punishment, the teacher told me to come and stand in front of the class. Once there, he took a ruler and struck it on my knuckles. This chastisement for no realistic reason seemed to be a method the teachers, like our host Mr. Menzer, used to channel the frustrations they felt from the war and the influx of needy people its aftermath had brought to their area.

Because of a government program aimed to feed schoolchildren, I ate better at school than at home. Some days for lunch we received a *brötchen*, or hard roll. We also got a bowl of soup to go with it. My classmates and I took the hearty bread roll, broke off pieces from it, and dipped the chunks in the soup.

Going to school created a sense of routine for me. After the upheaval of fleeing from our home, living in temporary housing, and being designated refugees, school helped establish a new kind of normalcy in my life. It did the same for Heidi and some of my other friends at the time as well.

I went to school in the mornings, and often had the afternoons free. After the bleak winter and rainy spring, the sunshine that summer invigorated me. Heidi and I spent hours playing with our friends in the street that ran past our homes. When I was with these children, I didn't feel the pressure of being looked at as a refugee, or someone who had drained the food and shelter supplies in Harksheide after the war.

Not all days were days to play, however. I also had to help Mutti with food and chores in our room.

If turnips were the sole food item that didn't run dry in those days, there was one industry (not counting, of course, the black market, which many benefited from illegally) still thriving. It consisted of the scrap metal market. In the early years of the war, Germany's factories cranked out helmets, guns, bullets, weapons, bombs, and other war equipment. After producing these items and waging war on Europe and Russia, those manufactured materials came back to haunt Germany. The Allies rained their own shrapnel and poured war-related equipment into the area. Then, during their retreat, German troops left behind supplies and uniforms.

All of this meant there was a vast amount of scrap metal in our area. And while some people found creative uses for old war supplies, others realized the scraps could be resourceful in another way. In fact, this hodgepodge of material could be used to rebuild Germany.

Soon an industry formed, in which some businesses collected scrap metal. They sold the metal to other companies. These companies, in turn, repurposed it for construction efforts in the city.

Our place in this chain lay at the very beginning. We hunted for scraps, and then turned in our findings to the local scrap dealer. In return, we received food stamps.

Heidi came with me to search for metal. For the task, Mutti asked the neighbors to lend us a wagon. They always agreed. Heidi and I set out together, pulling the wagon behind us.

We spent hours searching the area. Sometimes we found pieces of metal on the sidewalk near our home. We also hunted in the bombed-out crater, which was full of bits of hardware.

Other kids pulled a wagon and filled it with scrap metal too. Even adults went out sometimes to gather pieces. Any sort of metal that could be found was valuable, as it meant a chance to get more food.

While all metal was worth collecting, we received a better deal on the big sections we turned in. With that in mind, I kept a special lookout for sizable pieces. If I found a chunk of metal that was three or four feet long, I heaved it into the wagon. Then I held on to an end of it while Heidi pulled the wagon so it wouldn't topple out. We walked home that way, with the crooked, bent, or odd-shaped scrap balanced in the wagon.

Sometimes Wilfried came along to help. Occasionally Rainer joined us too. He sat in the back of the wagon, his little legs sticking over the sides, while we collected pieces. He, like us, had to be careful. Much of the metal we found had sharp edges. When we grabbed the pieces or touched them, we ran the risk of cutting our hands on the jagged sections.

Once we spotted a metal piece wedged in the ground. I could only see its top peeking out. To remove it, we dug around the object with our hands. Finally we pulled it out. Other times, we found small shells left over from bullets fired during the war. For fun, we took a hammer and flattened them.

When the wagon was full, we hauled our findings home and presented them to Mutti.

"This is very helpful," she said every time, looking over the metal.

Then she took the wagonload to a special place in Harksheide that collected leftover metal. I went along with her to take in the scraps. At the place, I always saw heaping piles of metal and junk. The more scraps Mutti brought, the more food stamps she received.

The extra stamps helped our family. Clearing out the area of scrap metal benefited Hamburg too. The land, once clean, served again for farmers to grow vegetables and grain, thus enhancing the food production cycle.

Collecting metal gave me a feeling of self-reliance. By picking up scrap metal and getting something in return for it, I sensed that we, too, could rebuild our lives. With each step and piece of metal gathered, we moved in a better direction, and the future held more promise than the past.

With food on our minds, Heidi and I searched for nourishment together. We looked through the potato fields nearby, even before the harvest was over and the rows were opened up to the public to scrounge for food. We did the same with turnips. Knowing we were desperate, our mothers allowed us to do this.

"Be careful that the farmer doesn't catch you," they always warned us before we left.

We tiptoed into the fields, and dug silently for potatoes and turnips. When I found one, I peeled it with my teeth and at it raw. Heidi did the same. The food helped calm the constant growling in our stomachs.

When the butcher down the street made sausages, Heidi and I stood in line at his shop. I held a little money in my hand that Papa gave me for such an occasion. When the butcher finished the sausages, he sold the water the meat had cooked in. The broth had a little fat in it, and also a little flavor from the sausages. We purchased the water. I loved drinking the sausage broth. It warmed my insides, and tasted delicious.

In 1947, my Uncle Hans, Mutti's brother, came to Harksheide. Two years earlier, before the war ended, he had been captured while serving in the German army and held as a prisoner of war in a French camp. He stayed in the camp even after the war ended. When the French finally released him, he found his way back to our family.

Mutti, always thrilled when family members came to Harksheide, rejoiced with the arrival of Uncle Hans. He carried scars from the war with him, including trouble with his eyes and one of his legs. Even so, the whole family celebrated the sight of him alive.

My Uncle Arnold, Mutti's youngest brother, also came to Harksheide. He had fled with his mother, my Omi, to get away from the Russians, and then stayed with a relative on a farm in the mountains to work after the war. In 1947, he came to live in our area.

Whenever someone we know arrived in Harksheide, Mutti invited relatives over to our place. So when Uncle Arnold and Uncle Hans showed up, many gathered in our small room. We were short on possessions, but overflowing with gratitude to see our family members. Even if she served only potatoes and water, Mutti smiled with contentment the entire visit.

Mutti taught me how to make our belongings last as long as possible. When a sock got a hole in it, we didn't throw it out. Instead, Mutti mended the sock, stitching up the hole. She showed me how to imitate the steps she took to fix a sock, and soon I could stitch an entire heel on a sock. I was proud of my new skills, and happy to help Mutti.

While we lived in the Menzer house, Mutti continued corresponding with some of our relatives in America. She got in touch with a cousin of hers, Pastor Arthur Fuerstenau. He served a Lutheran church in Grafton, Nebraska.

In one of his letters to Mutti, Pastor Fuerstenau mentioned the possibility of us coming to America. He noted we could attend a Lutheran church regularly there, and be actively involved members. He wrote of wide open fields, and the possibility of having work and plenty of food to eat.

Mutti longed for a place where we didn't have to worry about our next meal. She also wanted to go to church on a regular basis, an activity we weren't able to do in Harksheide.

Pastor Fuerstenau soon sent over details for Mutti to consider. He told of a refugee program geared to help folks like us. If we were interested, he offered, we might be able to move from Germany to America with aid from the church. If we wanted to come, he wrote, he would do whatever he could to make it possible.

At night, while lying on the floor where I slept in the room, I listened to Mutti and Papa talk about the letter.

"He says we could go to church every Sunday. Just think, every Sunday I could sing in church," said Mutti.

"What about our family here?" asked Papa.

"But it would be a better life, and food for our whole family."

Papa didn't answer.

"They say it is a land flowing with milk and honey," Mutti urged.

More food certainly appealed to me. I wondered, though, what a land full of milk and honey was really like. It sounded a little messy to get around in. Mutti seemed sure it would be a good thing. Given the bleak days in our one-room place, with bites of raw vegetables and sausage broth in our stomachs, heading to the country where the tantalizing care packages came from started sounding better and better.

"We should look into it," Papa said at last.

And with that, I closed my eyes. I dreamed of green fields, rivers of honey, and a table set with pitchers of milk, towering stacks of bread, and mounds of butter.

CHAPTER TEN: COMING TO AMERICA

"O beautiful for spacious skies,
For amber waves of grain,
For purple mountain majesties
Above the fruited plain!
America! America! God shed his grace on thee,
And crown thy good with brotherhood
From sea to shining sea!"
—Katharine Lee Bates, poem, 1910
—Samuel Augustus Ward, tune, 1882[108]

With America on her mind, Mutti looked into the paperwork needed to make the move. The process might have been an easy one, had she not stumbled into a roadblock early on. Since Papa had served in the German army, the *Wehrmacht*, he had been drafted to participate toward the end of the war. This made him ineligible for entry into the United States.

At the time, America let in some of those who, after the war, didn't have a place to call home. Its focus, however, centered on helping Eastern Europeans who had been brought into Germany by the Nazis and placed in prison camps or put to work. Now that the war was over, if they weren't able to return home, they could go to the United States. This was officially known as the Truman Directive on Displaced Persons of December 1945. It allowed 40,000 displaced persons to immigrate between 1946 and 1948.[109]

Those who married American soldiers or had close relatives in the United States left Germany and joined their loved ones on the other side of the Atlantic. The U.S. government also permitted scientists and technicians to enter. But no one who had been part of the *Wehrmacht* or was associated with the Nazi regime was welcome. This helped reduce the risk of Nazi officials fleeing borders to escape punishment for war crimes.[110]

Even though Papa had never faced trials for war crimes, and even though he didn't approve of the Nazi regime, he had been a soldier in the German army. Despite the generous offer of Pastor Fuerstenau, Mutti's cousin, to help, there was little that could be done to change Papa's official status—even if he loathed the Nazi policies.

After several months, the dream of going to America lost its shimmer. The hope of a new life took its place, quietly, in the corner of our refugee residence. Mutti didn't talk about it as much and instead, faced life, one day at a time, on our street in Harksheide.

For Germany, America, and the rest of Europe, 1948 brought many changes. One in particular, known as the European Recovery Program, launched that spring. On April 3, 1948, President Truman signed the program, which was commonly called the Marshall Plan. It aimed to boost Europe's recovery, and Congress approved $12.4 billion in aid for the plan.[111]

Eleven days later, on April 14, 1948, five American ships sailed from Galveston, Texas. They carried 54,000 tons of grain, and also fuel, food, feed, chemicals, fertilizers, raw materials, semi-finished products, and vehicles. They crossed the Atlantic, and became the first fleet to bring official aid from the European Recovery Program to Europe. More ships followed in the next days, weeks, and months, loaded in ports from Texas to New York, and carrying everything from wheat to mixed seeds, dry peas and construction equipment.[112]

The goals of the Marshall Plan reached beyond helping Europe's poor economic condition. It also sought to reduce the appeal of communism in Europe, and further expand U.S. commerce.[113]

The Soviet Union refused aid for its country and the German zones it controlled. So America sent funds to Western Europe, and in doing so, strengthened the growing divide between America and the Soviet Union. The United States tugged countries economically toward its own ideologies, while the Soviet Union sought to bring more nations into its own influence. As a result, the beginnings of the Cold War brewed.

Germany directed much of the aid it received toward rebuilding industries. The coal industry, for instance, took in 40 percent of the funds. After companies received money, they paid back the amount to the government. The funds could then be lent out to other businesses, who in turn repaid the government again.[114]

While the Marshall Plan made headlines, we didn't note any effects from it right away. Instead, for me, early 1948 brought a break from school. During it, I played with Heidi, collected metal, shot marbles, and pranced through the meadow. The vacation ended in April 1948, and we headed back to school.

My main teacher that year kept a branch on his desk. Students who disobeyed or caused a disturbance in class faced the switch on their hands, backsides, or worse—heads.

One day I sat at my desk in class. My hair hung in two braids down my back. I dipped my pen in the small inkwell perched on the ledge ahead of me, and wrote on my paper, following the teacher's instructions. My classmates on both sides dipped their pens in inkwells and wrote as well.

Our desks were formed of long benches with small ledges attached to the back of them. Rows of benches, each of them lined with students, filled in the room. Many kids paid close attention to the teacher. Some, however—especially those sitting on benches in the back of the room—bothered the students sitting in front of them.

During the middle of a lesson that day, I felt my braids move. Then something tugged on each one of them. I turned around to find the cause. As soon as I swiveled my head, the boy behind me laughed. He covered his mouth and pointed to the ends of my braids.

I swung my head back and grabbed my braids. I pulled them up to get a look at the ends. Black ink covered each end. It dripped on to my dress, forming small dots on my shoulders and collar.

Just then I heard the teacher. "Elfi, come to the front of the class."

It couldn't be! I was getting called on for an act I had nothing to do with. I reluctantly went.

"You are being disruptive," the teacher continued. "You shouldn't turn around in class. Hold out your hands."

The teacher slapped them several times with the switch, and then told me to return to my seat.

When I arrived home after school that day, I showed Mutti the wounds on my hands.

"What happened?" she asked.

"A boy behind me dipped my braids in ink!" I wailed. "And then the teacher punished me for it."

I showed her my ruined dress and colored hair. She took my hands in her own, studied them, and shook her head. Then she cleaned my braids. There was nothing to say to change the situation, and we both knew it.

* * *

In 1936, Hitler set up price controls so he could buy war materials at artificially low prices. Three years later, in 1939, rationing started. By 1948, the German people had lived under price controls for 12 years and rationing for nine years.[115]

After the war, the Allies kept price controls and rationing in place.[116] As shortages grew worse, many citizens turned to bartering to pay for items. They also used cigarettes as currency. Money was hardly used.[117]

To make money valuable again, the Allies proposed a new currency. This new form of money would replace the Reichsmark. In 1948, British, American, and French troops distributed 23,000 wooden crates around Germany. These containers held new money, which would have the name Deutschmark. The money had been printed in the United States. Exactly 10 billion, 701 million, 720 thousand Deutschmarks were delivered.[118]

On Friday, June 18, 1948, a special announcement came over the radio waves in Germany: "The military powers of Great Britain, France and the United States have passed the first law for the reform of the Germany monetary system. It will become valid as of June 20th. The old German currency will become invalid following the change."[119]

On June 20th, a Sunday, Mutti and Papa went to the same spot where Mutti usually picked up ration stamps. Instead of getting stamps for food, they each received the new currency. They got 40 Deutschmarks apiece. Every other German that went also received 40 Deutschmarks.

The new money symbolized power and change. Goods which few of us had seen for years, much less owned and enjoyed, appeared on store shelves. Clothing, shoes, and food were available and for sale without the need of a ration card.[120]

In addition to the new currency, the government cut tax rates. All of these changes had a nearly electric effect on the West German economy. As author Henry C. Wallich noted in his book, *Mainsprings of the German Revival*, "The spirit of the country changed overnight. The gray, hungry, dead-looking figures wandering about the streets in their everlasting search for food came to life." [121]

* * *

When I returned home from school on Monday, June 21, 1948, Mutti was nearly ecstatic. "Come and see," she said.

Taking me by the hand, she led me down the street, in the opposite direction of the way I usually walked to go to school. We arrived at the bakery, which usually had bare shelves in the afternoon. To my surprise, there was loaf after loaf, stacked on top of one another in the window.

"What is this?" I asked.

Mutti took me by the hand again in response. "Let's look at another one," she said.

Down the street we went. Store after store had more goods in it than I had seen the week before. With the new currency in place, shop owners were eager to sell items for money that was worth more than the previous marks. They chose to put their wares for sale in their own stores, rather than trading them for items on the black market.[122]

I was nearly dumbstruck at the sight. "Mutti this is wonderful," I stammered.

After a few more stops to peer inside windows, I had another question. "Can we buy any of it?"

"We don't have much money today, so no," said Mutti. "Soon, though, we may be able to buy more."

She was right. Within weeks, business picked up considerably in our area. Papa received the new currency in his wages. We bought our own goods, and didn't have to rely on ration cards any more. Shop owners preferred to receive money instead of ration stamps, and were motivated by the changes to sell whatever they could.

A month later, Mutti and Papa each received another 20 Deutschmarks at the same place where Mutti had gone for ration cards in the past. Other German citizens got this as well. [123] Over the next months, authorities removed the regulations on rationing in Germany. Sellers set their own prices for vegetables, fruit, eggs and almost all manufactured goods.[124]

Things were starting to look up in our area. Mutti and Papa suddenly had more options than what felt like ever before. Of course, the money they had to spend was very little, so our overall eating consumption didn't pick up right away. Still, there was a feeling of freedom and independence in the air that was contagious, even for young children.

On the other side of Germany, in the region the Soviets controlled, the economy was bleak. Something had to be done to keep the Reichsmark, which was the currency that had previously been used in the Western zones, from flooding the Soviet controlled region. As a result, the authorities on the Soviet side issued a currency known as the Deutschmark East.

At the beginning, the Deutschmark East was worth nearly the same amount as the currency the Allies introduced in the western zone. But that soon changed. At the end of July 1948, the Deutschmark East was worth approximately half the value of the western Deutschmark. This further separated East and West Germany.[125]

By September 1948, our living situation felt the effects of the currency reform and incoming aid. Some nights I crawled into bed without feeling hungry. During the day, Mutti loved having her brothers and other relatives over to our one-room place. Now she had more food to offer them at gatherings.

On September 22, 1948, for my eighth birthday, Mutti served a whole meal. And we had another reason to celebrate. Mutti's brother Lothar had returned. We had not received word from him since he left for the war.

My Uncle Lothar was Mutti's younger sibling who fell deathly ill as a child. He recovered somewhat miraculously after eating pickles, getting thirsty, and starting to drink fluids again. He remained healthy after that. He was drafted during the Second World War.

He was captured and spent years in England at a prison camp. Upon his release, he headed to Harksheide, where he joined the rest of the family. He was the last of the brothers in Mutti's family to arrive home after the war.

With Lothar's return, we had all of Mutti's brothers accounted for. On Papa's side, however, we did not know what had happened to his father, my Opa who stayed in Schneidemühl to care for the animals and wait for the Russians. We also had not heard from Uncle Willie, Uncle Erich, or Papa's two brothers-in-law.

* * *

In May 1948 the state of Israel appeared on the map.[126]

Also in 1948, Europe's East-West division hardened. Albania, Bulgaria, Romania, and Yugoslavia slid under communist control, along with Poland, Czechoslovakia, and Hungary. Greece resisted communist influence, in large part because it received aid from the United States. Essentially, though, Europe was divided between East and West, and would remain so for 41 years.[127]

That December, in preparation for the arrival of Christmas, Mutti managed to put together a small Advent wreath. She took pine branches and formed a circle out of them. She placed it on the table in our room and added candles to it. On Sundays, in the evenings, she lit a candle to mark the week of Advent. We enjoyed the wreath, but only on Sundays, as candles were expensive and we had to preserve them so they would last a long time.

On Christmas Eve, Mutti filled our plates higher than the year before. Then we went to a Christmas service at a large Lutheran church in Hamburg. When we got home, it was late, and I felt tired from the trip.

Mutti opened the door to our room, and I stumbled in, ready to fall asleep.

"It's not time for bed yet," said Papa. He pointed to a corner, where there were wrapped packages.

"For me?" I asked. Wilfried and Rainer dashed over to the gifts.

Mutti handed one of the gifts to me, the first one I had received since 1944, before we fled Schneidemühl. Wilfried and Rainer got a present too.

Eager to absorb the moment, I fetched my dearly loved rag doll from Heidi's mother. I perched her at my side, so she could be there for the special moment of gift unwrapping.

Then I began.

I tore away the brown paper wrapping, and gazed at the lovely figure inside.

I stared at the gift for several minutes.

"It's beautiful!" I finally managed to say.

Before me, looking directly into my eyes, was a doll. The figure had a porcelain face with fine features. I touched her hair; it was real. The doll was sturdy and stood nearly two feet tall. In an instant, it became my treasured possession.

I turned to Wilfried and Rainer. They hunched over a train set, deeply absorbed. Two open boxes sat next to them.

I wrapped my arms around Mutti and then Papa, hugging them tightly and thanking them profusely. Then I fixed my attention on the doll. I spent the remaining hours of the Christmas holiday gazing at the baby, softly touching her face, hands and feet, and smoothing out the lovely clothes she wore. It was a wonderful surprise and I couldn't wait to share the news with Heidi.

After Christmas, I played with the doll every day. In the evenings, I placed her carefully in a spot near the place on the floor where I slept. I never kept her too close to me in the evening. I didn't want to risk rolling on top and damaging her delicate features.

I showed Heidi and my other friends, and they adored the doll too. I loved combing the figure's hair, dressing her and changing her, but I never took her outside. Keeping her inside felt safer, as there was less chance of the doll getting dirty, lost, or broken.

In the spring of 1949, Wilfried, now six years old, started school. We walked to class together in the mornings, with Heidi, and returned side by side in the afternoons.

Like me and the other refugees, Wilfried often faced punishments. One day, the teacher had a violin bow on his desk to dole out punishments instead of the usual tree branch. He called on Wilfried for being disruptive. Wilfried stood before the teacher. In a flash, the teacher struck the violin bow on his head. Upon impact, it cut a large gash in his head. Blood poured out.

At home, Mutti was terribly upset when she saw Wilfried's head and cut.

The time we spent outside of school was generally more enjoyable. At home, larger portions of food crept in. My stomach grew less restless.

* * *

One of the first major international dilemmas of the Cold War, which involved Berlin, ended around that time. The Western Allies oversaw the western part of the city, and the Soviet Union controlled the eastern portion of Berlin. In an attempt to take over more of the city, the Soviet Union cut off access to the region the Allies supervised in 1948.

In response, the Western Allies flew in goods to Berlin. Known as the Berlin airlift, the drop offs began on June 26, 1948.[128]

The flights continued during the following months and into the next year. American and British planes regularly flew in 4,000 tons of food a day. At one point, they delivered 13,000 tons of food in just 24 hours.[129]

By the spring of 1949, the Allies had won the battle. They had proven they could support West Berlin, and continue flying in goods as needed. In response, the Soviet Union lifted the blockade in May 1949.

The Berlin crisis had significant consequences. Both sides, after three years of demobilization, started a vast and rapid buildup of their arms and military forces, including the reintroduction of the U.S. military draft in June 1948.[130]

The event also led to the creation of two separate German states: The Federal Republic of Germany (West Germany), and the German Democratic Republic (East Germany).

The Allies recognized West Germany, which consisted of 96,000 square miles and had a population of 56 million people. East Germany had a population of 19 million and was about 44 percent the size of West Germany.[131]

* * *

In the summer of 1949, Mutti invited some of my uncles over for a meal. After it was finished, Papa told the others of a new program he had heard about.

"We could build our own home," he explained to my uncles. "The government has it set up so that refugees like us can build a duplex. They provide the materials needed to build it, and we put in time to help construct the home."

"How much time?" asked Mutti.

"1,500 hours. It won't be that much if we all pitch in and work on it together."

And so it was settled. After school and on weekends, our whole family chipped in to build the house. Many times Mutti's brothers came to help too.

We spent most of the 1,500 hours of labor working at a factory nearby to make bricks for the house. The place took rubble gathered from around Hamburg, ground it up, and created new bricks.

The government provided land for the duplex on a street named Weg am Denkmal. This street ran parallel to Grootkoppelstraße, the road where Menzer's house was located. It was also just minutes, by foot, away from the school Wilfried and I attended.

I told my doll about the new place, and explained she could move to the house when it was finished.

Mutti continued to have family members in Harksheide over to visit on occasion. When others came, they always sat on the bed. It was a logical place to gather, as it was the only furniture in the room besides the table and chairs.

One afternoon, at a family gathering, several relatives perched on the bed. With my precious doll wrapped securely in my arms, I approached them. Together the doll and I sat down by the others. While they talked, I played.

After some time, I placed the doll on the bed. Not long after I set her down, I went to help Mutti on the other side of the room. While I was away, Wilfried pulled himself up and climbed onto the bed. As he sat, there was a terrible crunch.

He quickly jumped down.

I gasped and ran to the bed.

The doll's face was crushed to pieces.

I was speechless. The doll was destroyed.

"I'm sorry," Wilfried said, looking at the floor.

By then, I was crying too hard to respond. I had barely had the doll—not even a year—and already she was gone.

It was loud in the room. Everyone had scattered off the bed. Some looked on at the devastation before them.

Mutti, in the midst of them, quietly cleaned up the pieces.

I was torn apart. I knew the doll had been a special extravagance for my parents. Surely there wasn't enough money to buy a replacement doll right away. My precious toy was lost.

I cried for days over the doll. Even as life carried on, I felt sad for months.

And life indeed carried on. Work on the house took nearly a year to complete. When it was finished, I thought the home was beautiful.

It looked like many of the other houses in the neighborhood. It featured two stories, with brick and stucco on the outside. A tile roof topped the structure.

In our half of the duplex, the downstairs featured a kitchen, living room, and two bedrooms. On the second level, there was another bedroom. The upstairs room took up the entire second level of the house, creating a wonderful, ample space. It had an angled ceiling to match the roof.

We moved into the home in 1950. Omi, Mutti's mother, joined us. Prior to living with us, she had lived on her own and then stayed with some of my uncles.

In our new big house, there was now room for her. She moved into the bedroom upstairs. Mutti and Papa slept in one bedroom downstairs, and my brothers took up the other one. Papa set up a small bed for me in the kitchen, and I slept there.

After living in crowded, temporary spaces, the duplex must have seemed like a castle to Mutti. She hung delicate white lace curtains on the windows. Papa planted daisies, cornflowers, and lilies of the valley in the front yard. A fence surrounded the place, with a gate that opened to a walkway leading up to the door. We were officially in a home.

And it felt like it. Our family lived in one half of the duplex, and another family lived in the other side. The duplex had a spacious backyard. A fence running through the middle of it divided the yard into sections: one half for us and the other half for the neighbors. Even though I had spent my first years on a sprawling farm with so much free space to roam beyond its borders, after living in tight quarters for the past five years, our new yard felt abundant.

* * *

In 1950, the same year we moved to our duplex, North Korea invaded South Korea. The United States quickly jumped in to help South Korea, and another crisis began.

It was the Cold War's first hot war, and it came after nearly two years of skirmishes between North and South Korea. The Soviets backed North Korea, and so the war that followed was the first direct combat between the United States and the Soviet Union.[132]

* * *

By us, at home, Papa put in motion much of the outdoor expertise he had gathered while living on the acreage outside of Schneidemühl. A gardener at heart, he planted trees that soon produced cherries, plums, and apples. He wrapped white grape vines along the fence in the back. We also had raspberry bushes, boysenberry bushes, and even a *stachelbeere*, or gooseberry bush.

Papa created a garden with precise, straight rows. He kept it fully pruned, without a weed in sight. Soon we had carrots, beans, and snap peas for dinner. I loved snap peas so much that I often went out to the garden, before they had been picked, and helped myself to a few for a snack.

Papa also grew potatoes, and sometimes we had a meal of snap peas and potatoes together. We had kohlrabi in the garden and—of course—turnips.

That year, Mutti had exciting news: she was expecting another baby. I secretly hoped for a sister.

Several months after we moved into our new home, five years after Germany surrendered, we learned what happened to two of the relatives we hadn't had contact with since we lived on the acreage. One of these was Papa's brother Willie, Aunt Lydia's husband, who had run the restaurant back in our Schneidemühl days when I was small, and never returned from the war.

A man visited our family in Harksheide, and told us he spent time with Uncle Willie in a prison camp. He said he and Uncle Willie had been captured by the Russians and sent to a camp in Siberia. While there, Uncle Willie died of dysentery and starvation.

The report saddened Mutti and Papa. It devastated Aunt Lydia.

We also heard news of Opa, who had stayed on the farm until the Red Army came through that area. An acquaintance who also had remained in Schneidemühl, like Opa, told us what happened.

The fighting there started at the end of January 1945, right after we left. It lasted for more than two weeks.

On February 14, 1945, the Russians took over Schneidemühl. They captured Opa and put him in a line of men to be marched away as prisoners of war. At one point, a neighbor who ran a lumberyard stepped out of line. A Russian soldier shot the neighbor.

Opa was 75 years old at the time. He and the others with him walked for days in the cold with no food. The hard journey wore Opa down; he eventually stumbled and stepped out of line. When he did so, the Russians shot him. He fell in a ditch and they left him there to die.

As for Schneidemühl, the fighting destroyed three-fourths of the town; when the war was over, a full 90 percent of the city's historical center lay in ruins.

Papa had a brother-in-law who was also sent to a Russian prison camp. He was eventually released but died shortly after. We never heard from his other brother-in-law or his brother Erich.

* * *

If conditions for prisoners of the Western Allies were bad, those experienced by prisoners in the east were atrocious. Of the 3 million prisoners taken by the Soviets during the war, more than a third died in captivity. Prisoners taken in the east were 90 times more likely to die than those taken in the west.[133]

There were a number of reasons for this. First, resources were far scarcer. The Soviets and their allies had relied heavily on the Western powers to supply them with food and materials throughout the Second World War. They used their scant supplies first for themselves, and their army, before feeding prisoners. Also, considering how bitter the Russian winters could be, it was not a surprise that more prisoners died from exposure in Soviet camps than in Western ones. The biggest reason, however, was because virtually no one who looked after the prisoners in Russia cared whether they lived or died.[134]

Some lucky prisoners of war were sent home as early as 1947, but most remained in Soviet gulags until 1950, when Stalin issued an 'amnesty' for those Germans who had been 'good workers.'[135]

* * *

Papa was the only man in his family to be alive in 1950. In Mutti's family, all of her brothers, by God's mercy, survived. Just as they had come to visit us when we lived in the Menzer house, they came over to our new place.

We often had Heidi over for meals too. Before eating, we always prayed and thanked God for the food. Heidi noticed this was something she didn't do at home at the time.

In the spring of 1951, our whole neighborhood, filled with freshly built homes, sprung to life. Yellow and red tulips dotted the paths and yards, violets blossomed, and chrysanthemums and pansies of all colors grew amongst the other flowers. The bright shades of red, yellow, purple and other colors set against a solid green background of grass gave our streets a rejuvenating boost. Fruits and vegetables lined our yard. Harksheide, like other parts of Germany, was healing.

Perhaps the best part was that food was no longer as scarce as it had been. For birthdays, we now held parties and invited friends and relatives to the new house. Many of my uncles often joined us. For special occasions, Mutti always served *Kalter Hund*, (Cold Dog), a layer cake that didn't have to be baked. To make it, she took plain cookies, or butter biscuits, and lined a bread pan with a layer of them. Then she created a sauce by mixing together chocolate and coconut fat, a type of fat made from solidified coconut oil.

Often sold in Germany under the brand name Palmin, it resembled lard or vegetable shortening. On its own, coconut fat didn't have any flavor.

She spread the chocolate and coconut mixture over the cookies, and then repeated the layers several times. When she finished, she had a cake made of rows of cookies, with the chocolate and coconut mixture serving as a filling between each layer and also coating the top and sides.

After assembling it, Mutti put the tart in the fridge to chill. After a couple of hours, she took it out and removed it from the pan. The cake stood on a plate, looking lovely and tall. It tasted delicious every time she made it.

"Have another slice," Mutti always urged guests and our family.

The dessert was wonderful, but it was very rich, so we could only eat a little. If we ate too much, we felt sick. An overdose of the heavy sweetness caused a stomach ache that lasted for hours.

Two of my uncles—Arnold and Lothar—became butchers in Harksheide. One day, they showed up at our house with a little lamb. It was a lovely creature, and so gentle. I hadn't had a pet since the rabbit on the acreage before the war. I fell in love quickly with the animal, and cared for the lamb as a pet. I fed it regularly, gave it water, and played with it.

Several weeks later, Uncle Arnold and Uncle Lothar came over to visit again. They wanted to see my beautiful pet lamb. I happily went for it.

I brought the creature to them and started petting it. After admiring it, they took it from me. They led it to the backyard and got out a knife. Then they began the preparations to butcher it.

I ran to the kitchen in tears and stood there, listening to the ongoing butchering outside. I grew hysterical, horrified at the miserable ending my beloved pet had met. Mutti came in to comfort me, but it was no use. I was too distraught and soon she was called to help my uncles with the slaughtering.

After that, I refused to eat lamb.

The arrival of meat and more food pleased Mutti and Papa, but there were other issues they were dissatisfied with. For starters, Papa worked as a welder, helping to rebuild Hamburg, and got paid very little. We had a home, but money remained tight.

Perhaps more importantly for Mutti, the nearest Lutheran church was very far away. Since going to church still involved a full day's trip, we hardly went.

We had spent long years without the right vitamins and nourishment, and that deficit took a toll. Wilfried broke his arm while playing at school one day. It wasn't properly set, and he broke it two more times. The fractures were a result of poor nutrition, the doctor said.

Wilfried and Rainer, who turned eight and seven, respectively, in 1951, often polished bikes to make a little money. Uncle Reinhold and Uncle Arnold were two of their best customers. Whenever they came to visit, they let the boys clean their bicycles.

Wilfried and Rainer liked to polish the rims and spokes with oil. With the money they received, they were able to pay the entrance fee to soccer games. Sometimes Papa took them to a game, and they paid to get in with the money they had earned.

Once when Wilfried took a bike out for a spin after oiling it down, he fell and cut a gash six inches long in his leg.

The wound was deep, and Wilfried needed stitches. A doctor came over to the house, and put a rag in Wilfried's mouth. Then he put the stitches in. There was no pain killer to give Wilfried or anything that could be done to numb the pain. The rag was simply used to keep him from screaming.

Rainer and I looked on. The scene disturbed me, and I felt terrible for him. Rainer and I both cried as they treated him.

* * *

In those years, other changes took place around the world. In the United States, the Displaced Persons Act came into being in 1948. This law allowed an additional 205,000 displaced persons to immigrate between 1948 and 1950.[136]

Then in 1950, the law was amended to let even more immigrants come over. Those that did so had to have an American sponsor. Potential sponsors included individuals such as relatives or voluntary organizations such as churches. These sponsors needed to demonstrate they were in a financial position to support the immigrant. A statement from the sponsor pledging support for the newcomer had to accompany the visa application submitted to American consulates.[137]

The biggest change that affected us, however, was that starting in 1949, ordinary Germans, including members of the former *Wehrmacht*, were free to leave.[138]

Uncle Herbert, Mutti's brother, left Harksheide and went over to America in 1951. Pastor Fuerstenau, Mutti's cousin who had offered to help us, made arrangements for Uncle Herbert. He settled in Grafton, Nebraska, where Pastor Fuerstenau lived. He got a job at a gas station there, and wrote letters urging Mutti and Papa to join him. He said it was a good place to live. He told of how he had settled in the small town and was comfortable.

After considering the options, Mutti wanted to go too. Above and beyond the prospects of better jobs, she wanted to worship on a regular basis.

In August 1951, Mutti had her baby: a boy they named Detlef. I was asleep when he was born, and when the others woke me to tell me I had a new little brother, I was upset. I had no desire to see him, let alone hold him.

"I wanted a sister!" I told them, adding, "I will never take care of him. I'll never take him for a walk!"

During the next days, however, I softened somewhat. Over time, I grew fond of the new little bundle. He wasn't a sister, like I originally dreamed of, but he was a fun addition to the family. I enjoyed taking him for walks and showing him off to my friends. They liked playing with him too.

After Detlef was born, Mutti revisited the idea of going to America. She quickly learned the process of getting a visa was complex. Those who wanted a visa had to apply by letter accompanied by a self-addressed, stamped envelope. In addition to filling out the application form and other paperwork, we needed a letter from a sponsor. We also had to have medical exams and interviews.[139]

Finally, anyone who wanted to leave Germany and travel to America had to pay for the expensive trip. Both flying and traveling by ship had high price tags attached to them. Furthermore, tickets to ride on foreign ships had to be purchased in dollars, and there were no German ships available. Nearly all who left Germany needed an organization or person abroad to fund their trip.[140]

Mutti wrote Pastor Fuerstenau to let him know we were thinking of coming over, now that Papa could join us there. She explained our situation and the need for a sponsor. He responded in a letter, "Let me see what we can do from here."

While we waited in Germany, one Sunday, at the Lutheran church he served in Grafton, Nebraska, Pastor Fuerstenau addressed the congregation after the service.

"Would anyone be willing to sponsor a German family of six to come and settle here?" he asked.

One man, sitting a few rows from the front, stood up. He was tall and kept a hand on the pew ahead of him to steady himself. "I'll do it," he said, bowing his head slightly.

The man's name was Mr. Alton Workentine, and he was a prominent farmer in the area. At the time, he was single and had no immediate family to support. As a sponsor, his responsibilities included paying the costs of our visas and trip by boat. He also agreed to find a place for us to live and secure a job for Papa.

Taking on our family was no small task. It would cost about $1,000 for us to come. Mr. Workentine sent money over to Germany—it was enough to cover our visas and ship fares.

Mutti was nearly overcome by the generosity showered on us from Nebraska. While Papa was less inclined to leave Germany, Mutti was firm in her desire to worship often and freely. She had spent several years not going to church regularly during and after the war, and she didn't want to continue living that way. She wanted worship to be a central activity for the whole family, and not something we did once or twice a year.

Furthermore, Mutti worried about what would happen to our faith if we stayed in Germany. She was convinced that going to the U.S. would be the right thing to do for our spiritual upbringing.

After talking about it, Mutti and Papa decided that moving would be best for all of us.

The other family members in Harksheide found it hard to understand our intentions of leaving. They asked, "Why are you going to America?"

Not many people in our area were leaving, and some relatives wanted us to stay.

But Mutti wished to go live with the people that showed such kindness to us. She wanted to worship at a Lutheran church. And she thought America would be a better place for our family.

To take care of the paperwork involved, Mutti and I started making trips from Harksheide into the city of Hamburg. Omi watched my younger brothers when we went. We took the train in to the city, and then walked for blocks and blocks to get to the government offices.

Our route always took us past a bombed out section of the city. Rubble still lay in the streets and sidewalks. We avoided the fallen bricks and stepped around the debris in our path.

Hollowed out buildings lined the streets. They all held their own tales of misery and suffering from the particular moment—years before—that a bomb landed on their structure. I knew many people had lost their lives right where I was walking.

Every time we went to the U.S. embassy and other government buildings in Hamburg, the trip took the entire day. Mutti and I arrived back home late in the evening, tired from walking.

A number of times when we went, the officer dealing with us looked at Mutti with a questioning expression. "All six of your family members are going?" he said one day.

"Yes," replied Mutti.

"And you are not paying for it?"

"No, our sponsor is covering the cost of the trip."

"You are very lucky," the officer said. "There are very few who would do that. In fact, you are the only family we have dealt with here that is so large and has a sponsor paying for the trip."

"It is not luck," Mutti replied. "It is God directing our path."

Every time we walked past the American embassy, Mutti and I noticed the American flag waving in the breeze. We loved the design and the red, white, and blue colors. Most of all, I loved it when Mutti said what it represented.

"It symbolizes freedom to live and worship as we please, and it will be the flag of our new home," she explained.

Like many others headed to America, we had to get shots before going. We also had to be checked over for diseases and deformities. For that process, Mutti and I went to a large building in Hamburg. We stood in line with hundreds of other women and children waiting to get inspected.

It was done on a scale of mass production. It took place in a large, open building. Once the whole group was lined up in the crowded area, the authorities asked everyone to strip down. We took everything off, and got shots just like the others.

We passed the tests, and once we had our shots, we were given the all clear to travel out of Germany. Papa and the boys went through the same ordeal to get cleared.

That winter, in December 1951, we had the loveliest Christmas since before the war. We went to church on Christmas Eve. On the way home, it started snowing. Big, beautiful, lofty flakes meandered their way from the sky to the ground. Christmas trees glittered in many of the windows that year. We had a Christmas tree in our home too. It seemed people everywhere sang that night.

To prepare for living in America, Mutti found a tutor to teach me English. I was in my fifth year of school at the time. The English classes were held in the same building I went to for school. I attended my regular classes in the morning, and then stayed an extra hour after school let out for the English lesson.

I began studying English in April 1952, and learned a smattering of words. I knew how to say "table" and "chair" and some other basic vocabulary. I didn't know enough, though, to string a whole sentence together in English. I also studied both the hard and soft "th" sounds. In German, the "th" sound does not exist, so the teacher helped me practice the sound again and again, until I could make out a fair "th" if I tried hard. I pronounced words with the hard "th" sound such as there, than and them. I also practiced the soft "th" in words like thin, nothing, and month.

I enjoyed learning English, but after three months, the teacher fell ill. We couldn't find another one, so I didn't continue with the lessons.

A couple of months before leaving, Papa got a new job. It was a position in Hamburg's harbor. Through it, he could help rebuild ships. It was a much better job than he had before, and paid well.

In his new line of work, Papa sometimes brought home items the ships brought in to the harbor and had to be disposed of. Instead of throwing the goods away, he and his coworkers often divided them up.

One day Papa came home from his shift at the shipyard with a strange looking fruit. It came in bunches, and each piece was long and curved, covered by a thick yellow peel.

"Try it," he urged us.

"Papa what is it?" I asked.

"*Bananen,*" he replied, meaning "bananas."

He peeled the skin away.

Wilfried, Rainer and I inspected the fruit curiously. We had never seen or eaten bananas before. After one taste, though, we were convinced. We devoured them all in one sitting.

"Papa what a treat!" I exclaimed when I finished mine.

With Papa bringing in more income, there was now more money for items—even extra things. This included a doll, which served as a replacement for the porcelain doll that had shattered earlier. The new doll was made of a plastic called celluloid. This type of material was practically unbreakable. I could easily move the arms and legs, and even the head. The doll had hair made of the same plastic. It was dyed blonde and formed in waves. Her eyes were blue and looked real. Her hands were open and had individual fingers. The doll could stand by herself, and could also be posed to sit down. She was very lightweight and stood about 16 inches tall. Mutti crocheted a beautiful green dress for the doll, and she wore white socks and shoes that I took on and off.

The company that made the doll, Schildkröt (which means "Turtle"), had been making dolls in Germany since 1896. Each doll sported a trademark on its neck. The trademark consisted of a diamond with a turtle inside of it, and a number for the doll.[141]

Mutti finished the paperwork needed for us to leave Germany and go to America at the end of the summer in 1952. With that in order, and the money Mr. Workentine had sent over, the time to leave our house in Harksheide was fast approaching.

"You won't be able to take much," Mutti told us when we started packing.

She handed us each one suitcase. "Everything you take will need to fit in there," she explained.

I packed a couple of changes of clothes and the new doll. Mutti added a feather bed. She also packed the family Bible. It reminded me of some of the very things she took when we left Schneidemühl.

I was sad about leaving many of our belongings behind in Germany. I was especially upset about bidding farewell to the furniture we had accumulated during our time in Harksheide. Mutti and Papa had managed to put a *schrank*, a beautiful, heavy, wooden cabinet, in our dining room. It was large, dark in color, and covered nearly an entire wall of the room.

In September 1952, on one of the last Sundays before we left for America, we had a family gathering at our home in Harksheide. At the get together, I had jumbled feelings about the trip. I was excited to go and experience the adventure ahead, but also pretty scared. We had just settled into a normal, regular life in Harksheide, and I didn't want to leave the family we had there. We had to say good-bye to many of Mutti's brothers, and also Aunt Lydia, Ruthchen, and Oma. I wouldn't get to play again with Heidi, or the other friends I had made in the neighborhood.

I didn't know what would be waiting for us in our new place. I hoped things didn't go wrong and lead us back out on the street in America, without a home to call our own.

When it was time to say good-bye, we shed many tears. I didn't know when—if ever—I would see our loved ones again.

Mutti saw my tears and put her arm around me.

"God knows what lies ahead," she said. "Remember, he will always take care of us. His angels will be with us on the trip."

As before, her words helped calm my fears, and made the tears stop. I trusted everything would be alright.

We had lived in the duplex built through the government program in Harksheide for about two years. When we left, we gave the house to Uncle Gottfriedt. We also left all of the belongings inside to him.

On the morning of Friday, September 12, 1952, we left our home for the last time. To get to the harbor, one of Mutti's brothers took us to the train station. We rode to the harbor in Hamburg, where our ship waited for us.

When we got out at our stop, the place was bustling with people. We made our way to the ship we were to board, the *Italia*. It was a big passenger ship, and its presence loomed magnificently in the harbor. The sky was clear and bright. A soft breeze, originating from the water, wafted over us.

I wore a nice dress that day. My brothers had on short pants Mutti had sewed for them. As we walked up the gangplank to get on board, I peered into the water below.

Once we were on board, we went to the upper deck to wave good-bye. We found chairs stacked along the edge of the ship, by the railing. Wilfried, Rainer, and I climbed up the stacked chairs to get a better view of the harbor. It was interesting to be so high and see so many people back on the land.

But it was also worrisome. We were headed to a new land, on a different type of trip than I had ever experienced. This one would include food and regular meals. It wouldn't be filled with bomb shelter stops and a constant fear of what lay ahead. No, we were not fleeing from an advancing army. We were not hoping to save our physical lives. We were searching for a place to settle, work, and go to church. We wanted to belong to a land fit to fill our souls.

Regardless of what we found on the other shore, we all knew we would not be returning to Germany to live. The ship's departure was our final farewell to the place, our homeland.

A band struck up and its tones broke into my thoughts. I looked around. Many people cried and waved good-bye. Mutti was in tears. My cheeks were wet too.

And then, slowly, the ship pulled away from the harbor. We waved good-bye for the last time to the crowd back on shore. The ship left Hamburg, and set out to take us on our next journey, to our new home, new country, and new life.

CHAPTER ELEVEN: A NEW LIFE

"Through many dangers, toils and snares
I have already come;
'Tis Grace has brought me safe thus far
And Grace will lead me home."
—John Newton, 1779[142]

We brought so much emotional luggage on the boat with us. Memories of a free life, with my white rabbit, danced in my mind. Dark clouds, sirens signaling air raids, and bombs exploding leapt through my thoughts. And, of course, I anticipated the future. I wondered if America would deliver as promised.

Like us, the ship we traveled on, the *Italia*, bore a history marked with ups and downs. In 1928, Blohm & Voss, a German shipbuilding company, built the vessel in its shipyards in Hamburg. The ship's original name was *Kungsholm*.

The Swedish American Line owned the craft from 1928 to 1941, and used it to carry passengers back and forth across the Atlantic. It also went on some cruises. Parts of the vessel were luxurious, and many thought its first class lounge was one of the most beautiful rooms afloat.[143]

Then in 1941, during the Second World War, the United States Government's War Shipping Administration took control of the boat. It also gave it a new name: *John Ericsson*. To help with the war efforts, it carried troops in the Pacific Ocean and Mediterranean Sea. Needless to say, the ship took on a new look, complete with bunks and war equipment. The vessel even participated in the invasion of Normandy on D-Day, 1944.[144]

After the war, the ship underwent changes to carry passengers again. The Swedish American Line, the boat's first owner, actually bought it back, but then sold it to a different company. This firm, called Home Lines, named the boat the *Italia*. Soon it set out on its new career, carrying passengers back and forth between Italy and South America, and then between Italy and New York.[145]

In 1952, the boat took on a run that traveled from Hamburg to New York.[146] And that's the year our lives and the ship crossed paths.

During our trip, the ship captured my full attention. It had a big, wide staircase that wrapped down to the dining room. Round tables, covered with gleaming tablecloths, filled the eating area. The waiters wore sharp black suits, and for fancy dinners, they also sported a stand-up, or mandarin, collar.

Thanks to Mr. Workentine, we were paying passengers—and not refugees anymore. We felt the change. At mealtime, and throughout our days at sea, the crew treated us very well. Our passages were not first class, but I felt we received top-of-the-line service and accommodations.

Some of the passengers on the ship were taking vacations to America, but the majority on the boat were like us, embarking on a one-way trip to what we hoped would be a better life.

The other passengers, like us, had access to a wide variety of facilities on board. In addition to the restaurant, there were gift shops, and also a bar, dance hall, movie theater, and swimming pool. I watched a children's film with my brothers; I also waded into the shallow end of the swimming pool, as I didn't know how to swim. When we wanted to rest, we sat on chairs and enjoyed the view from the ship deck.

The *Italia* had spacious individual rooms for first class passengers. Those who had paid for a lower class ticket, as we had, slept among the masses. Mutti and I found ourselves in a cabin that fit a total of 24 women and children. To accommodate us all, there were eight bunk beds. Each bunk bed had three beds on it: one on the bottom, one in the middle, and one on top. The spaces where we could lie down were very narrow, and only fit one adult or child per bed. I slept on the very top bed of one of the bunks. Mutti took the bunk below me, in the middle. Another person slept in the lower bunk. Papa and the boys were in another section on the other side of the ship.

Of all the luxuries, the food was the best. For one of the first dinners, we ate oxtail soup.

"Oh my goodness," cried Mutti when it arrived. She considered it such a delicacy. It had a clear broth with small bits of meat and barley sprinkled in it.

Indeed, there was a bounty of food, and heaps and piles of goodies that surpassed even what I had dreamed of during our years of hunger. We dined on red cabbage and sauerbraten, dumplings, and thick bread. We ate sandwiches laden with luncheon meat. We spread a thick layer of butter on the slices of bread, and topped them off with an array of colorful jams and jellies.

One dinner, several days after we left Hamburg, we sat at a table with bowls of soup laid out in front of us. The ship hit some rough water just then. The vessel tipped in one direction, and the bowls followed, sliding down the table. The boat shifted in the opposite direction, and the bowls slid back.

A storm was brewing.

The ship swayed back and forth. Within a few minutes of rocking, other diners moaned. I clutched my stomach and looked at Mutti. She hunched over and grabbed the table to steady herself.

Ready to wait out the storm, we left the supper table and headed to bed. The night passed, and another day began. It was still storming. That day came and went, and then another passed. The sea remained rough.

I laid in the top bunk, with Mutti below me, seasick. The rocking went on and on. The close quarters of our room, and the fact that many in our cabin got sick, set the scene for several long, agonizing days.

When the vessel hit the worst of the storm, the winds pushed the waves right over the ship's rails and onto the deck. Most of the passengers stayed in their assigned cabins because the sea was so violent. I continued to feel poorly, and remained in bed for the next three days. Stuck in our tight sleeping quarters, intense feelings of claustrophobia washed over me.

While Mutti and I felt miserable, Papa and the boys didn't get sick. Wilfried and Rainer, who at the time were nine and eight years old, spent long days meandering around. They also helped Papa watch 13-month-old Detlef, who was learning to walk.

My brothers made friends with various crew members. The steward in charge of their sleeping cabin was also a waiter; he brought food to Wilfried and Rainer in their bunk area whenever they were hungry. Sometimes he gave them ice cream and oranges as treats.

The captain ate at a different table in the dining room for each meal. This allowed him to meet and chat with passengers on board. One night, he sat and ate with Papa and the boys for supper. It was so exciting to see the captain up close, and they took a picture with him.

Five days after the storm started, the winds died down. As they quieted, my stomach did too. Soon Mutti felt better.

I ventured out of the room, on to the deck to take in the lovely views of the now-calm sea. During the next days, we had good weather. I enjoyed the peaceful waters and beautiful ship, and soaked up every minute of the journey.

Sometimes when I stood on the deck, a cool breeze blew over me. Wilfried, Rainer and I watched whales and dolphins swim and play in the ocean. We took turns caring for Detlef, who was fascinated with the ship. Despite the movements of the sea, he took his first steps while aboard the craft.

One of the stewards showed Wilfried and Rainer how to fold a paper airplane. The boys took the plane when it was ready and launched it over the ship. It flew so well that it glided for a long time. It cruised the equivalent of several blocks over the water.

One morning, while wandering on my own, I saw iron steps going down a stairwell I had never explored before. Curious, I followed them. At the bottom of the stairs, I found an opening in the side of the ship. It looked as if someone had pushed a big freight door open. There was quite a bit of machinery nearby.

Peering out of the large window, I could see straight into the ocean. It was very still that day, and the water was as smooth as glass. It was so calm that I reached down with my hand and touched the water. It was incredible to be so close to the open sea. I had no idea why the door was open, and there was no one around to ask.

I could have jumped right in. Before someone found me, however, I climbed back up the stairs.

On September 22, 1952, we had been at sea for 10 days. It was my birthday, and I turned 12 years old that year.

The morning of my birthday, Mutti and Papa presented me with a big bar of Hershey's chocolate. Since I no longer felt seasick, the gift looked especially appetizing.

"But where did you get it?" I asked Mutti.

She shrugged and smiled.

"From one of the shops?" I asked.

She nodded. *"Herzlichen Glückwunsch zum Geburtstag* (Happy birthday), Elfi," she said.

That evening, the sky was clear. From the deck of the ship, we looked out toward the west. There, far in the distance, on the edge of the horizon, dots of light shone.

As night fell, the specks of brightness grew. Soon they scurried back and forth, here and there. I also spotted fuzzy shapes that resembled tall buildings.

"It's the Manhattan skyline," a nearby passenger told us. The moving lights belonged to cars, traveling down a road that ran alongside the ocean. We also saw lights from the skyscrapers in New York, and other buildings on Long Island.

The next day, September 23, 1952, we reached the New York Harbor. As we maneuvered into it, a tall green statue came into view. The boat slowed as we neared the monument.

Our whole family stood on the deck, gripping the railing and taking in the bright, nearly glowing structure. I glanced sideways at Mutti. "It's the Statue of Liberty," she explained.

Within minutes, hundreds of passengers joined us. A hushed silence fell over the crowd.

We didn't see the words of poet Emma Lazarus in the inner walls of the statue's pedestal, noting "Give me your tired, your poor, your huddled masses yearning to breathe free," but we felt the invitation. All around us, tears started to flow. Mutti and I cried too. We were all keenly aware we were about to enter a new country. It had taken 11 days to cross the Atlantic.

The ship docked early that morning. We ate our final meal, a big breakfast, in the beautiful dining room.

Then it was time to disembark. Loaded down by our suitcases, we shuffled with the crowd toward our next stop: a large immigration building. At the entrance, a woman met us. She must have wanted to help us proceed, but she didn't speak German and we didn't know enough English to communicate.

So we went in on our own, along with about 2,000 others, to start the process of entering America.

Officials in the building checked the papers we carried, and verified that we had received the required shots. They also went over our visas and birth certificates. We stood in line for each step of the process; once we were approved in one spot, we went on to wait at another station.

Noon came and went. We waited in more lines. The minutes passed slowly, and my stomach growled loudly. There were no other choices, however, except to sit on our suitcases, wait, and move along when the line shifted.

Finally, in the late afternoon, we finished all of the paperwork. We were all hungry since we hadn't had anything to eat since breakfast.

Mutti spotted a small store selling deli meats, cheeses, and sandwiches, and led us toward it. Once inside, she motioned for me to do the talking. Since I had taken a little bit of English in Germany, she wanted me to put in our order for food.

Unfortunately, I only knew a few words in English. I had no idea how to form a sentence.

"Bananas," I said, and then pointed to my stomach. This was an exciting find, as I remembered the special fruit Papa had brought us once in Hamburg.

The shopkeeper looked at me, a blank stare on his face. My pronunciation must have not been correct.

"Food," I tried. Then, "Apples."

We weren't getting anywhere.

I looked at Mutti and shrugged my shoulders.

Then the shopkeeper leaned toward us. "*Wo kommen Sie her* (Where are you from)?" he asked in German.

Now it was my turn to have a blank stare.

"I am from Germany," he quickly explained in German. "I am Jewish, and came over to the United States. What can I help you with?"

Everyone was at once relieved, and me doubly so. Quickly the kind gentleman helped us pick out a meal. We walked out of the shop, hands full of sandwiches and fruit, hearts filled with gratitude.

We stepped outside of the building and into the freedom of the United States.

I couldn't believe we were really in America. And our point of entry into the country—New York City—was startling. There were no bombed out buildings to be seen anywhere. Everything looked new and modern.

For the next leg of our trip, we needed to find a railroad station.

Papa hailed a taxi using sign language outside the immigration building. Soon we were in for the ride of a lifetime, cruising down streets lined with towering skyscrapers. The driver talked a mile a minute. None of us understood much of what he said. I did catch one phrase, "Fifth Avenue," several times. I pressed my face to the window, absorbing everything. I had never seen high rises like the ones lining the streets.

The cab took us to the railroad station. When we arrived, it was evening.

Now we had to find a train. Our destination was Omaha, Nebraska, where Mr. Workentine and Pastor Fuerstenau would be waiting for us. After some meandering, we ran into a worker who also spoke some German. She didn't know as much as the shopkeeper, but between her broken German and my few English words, we found a route to take.

First we were to head to a place called Chicago. There we would switch trains and get on one that would take us to Omaha.

We found the first train and boarded. Once inside, Mutti and Papa found a place for us to stand. There was seating available, but they didn't want to sit down and risk missing our stop.

Minutes later, the train blew its whistle, signaling the start of our railroad journey. We rolled out of New York. Standing, we watched the city disappear. The train went on, and we remained on our feet.

Night fell, and a deep blackness outside surrounded us. Other passengers on the train sat, but we didn't join them.

None of us knew we had to travel nearly 900 miles to get from New York to Chicago, and then another 470 miles to go from Chicago on to Omaha, Nebraska.

Hours later, my feet ached from standing. I didn't want to complain, so I remained in the same position. I glanced at the nearby vacant seats.

Mutti caught my gaze. She looked over the seats, at the other passengers bedded down for the evening, then to the door and darkness, and back again. She studied several empty seats next to me for a long moment.

"Okay, we can sit down," she relented.

She laid baby Detlef on a seat to sleep. Wilfried, Rainer, and I sat in seats, rested our heads on the back of them, and soon dozed off. It had been a long, exhausting day.

The following morning, shortly after the sun came up, the train stopped. I looked out the window for a station, ready to jump to my feet.

Except there was no train station. In fact, there wasn't much of anything. Fields of corn and wheat stretched out before me. They went on and on.

There was no person, road or vehicle in sight. We were in the middle of nowhere.

Inside the train, a man's voice came over the intercom system, speaking fast in English. I couldn't understand a single word he said. I looked over at Mutti and Papa, who exchanged glances with each other, questions filling their eyes. We had no idea what was going on.

When the voice over the intercom stopped, the other passengers stayed in their seats. We remained sitting too. We waited that way for a long time.

Then, without warning, another train approached. It came up along a parallel track, headed in the same direction. It slowed and came to a stop beside our train. When it was at a complete rest, others on board our train started shuffling and moving.

The same rapid voice came on over the speaker again. When the announcement ended, passengers in our car got off the train. We followed suit.

Everyone else moved over to the other train. We did too.

The other train was crowded, and most sections were completely full. Our family shifted through until we found an open spot with four chairs. Mutti, Papa, Wilfried, and Rainer took a seat. Detlef sat on Mutti's lap. There was no place for me.

Across the aisle, there was a group of U.S. soldiers. They took up most of the chairs in the section, but one seat was open. It was along the aisle, and not too far from Mutti.

Mutti looked at the unoccupied seat, and motioned for me to take it.

I hesitated. The soldiers were large, and I had no desire to sit close to them. But there were no other sitting options on the train. Slowly, I shifted toward the seat and then settled into it as best as I could manage.

After several minutes, the soldiers smiled at me. They said something in English I didn't understand. Then they pulled out sandwiches, and started to eat.

I was so hungry. The bread smelled exceptionally good. Our own sandwiches and food from the shop near the station in New York with the Jewish owner were long gone.

One soldier, with dark features and ebony-colored skin, leaned toward me. He held out the sandwich, offering it to me.

I was terribly scared. I hadn't been this close to a soldier since the night we fled from the refugee train in Germany to escape the bomb raids and a German trooper carried me to safety. And I had never seen an American soldier before.

I looked at Mutti for help; she nodded. "It's okay," she reassured.

Hesitantly, I reached out and took the sandwich, and then tentatively took a bite. It was delicious.

This action seemed to delight the soldiers. Soon they paid more attention to all of us, talking and leaning over the aisle to play with my brothers.

Even though they only spoke English, the words sounded kind and they smiled frequently. Slowly, as the train rolled on, my fears subsided. I settled in again, this time with a full stomach, and decided this ride would be a good one.

Through hand motions and some explaining, we gathered that the first train we had been on had broken down. It had stalled out in a place called Ohio. After stopping in the middle of farm land, it waited until another train came along that could take us on. The good news was that it appeared the train we had transferred to, and were currently on, would take us to Chicago.

As the train moved along, I looked out the window and again saw field after field of corn and grain. The vastness of the country, and the wide open spaces, amazed me. In Germany—a smaller, more densely populated country—I never saw such immense expanses of nothingness.

Occasionally we passed through a bigger city, but even then, I hardly saw any people moving around. The streets were nearly bare, and everything was so spread out. It wasn't like Germany, where people lived very close together and often walked on the streets.

At midmorning that day, the train came to a stop. Anxious, I turned to the friendly American soldiers. "Chicago?" I asked.

"No," they replied, shaking their heads. One of the soldiers talked some more, probably explaining where we were, but I didn't understand what he said.

Hours passed, and the train stopped again. This time, the soldiers turned to me. Before I asked, they shook their heads. "Cleveland," they said, pointing out the window at the city.

The day ended, and night fell. The train ambled on through the darkness. I was hungry again, but also tired from the travel, strange sights and foreign language. Exhaustion soon settled in, and I fell fast asleep.

The following day, our train stopped once more. This time, the soldiers pointed out the window and informed us, "Chicago."

It was time to get off.

The station was hopping. We had no idea where to go. Our family stood together and observed the scene. It seemed like we were the only ones who didn't know what to do. Other passengers zoomed past, occasionally brushing their suitcases against ours.

Papa set out to look, and through some hand motions found a helpful person who led us to the right train.

This time, when we got on, we didn't stand for hours. Mutti promptly placed our family together on seats in our car.

Soon the train rolled away from the station. I was glad to sit with my family for this stretch, but our car was very warm. All of the windows were open for ventilation, but as we headed out of Chicago, the temperature seemed to rise even more.

A slight breeze came in through the windows. Even so, it was sweltering in the train. I was used to the cool temps of Hamburg, with clouds and rain dominating the sky most days.

The sun beat down and this train, unlike the previous one, started swaying slightly as it teetered along the track to Omaha.

Soon I felt queasy. The feeling resembled the seasickness I had felt aboard the ship on our way over from Germany to New York. It was miserable.

To help ease the motion sickness, Papa directed us out of our seats from time to time. He opened a door that led to an open space between our car and the next one. I stood on a small platform and clung to the rail, gulping deep breaths.

The action took away a bit of the nausea, but soon the waves of sickness came raging back. The temperature outside seemed to rise by the hour. The heavy wind, dripping with heat, made me feel worse than I had felt on the ship.

Finally, after what seemed like an awfully long ride, we arrived in Omaha. It was late evening on September 25, 1952. It had taken two days of traveling by train to get from New York to Nebraska.

As planned, Pastor Fuerstenau and Mr. Workentine were there to meet us.

Pastor Fuerstenau was dressed in a dark blue suit, stood very erect, and best of all, spoke German. What a wonderful respite! As soon as she saw him, Mutti thanked him profusely. His aid in helping us come over and lining up a sponsor had been a pivotal step to our arrival in America.

To greet Mr. Workentine, we all looked up. He was tall, and easily cleared six feet.

In addition to his height, Mr. Workentine's outfit immediately caught my attention. He wore some sort of pants that went all the way up to his chest. Thick straps connected the top of the front bib to the back, which was also very high. Underneath the concoction was a plaid shirt. I had never seen anything like it.

Noticing my gaze, Mr. Workentine pointed to his attire. "Overalls," he said. Then he smiled. He had a friendly looking face and warm smile. I liked him on the spot.

Mr. Workentine had driven his car, a 1952 Chevy, to pick us up at the train station in Omaha. We piled our suitcases in, and then climbed into the car. The three men sat in the front. Mutti and us kids sat in the back. I wondered if we were close to what would be our new house.

Mr. Workentine first took us to a restaurant. We were equally starving and thankful. Then, with full stomachs, we returned to the car.

Several hours later, after dropping Pastor Fuerstenau off at his house in Grafton, Mr. Workentine's vehicle slowed and turned into a driveway. I couldn't see much since it was the middle of the night. We had spent a week and a half traveling across the ocean, aboard trains, and in a car to get to it.

But we had arrived. I craned my neck to look out the window. In the moonlight, I saw the outline of a big farm house just off the road.

Mr. Workentine led us into the dwelling. Speaking in English, he pointed to the different rooms and indicated where to go next.

Within moments of stepping inside the house, it was obvious many preparations had been made for our arrival. The place was fully furnished, complete with a living room set, dining room table and chairs, and a kitchen with a refrigerator and stove. A pretty tablecloth covered the kitchen table, and a vase full of flowers sat in the middle of it. What a different kind of welcome than some of the ones we had received while fleeing during the war!

We didn't know what to say. Everything about the place was overwhelming.

Someone had put a lot of thought into the sleeping arrangement we would need. Upstairs, we found two bedrooms: one set up for the two older boys, and one made for me. A crib for baby Detlef was waiting downstairs, in the bedroom where Mutti and Papa would sleep.

There was so much to see! We peered from one room to the next, wide-eyed and tongue-tied. To think that we were being given a place, just like that, without having to pay for anything—it was like a touch of heaven.

Mr. Workentine had set up the living arrangements, but as he pointed to the different things—the flowers, the beds, and the spotless interior, he repeated two words: "Mrs. Fuerstenau."

By the third time he said it, I realized it must have been that the pastor's wife, Mrs. Fuerstenau, had made sure all the details were set for us. Even after the explanation, I remained in shock. It didn't seem real that others would do so much to help without even knowing our family. Surely God's hands had directed our path over the ocean, in the same way his hands had guided our steps in Germany.

We settled in for the night, exhausted not only physically but emotionally too.

Even though I was tired, when I crawled into bed, my mind raced with thoughts. I wondered how our new life in America would begin. I also thanked God for Mr. Workentine. Even though his German and our English were limited, thus far we had been able to communicate with simple words and much hand pointing. And his outpouring of kindness, which had paid for a family of six he didn't know to travel to his home and live in it, spoke a thousand more words than any conversation.

The next day, we surveyed the area. The main two-story house, our new home, stood on Mr. Workentine's property. He also had a trailer home set up south of the house, where he stayed. A garage sat between the two structures.

To the west of the trailer, there was a storage barn. It was filled with large equipment. There Mr. Workentine stored his corn sheller and tractors.

There was a barn to the southwest of the house. On the south side of this was a pen, and then a cornfield. To the north lay an alfalfa field. Everything was expansive and so, so flat. We could see for miles, and what we saw was mostly fields of crops.

That afternoon, Pastor Fuerstenau stopped by. After making sure we had everything we needed, he talked to Mutti about coming to church the following Sunday. He asked if she was going to bring the children along.

"No, not the baby," she said, nodding to Detlef, who was toddling around the kitchen.

In Germany we never took babies to church. They always stayed home, where they could fuss and cry all they wanted. That way the little ones didn't disturb worship.

"No, you bring the baby too," Pastor Fuerstenau countered.

Mutti was terrified Detlef would make too much noise. Yet she didn't want to go against Pastor Fuerstenau's wishes. So that first Sunday, Detlef came to church with us.

The church, called Trinity Lutheran, consisted of a small, white building located in the town of Grafton. It sat on a plot filled with lovely, neatly trimmed green grass. Inside it felt immediately cozy.

In addition to the baby, Mutti took her German Bible to the service. When Pastor Fuerstenau announced a reading, Mutti opened her German version. She followed along while the pastor read the lessons for the day in English.

Singing, as usual, came readily for Mutti. Most of the hymns had a familiar tune. Mutti had learned these melodies in Germany years before, and had taught many of them to us. We sang the same tune, and tried out the English words.

During that first service in the Lutheran church in Grafton, I sat quietly in the pew. I watched Pastor Fuerstenau stand tall and proper in the front of church. His loud voice filled the building each time he read from the Bible. And his gaze meant no-nonsense. Even I didn't need an interpreter to translate the stern expression etched into his face. No one had to tell Wilfried, Rainer, or me to behave in church. Detlef, however, oblivious to the order of service, scurried around, just as Mutti had feared.

After church, the members greeted us warmly. We didn't understand their words, but their faces and expressions shone with sincerity. I felt truly blessed to be right where we were at that moment in time.

In Germany, just before we had left for Nebraska, I had been in the fifth grade. Here in America, right after we arrived, with the help of Pastor and Mrs. Fuerstenau, Mutti and Papa enrolled me in sixth grade. They registered Wilfried and Rainer as well. We were set to attend a public elementary school in the town of Grafton, a mile and a half from Mr. Workentine's farm.

To help us prepare for school, Pastor Fuerstenau instructed us regarding how to answer questions. "If someone asks, 'What is your name?' tell them your name," he said. "After that, say 'I don't know' if they ask you more questions."

On Monday, October 6, 1952, we started school. The morning of our first day, the three of us went outside the large farmhouse, right by the road. Mr. Workentine and Mutti came out with us. We waited 15 minutes, and then saw a big yellow school bus roll down the country road. It pulled up to us, and stopped in front of the house.

We got on, and the bus took us down the stretch of road that led into Grafton. Along the way, we passed more farm country. It was harvest time, and we spotted acres and acres of green and golden crops, waiting to be brought in. Some of the fields had already been harvested. I didn't see any children raking those fields in search of a few leftover potatoes or a couple of misplaced turnips.

The bus drove into town and dropped us off in front of a tall, brick building. Vast open space surrounded it.

I stepped out with wide eyes. It had been my first time on a school bus, since I had always walked to school from our home while living in Germany.

Almost as soon as I found the right classroom and sat down with the other students, the teacher introduced herself to me. I repeated her name in my head: Mrs. Jessie Helzer. She stood by her desk in front of the class. She was the teacher for 5th grade, 6th grade, 7th grade, and also 8th grade. She had short brown, curly hair and a small build. She wore glasses and had a kind face.

Moments after this introduction, she spoke again.

"Elfi," she said, looking at me from her desk. She motioned for me to come to the front of the room.

I looked around. Surely she meant someone else! All of the other children gazed right at me. No one else moved.

I glanced back at Mrs. Helzer, and she was still looking at me and indicating I should come forward.

Getting up, I moved to the front of the classroom. Mrs. Helzer held out a book for the class to see.

"This is a third grade reading book," she explained. "I'm going to ask Elfi, our new classmate, to read from it to us."

She handed me the book, and pointed to where I was to start reading.

I was mortified. I knew only a handful of words in English, and had never before read or spoken an entire sentence in English to anyone, let alone a classroom full of peers.

Not wanting to upset the teacher, I began. And stumbled. And stumbled again. I had no idea how to pronounce most of the words.

Amazingly, despite my general battering of the text, not a soul laughed or even snickered. All of the kids sat quietly at their desks, ears attentive. I finished, and then remained standing, puzzled at the silence.

The quiet lingered. Then, mercifully, Mrs. Helzer spoke and broke the stillness. Her words seemed to indicate I could be done. She waved her hand toward my seat.

Hastily I sat down.

I didn't know if the teacher had told the children prior to my arrival that I couldn't speak English, or if she had simply trained them to be well-behaved in awkward situations. Whatever the case, I was intensely relieved that the other kids didn't mock me. I was also more than ready to head home when the school day was over. My head hurt from the language struggles and newness of the whole ordeal.

The following week, in school, Mrs. Helzer lined up language help for me. Every day after lunch, I went to a small room in the school building. The space had a baby grand piano in it, a window, and a couple of chairs. It was very quiet.

Another girl at school, who was a couple of years older, joined me. We both sat on chairs in the small room. I opened a book Mrs. Helzer had lent me, and began to read aloud from it while she listened.

It must have been difficult to hear me flounder through words, but the girl was kind. She always smiled at me. "Well done," she said if I got a word right.

When I couldn't get through a sentence, she simply corrected me and demonstrated how to say it. The ongoing practice helped me immensely. We read together for an hour each day.

My classroom consisted of students from the fifth to eighth grade. Wilfried and Rainer were in a separate area of the school. Both of them swiftly assimilated to the changes.

While the three of us attended school, Papa worked on the farm. Part of the agreement that had been made regarding our move to America and Mr. Workentine's sponsorship was that he would help Mr. Workentine, who had a very large farm, care for the property.

In addition to operating his farm, Mr. Workentine owned a corn sheller which he used to shell corn for other farmers in the area. Surrounding neighbors, near and far, called to line up appointments for Mr. Workentine to come and shell corn for them. Others phoned to line up times when they could use the corn sheller.

Mutti took care of answering these incoming calls. By talking on the phone, Mutti had a crash course in English. She also looked after Detlef.

On one of our first Saturday nights in Nebraska, we went grocery shopping. For the food run, Mr. Workentine drove Mutti, Papa, and us kids to the nearby town of Geneva, where there was a small grocery store. Mutti gathered items, including staples like flour, butter, and bread. When she finished, and everything was rung up, we piled the food into four big paper sacks. It looked like a huge haul to come home with, and made the meager rations we had lived on for so long in Harksheide seem ever more scant. The total bill for the groceries came to $11.

"So much for so little," Mutti said in awe.

I couldn't believe the final cost was so low.

A different time, we went to another nearby town called Sutton to shop. Again, Mr. Workentine drove our whole family to a small grocery store there. Mutti walked the aisles and peered at the shelves, eyes popping at the wide selection and quantity of goods. There were so many options to choose from and the prices were amazing.

Mutti trolled the entire store, raking each aisle with her eyes, searching for familiar looking products. When she couldn't find *grieß* (semolina, or the meal used to make cream of wheat), she asked the store owner for help.

"*Grieß?*" began Mutti. The pronunciation of the word came out as "grease."

"Hmm, let me see if I can help," replied the shopkeeper, heading toward a shelf. He held out a container of lard.

"No, *grieß*," Mutti replied.

"My last name sounds like that, are you looking for someone in my family?" he asked.

Mutti tried once more, pretending to spoon a substance into her mouth for emphasis. It was to no avail, as the owner didn't know German.

And Mutti, in turn, couldn't explain any more in English.

Instead, she opted for the lard the owner pointed out.

One of the next times, Mutti tried to plan her trip to the store more carefully. At the farmhouse, she studied one of the items she wanted to get, which was a replacement for a 5-pound bag of sugar that was nearly gone. She saw the label "5 lbs." and sounded it out.

When she got to the store, Mutti announced to the man inside, "I want five lips of sugar."

That time, after some back and forth, the owner realized by "lips" Mutti meant the *lbs* abbreviation for "pounds."

Fortunately, Mutti had a gift of not taking herself too seriously. She soon shared the story with others, and laughed along with them at the tale.

Despite the language battles, Mutti was convinced we had made the right move. We all felt at home at the church in Grafton. Pastor and Mrs. Fuerstenau kept us under their wing, visiting often and bringing us meals and other items, such as a butter churner, for the household.

During down moments, or evening battles with homework, Mutti reminded us of God's grace and ongoing mercy. "Don't be afraid; God is with us," she often said. The words consoled my soul just as they had in Germany.

Pastor Fuerstenau took Mondays off, and on those days, he and Mrs. Fuerstenau drove over to our house. They picked up Mutti and baby Detlef, and together, the four of them drove around the area, admiring the countryside, stopping in nearby towns, and occasionally grabbing an ice cream treat. Detlef spent the time during the drives watching for horses. Mutti loved exploring the region, and looked forward to Mondays each week.

When we had been in Grafton for a little less than a month, Pastor Fuerstenau offered to take us to a mission festival. Mission festivals were held in neighboring Lutheran churches in the area during the fall, after the harvest, and almost always on Sunday afternoons. We agreed to the outing.

The Sunday of the mission festival began as a hot day. In fact, the fall of 1952 was unusually warm for parts of the Midwest. Temperatures ranged from the 90s to more than 100 degrees Fahrenheit.

For the occasion, we first went to worship at the church in Grafton. After the service, we piled into Pastor Fuerstenau's car. Our family, Pastor Fuerstenau, and Mrs. Fuerstenau headed for Clatonia, a town located about 60 miles east of Grafton.

As we drove, I stared at the countryside. The ample, rolling fields stretched on endlessly, stopping only when they hit the horizon. Houses resembling small dots on a sea of grain popped up occasionally. Never before had I lived in a land with so much space to move about, and so much food for the taking. The cramped spaces of Germany, the tight cottage quarters we lived in after the war, the bed in the kitchen of our duplex where I slept—it was all a world away.

The sun too was different. Here it shone so brightly. Gone were the damp, dreary days of Hamburg and its frequently cloudy skies. The sun shed so much light on the pastures and countryside that everything glowed.

Once the festival service ended, the congregation at Clatonia invited all who had come to stay for a lunch in the church basement. I was thankful to go down the stairs. It was much cooler on the lower level.

First everyone ate a small meal. Then, some of the women from the church set out a dessert. When it was announced that the sweets were ready, I scuttled with the others to stand in line for it.

The sight that met my eyes that afternoon, when I got to the front of the line, made me stop in my tracks. Before me was a long table covered with individual plates. Each plate was small, and held a triangular-shaped pastry on it. Some of the pastries had a bright red middle, others a light peach hue, and still others were a light yellow. A few looked especially unappetizing, as if someone had merely pushed a pile of brown mush together and molded it onto a plate.

In spite of the foreignness, the abundance of dessert boggled my mind. For years my stomach had grown accustomed to only dreaming about food and my next meal, and hunger was a constant companion. Now I stood and my eyes raked in the rows and rows of plates, the bountiful display of food, free for the taking.

Mutti joined me, and stared, dazzled, at the array.

After studying the display for some time, not knowing what to do or take, we decided to ask Pastor and Mrs. Fuerstenau for input.

"What are all of these things?" Mutti asked Pastor Fuerstenau.

"It is called pie," he explained. "There are different flavors. Come, I will show you."

He pointed to the array. "This is cherry pie. We also have peach, and lemon meringue. This deep colored one is pumpkin pie."

"I have never had pumpkin before," I told him.

In Germany, we had delighted in desserts with fruit, like raspberry filling in a torte. But this thing called pie was a novelty.

Carefully I took a plate with a piece of pie that had red filling in it. I carried it to the table where we had been seated. I took a bite, and rich dough and cherries filled my mouth. The pie went down easily. After that single slice, my stomach was filled to the brim with sweetness.

It was then that I knew we had indeed arrived in the land of milk and honey.

CHAPTER TWELVE: ADVENTURES IN GRAFTON

"The Lord's my Shepherd, I'll not want;
He makes me down to lie
In pastures green; He leadeth me
The quiet waters by."
—*Francis Rous, 1650*[147]

Every Sunday after our arrival in Grafton we went to church at Trinity Lutheran. Worshipping consistently was a treat. The members of the congregation spoke kind words and had welcoming, patient hearts. They came to feel like family.

At home, Mutti settled in to life on the farm. She found some of the same basic foods she used in Germany on the shelves of nearby grocery stores. With those staples, she often cooked German cuisine familiar to us. We had potato pancakes and potato soup, potatoes with cottage cheese and chives, and whole potatoes that Mutti cooked, quartered, and served with gravy and onions. She baked bread almost every day, and served it with fresh butter. Sometimes she made a roast and then created a gravy from the drippings. She mixed the drippings with flour and water, and added sour cream at the end to make a rich sauce.

In school, we ate the hot lunch served through the school's food program. Each meal cost 25 cents. Unlike the familiar food we ate at home, the trays at school often held new and different items.

Mutti, frugal and conscientious from her upbringing in poverty during the war years, wanted to make sure we got our money's worth from the school program. She instructed us to eat all the food on our plate for hot lunch. True to her words, I always ate everything I was served, even when I couldn't tell what it was. This principle was engrained in my mind after so many years of having very little food to eat.

One day as I went through the line, a server scooped a heap of yellow bits on to my plate. I looked down. There, in a small section of the tray, off to the side, lay a pile of golden kernels.

"It's corn," the woman with the scoop said, and smiled.

I nodded and took the tray to a table.

I stared at the kernels. In Germany, corn was only fed to the pigs. Curious, I glanced around. Many of the other students also had a mound of corn on their plates. They weren't shying away from it. Instead, they eagerly spooned the substance into their mouths.

My eyes went back to the corn on my own tray. I thought of Mutti's guidelines regarding new foods. I also thought of the many days I went without enough food to stop the gnawing in my stomach.

Slowly, carefully, I took a spoonful and put a few kernels of corn into my mouth. The yellow grains were tender and soft. They had a nice, satisfying flavor to them.

That day, after school, I rushed into the farmhouse.

"Mutti, Mutti!" I called.

"In here," came a reply from the kitchen.

I found her busy stirring a pot of potato soup on the stove. It would be our supper in a couple of hours. "You'll never guess what I ate," I rushed.

"I don't know, there are many strange foods here."

"Animal food!"

"What do you mean? What are they serving at that school?"

"Corn."

Setting down the spoon for the potato soup, Mutti stared at me. "Corn," she repeated. "To you, not the animals."

"Exactly!"

She looked me over for another minute, and then returned to the potato mixture. "Well, it doesn't look like it made you sick."

"No, it was actually pretty good."

And with that, I started helping Mutti get supper ready.

In many ways, we were starting our lives—from scratch—again. Some of the earnings Papa made on the farm went to pay Mr. Workentine back for the money he had sent to sponsor our trip to America. The remainder of Papa's income went toward food and other essentials.

In addition to the wages he paid Papa, Mr. Workentine made sure we received a steady supply of meat. To do this, he periodically bought a butchered cow and then stored it in a locker in Grafton. The locker was located, along with many other lockers, inside an insulated building. These spaces served as large freezers. When our meat supply ran low, he drove to the locker and pulled out more cuts of beef for us. We also received meat from others in the area as gifts.

We were far from wealthy, but we woke up every day feeling immensely rich. We had warm places to sleep, a sprawling home to live in, and so much food that after every single meal, our stomachs were full.

We each had brought several changes of clothes in our suitcases from Germany. What we owned was enough to get us through a couple of days, and Mutti washed all of our clothes frequently. Besides the attire that had been packed in our suitcases in Germany, we had nothing else in our wardrobes.

One day, not many weeks after we arrived, members of the Trinity congregation in Grafton donated a large bag of hand-me-downs to us. Inside, we found jeans for Wilfried and Rainer. The boys had never worn jeans before. I received enough dresses to nearly triple the size of my wardrobe. The gift thrilled all of us, and Mutti especially.

The majority of girls my age wore slacks at that time, but I didn't care. I was comfortable in dresses. That's what the custom had been in Germany.

Grafton was a small place, similar in size to many others in the region. It had a main restaurant and service station owned by a local family whose last name was Baumann. Since Mr. Workentine was a bachelor, he often went to the restaurant for lunch or dinner. He stayed in contact that way with the other farmers. Plus, he said the food served at the restaurant was delicious, and he could always count on a good meal there.

For groceries and other basics, we went to nearby towns.

Sometimes in Grafton I heard, "Those used to be mine!" or "She's got on what I used to wear!" This was followed by giggles and laughter.

One time as I walked down the street in Sutton, a city eight miles from Grafton, I overheard someone say, "She's wearing my dress!"

The old clothes may not have been of the latest fashion, but it didn't matter.

"At least you have something to wear," commented Mutti.

I did, and I wore the clothes with a thankful heart.

Regardless of the snickers, I enjoyed going to Sutton. There we could catch a glimpse of television sets in the store windows. We didn't have a television set at home in Grafton. Instead, through the glass of the store windows in Sutton, we watched people move on the new machines.

Every Saturday morning, I went to see Mrs. Fuerstenau. The Fuerstanaus lived in a parsonage next to church. It was a cozy and simple home. Inside, Mrs. Fuerstenau sat with me at the kitchen table. Together we worked on English for an hour. Mrs. Fuerstenau, never in a hurry, slowly went over each lesson until I fully comprehended everything. This extra help, which came in addition to the tutoring I received at school, made a noticeable difference in my language skills. I looked forward to every class.

After the Saturday morning English lesson, I went to the church for confirmation class. Pastor Fuerstenau taught the group. There were four of us in class: Wilfried, myself, and Harlan and Mary Ackerman, a set of siblings in the congregation. Every week we dug into Scripture, and I always learned something new.

In addition to Mr. Workentine and the congregation, the Fuerstenaus became one of our biggest blessings. They didn't have children of their own, but they offered us plenty of their time and attention. As a result, Wilfried and I picked up a growing vocabulary of English phrases and words. We tied bits and pieces together to form real sentences.

One particular Saturday in late October 1952, several weeks after we began confirmation classes, Pastor Fuerstenau approached Wilfried and me.

"I was hoping you would both participate in the Christmas program this year," he told us.

"I've never been in a program before," I answered.

"Practices start this week. You'll both have plenty of time to learn your lines and get ready."

It was hard to disagree with someone as strong and straight-postured as Pastor Fuerstenau. So Wilfried and I simply nodded our heads "yes."

Every Saturday, from October to December, the children of the congregation in Grafton rehearsed together for the Christmas program. There were about 30 kids in all.

To prepare, we practiced songs. Then, at one of the Saturday sessions, Pastor Fuerstenau explained that each of the older children in the group would individually say a small portion of the Christmas story. This meant Wilfried and I needed to learn a part to speak on our own too.

Armed with our lines, Wilfried and I diligently reviewed our parts. At home, we rehearsed until we knew our sections by heart. Here I was, just two months into life in America, and I was already going to have my second public English performance!

Even after I had memorized my part, I kept repeating it. I didn't want to be gripped with the same fright and embarrassment during the Christmas service that I had felt while reading in English to the entire class my first day of school in Nebraska.

Before long, it was nearly Christmas. As the big day approached, the effects of new foods, a new home, and a change of life began taking a toll on our family. Almost everyone fell sick. Everyone, that is, except me.

On Saturday, December 20, 1952, four days before the Christmas Eve program, Wilfried got so ill he couldn't go to confirmation class. I went on my own, and upon arriving, told Pastor Fuerstenau of Wilfried's condition.

After listening, Pastor Fuerstenau nodded his head. "Hmm," he said.

Then he added, "That means you will have to memorize your brother's lines. You can take his place and fill in during the service."

I nearly fell over. I had been so nervous about my own predicament, and now I would have to cover for Wilfried?

During the next days, I studied my brother's part and practiced it again and again.

When Christmas Eve came that Wednesday, I felt ready.

I headed to church with Papa, who by then was feeling better. Mutti stayed home to take care of Wilfried, Rainer, and Detlef, who were still sick.

At the program, I said my own lines and also Wilfried's portion in front of the congregation. I made it through, a feat that seemed to surprise nearly everyone there, including myself.

When it was over, I breathed a deep breath and exhaled, happy to be done.

After Christmas and the New Year passed, Mutti found a program for me to join.

"It's called 4-H," she said when I asked about it. "It will teach you to cook, sew, and do other things around the home."

"But I can learn that from you," I countered.

"This will be better," Mutti said. "It's a national organization, they say. It has groups all over the country. And it will teach you the American ways."

The organization was divided into districts, and each section had an instructor, or teacher, assigned to it.

For my first session, I walked to the home of the instructor for my area. Her name was Mrs. Dorothy Otte, and she lived on a farm just one mile down the road from us. I knew the Otte family from church, as they also went to Sunday services at Trinity Lutheran. We could even see their farm from our place during winter months, when the trees were bare and provided a view between their branches.

Mr. and Mrs. Otte had two children. One of them, a boy named Jerry, was close to my age. The other, a girl named Judy, was a year older than me.

When I arrived at the nice-looking, two-story farmhouse that day, Mrs. Otte met me at the door. "Welcome," she said, with a warm smile. Mrs. Otte was tall and very slender, with dark hair. She wore her hair down to her shoulders. She led me to her kitchen, where her daughter Judy and several other girls waited. The space was lovely and ample.

"Let's get started," Mrs. Otte announced shortly after I arrived. "Today we are going to learn about sewing."

And so began my first 4-H class.

Sessions for the program were held once a month. At each one, we learned a home-related activity or craft. I absorbed every minute of it.

From the time I met her, I felt comfortable in Mrs. Otte's presence. Her ways were gentle; her instructions, kind. I enjoyed 4-H so much that I often stayed, even after the class ended and everyone else left. I didn't know how to do many of the things the other girls already mastered, due to my years in a different country living under difficult conditions. But it didn't matter to Mrs. Otte. She was patient, and reviewed the day's lesson once or even twice to help me understand.

One day, after the others went home, I presented Mrs. Otte with a special request. "Will you show me how to make a bed?" I asked.

Until then, I only knew how to make feather beds in Germany. For a feather bed, we first put a bottom sheet on over the mattress. This sheet didn't have any elastic trim to tuck in. It was a simple, straight piece of material, and we folded it to fit the bed being made.

On top of that we folded and placed the feather bed, which was similar to a heavy duvet. There were no other sheets or bedspreads involved; at night, when it was cold, we spread out the feather bed and slept under it. During the day, we folded it back up and placed it on top of the single bed sheet again.

Mutti brought a feather bed to America, but the other sheets in the house had confused us for months. I wanted to learn the American style of bed making.

Without hesitating, Mrs. Otte led me to one of the bedrooms of her home. She showed me how to put a fitted sheet on the mattress. Then she taught me to put another sheet over that first one, fold it properly, and add a blanket on top. "You could also put a top comforter on, if you like," she added.

I stayed busy with school and 4-H. Soon winter in Grafton faded to an end. As the temperatures rose, Mr. Workentine bought a brand new Chevrolet. It had a light blue body and a white top. It was a very pretty car.

After purchasing it, Mr. Workentine decided he would not be the only one behind the wheel. He came up to Mutti one day and said she should learn how to drive too.

"It will help you get around more easily," he explained.

"I've never driven a car," Mutti said. "And to learn on your new one?"

"Exactly!" Mr. Workentine's mind was made up. "It's easy. You're a quick learner. Besides, all it takes is a few lessons."

Stunned by his benevolence, Mutti didn't reply.

Mr. Workentine set up the first driving lesson. Papa and Detlef, who was three years old, would accompany Mutti on a shopping trip to Geneva, about 15 miles away. Papa would drive there, and then Mutti would drive home. Papa already knew how to drive, as he used machinery and equipment for his work on the farm.

The trip from Grafton to Geneva went well. Mutti, Papa, and Detlef went inside the store in Geneva, purchased the groceries they needed, and then set out for home.

On the way back, Mutti got behind the wheel. Initially, the drive went well. Then, while going down a county gravel road, Mutti came upon a sharp curve. The road veered left, and to the right of the curve lay a deep ditch. Mutti took the turn too hard and with too much speed. She lost control.

The vehicle swerved and then flew off the road.

It dove down the ditch to the right of the road, which was about eight feet deep. The car rolled several times and then came to a stop, landing on its top.

During the crash, Mutti was thrown from the vehicle. She landed hard on the ground, a short distance from the car, but was not injured severely. Quickly she turned to scout out Papa and Detlef.

Papa was stuck in the car, upside down, with his head against the interior roof of the vehicle. Mutti couldn't tell if he was alright or not. And Detlef wasn't inside the car.

Mutti looked some more, and found the toddler tucked in a small pocket of space directly under the windshield. The car landed on an incline, creating a spot between the dirt and slope of the windshield. The space was just big enough for a child to fit inside.

The incident happened on a gravel road between Geneva and Grafton, where other cars regularly passed through. Some of those who drove by the ditch that day saw the car and notified the authorities. Others stopped and tried lifting the car up, unsuccessfully, to get Papa out.

Soon the paramedics arrived in an ambulance, coming in response to a call a passerby had placed. The workers found a hysterical Mutti. They tried to give her a shot of medicine to calm her down and get her into the ambulance. She refused to have a shot or go inside the emergency vehicle. Instead, she tried to explain that Papa and Detlef were the ones who needed help.

She was so shook up that talking calmly in English was impossible. Instead, Mutti flailed her arms and talked animatedly in German. The paramedics answered in English.

The scene would almost have been comical, if it hadn't been so frightening at the time.

Finally, through a series of hand motions, Mutti directed the medical team to Papa and Detlef. Carefully they pulled Papa out of the car. They also retrieved Detlef from his little bubble of safety.

The paramedics loaded Mutti, Papa, and Detlef into the ambulance and headed for the hospital in Geneva. After checking them over thoroughly, the doctors at the emergency room confirmed Mutti and Detlef had only suffered bumps and bruises. Papa, however, had a concussion.

The driving lesson had been Mutti's first, and it would be her last. Even after Mr. Workentine replaced the totaled car, she refused to get behind the wheel again.

In addition to the crash, we faced other injuries in Grafton. Many of these were the result of a soft bone structure, developed during the years of malnutrition in Germany. Our bones were brittle from those days, and snapped easily.

One day in early 1953, while in recess at school, I joined a game of leap frog. When it was my turn, I went to jump over a girl's back. On the way down from the leap, I stumbled and fell to the ground. My right arm hit first, and immediately deep pains shot through my body.

I was in bad shape, and it was determined I needed to go to Sutton for medical treatment. The school called the farm, and Papa drove over with Mutti. They took me the short distance to Sutton.

There I met Dr. Nuss, a man who appeared to be in his mid-40s. He would be the one to investigate the injury. He ordered X-rays, and confirmed the upper arm, above the elbow, was broken. The section of the arm was shattered in various places.

Working steadily, Dr. Nuss set my right arm. First he put plaster in the upper section where the break occurred. Then he put the arm, bent at the elbow, in a wooden apparatus. This held the arm in the correct position to heal properly and not dangle at my side. I tried to sit quietly while Dr. Nuss got the cast in place, but pain seized my arm. Mutti and the nurse held me while the doctor carried out the procedure. I let out loud cries from the pain.

Once on, the cast fit well. At home, we cut the sleeves out of the right arm of most of my dresses. This way, I could wear them and still keep the cast in place.

I wore the cast for eight weeks, and then Dr. Nuss took it off. When he removed the plaster and wooden apparatus, everything was in the right place. My arm felt and looked brand new.

The healing had taken place just in time for spring. Soon the warmer temperatures and rain brought in a new season on the farm. The days lengthened, and our school year came to an end. This cycle was different than the schooling we had gone through in Germany, which started in April and went year round, with scheduled breaks around harvest times and holidays. Now, instead of studying during the warm months, we helped with chores on the farm and in the house.

At the end of that first school year, I received my report card. In Social Studies and Arithmetic, I got a D as a final grade. In Spelling, Writing, and Citizenship classes, I finished stronger, with A's in each. In Music I got a B+, and in Reading I got a C+.

During summer, under the bright sun, we received our fill of vitamin D and then some. Mutti, unaccustomed to living under such strong rays, didn't know of any precautions to take. At the beginning of summer, after several days in the sun, our skin turned bright red. We didn't have air conditioning in the farm house, and in the bedroom upstairs where I slept there wasn't a fan. I went to bed aching and burned, then sore and peeling. I slept very little until my body healed.

On the farm, Mr. Workentine had acres and acres of alfalfa, wheat and corn. After planting the fields in spring, the crops needed to be watered. This included irrigating them.

Long, heavy irrigation pipes lay in the fields. These pipes had sprinklers set up on them. The sprinklers sprayed water in wide circles, covering the ground and crops within their reach.

In the mornings, I headed out with Wilfried, Rainer, and Papa to move the irrigation pipes. The tubing lay in between the rows of new crops. Working together, we took hold of the pipes and shifted them over a few rows, to the next area. The ground was always wet near the pipes, and we often got knee deep in mud during the process.

Once the pipe, which was about 50 feet long, was in its new place, it stayed there for 24 hours. Then, early the following day, before the heat struck, we moved the apparatus to the next spot.

* * *

While we rose each day and worked on the farm, on the other side of the world, the Korean War came to an end. This war had first started around the time we moved into our duplex in Harksheide in 1950. In July of 1953, an agreement was made to set up new borders between North and South Korea.

Another type of war, however, was in full swing. The United States, which had supported South Korea during the war, was still at odds with the USSR, a North Korea supporter. The Korean conflict was over, but the fight between the two superpowers raged on.

Soon the entire mainland of China fell within the Soviet orbit, while Japan sided with the Western camp. Germany and Europe had become divided, and anticolonial revolts erupted in Asia and the Middle East.[148]

* * *

At that time, our life was a simple one, unaffected by the global debates. And our help, while not much in terms of human strength and might, was needed on the farm.

Mr. Workentine was kind and generous, but he was not in perfect health. When he walked, he didn't have a normal gait; rather, he sort of shuffled along. It often appeared he was dragging a foot as he walked.

His condition was the result of a surgery. Mr. Workentine had been born with a tumor on his spine. As an adult, he had an operation to remove the tumor. During the surgery, a nerve was cut and as a result, he had very little strength in the lower half of his body. When he walked, Mr. Workentine used his upper body to move.

In addition to the heavy lifting of the irrigation pipes, we helped with other jobs, like driving. That first summer, Rainer was nine years old, and learned how to drive a truck. When the grain was ready, Mr. Workentine and Papa loaded it onto the back of a three-ton grain truck. Rainer drove the vehicle, heading north on the gravel road that went past the farm toward the grain elevator. He couldn't reach the pedals when seated, so he stood to drive the vehicle.

To get to the grain elevator, he crossed a busy intersection. At the intersection, the gravel road running past the farm met Highway 6, a main highway that went through Grafton. Cars always drove down it, fast, speeding to their next destination. After passing the busy highway, Rainer reached the elevator, which was located on the other side of the crossing.

Much of the farm was not only our work area; it was also our playground. One creature in particular fascinated me: the bull. Mr. Workentine kept him in a pen attached to the barn.

After chores, my brothers and I went to see the bull. We leaned on the wooden fence that enclosed the pen and peered inside. The fence formed three sides of the pen. Each length of fence was about 10 feet long. The barn wall formed the fourth side. Along the wall of the barn there was a door. Mr. Workentine used this entrance to move the bull from the barn to the pen, and then back again.

Curious about the animal, and oblivious to the grave dangers of pulling pranks on a bull, we invented a game to play with it. When it was my turn, I perched on the side of the fence that was closest to the barn door. I waited until the bull moved to the side of the pen that was furthest from the barn. Then I climbed over the fence and jumped into the pen.

As soon as he saw me move, the bull charged toward me. Pumping my arms and legs as fast as I could, I dashed for the door of the barn. Once I reached it, I yanked it open, ducked inside, and shut it again. Heart pounding, I leaned against the safe side of the door to catch my breath.

Then I headed back out, through a different door of the barn, and returned to the fence to start the game again.

Had Mutti seen me, she surely would have scolded me severely. But she didn't see me. Neither did Papa or Mr. Workentine. Mutti spent most of her time on the farm in Grafton inside the house, cooking, cleaning, and answering the phone when Mr. Workentine's farm clients called to inquire about his corn sheller. She came outside in the early mornings and evenings to milk one of Mr. Workentine's cows, and then carried the milk back to the farm house. She also planted a small garden close to the house. She tended the vegetables in it in the morning and occasionally in the evening too.

Taking calls about the corn sheller schedule worked well for Mutti. A natural conversationalist, she easily talked to others and helped them out. Mr. Workentine taught her some phrases to communicate over the phone. Learning and adapting were simply in her blood. Within the first year, she spoke and understood English over the phone and needed very little help lining up appointments.

In addition to talking on the phone, Mutti learned English in church. She eagerly sang the hymns and joined in the speaking sections of the service. She loved that we worshiped every Sunday.

Papa learned English too, but at a much slower rate. He spent his days on the farm, and not surrounded by other people speaking English, so it took him longer to pick up on words and phrases.

One morning Papa was working in the alfalfa fields located on the north side of Mr. Workentine's farm. The alfalfa had already been cut. Papa and Mr. Workentine were on a tractor, pulling a baler behind to make the alfalfa into bales.

Papa stood on the back of the tractor, watching that the alfalfa was getting baled correctly. As the vehicle crossed over the field, it struck a hole. It went down, and in the process, Papa's foot slipped too. The abrupt movements caused a fracture in his foot.

Life and work on the farm was tough, but Mr. Workentine treated us well. He was fun-loving, and Wilfried and Rainer often went over to his trailer for a rousing round of hide-and-seek. Sometimes I joined in on the fun; other times, I stayed home with Mutti.

Not long after Papa broke his foot, I was called on to help with the handling of the alfalfa. Once the crop had been formed into square bales, the bales were hauled to the barn and laid out in front of it. The next step was to get them from the ground to the upper level of the barn, to be stored and used later for the animals.

Mr. Workentine had just added a John Deere 70 tractor to his collection. It was the latest model in that line at the time, and very shiny.

Mr. Workentine asked me to sit behind the wheel of the big, green vehicle. It faced away from the barn, toward the road. Mr. Workentine secured a rope to the back of the tractor. Then he slung the rope through a pulley close to the roof of the barn, just over a section of the second floor that could be opened up to let in bales of hay. He attached the other end of the rope to a fresh bale of hay.

My job was to drive the tractor. Mr. Workentine showed me how to put it into first gear. Once it was in gear, I needed to drive forward slowly, toward the gravel road that ran past the house. He also showed me how to step on the brake to stop it, and put it in reverse too.

I put the tractor in first gear, as Mr. Workentine had shown me. As the tractor moved forward, the rope, through the pulley, lifted the attached hay bale up along the side of the barn. Mr. Workentine, Rainer, and Wilfried stood at the edge of the upper level of the barn, ready to direct the bale of hay inside the open door.

When the bale reached them, I stopped the tractor. They pulled the bale inside, removed it from the rope, and placed it in the barn. Then I put the tractor in reverse, backed up to give the rope some slack, and waited while Papa, who with his injured foot stayed on the ground, attached another bale of hay to the rope. I drove forward again, carefully, until Mr. Workentine and my brothers grabbed the hay bale.

One time after Papa attached a bale of hay to the rope, I put the tractor in gear. Then I drove forward and, instead of slowing as I neared the road, I sped up. Soon the tractor moved fast—too fast. I couldn't stop it, even as Mr. Workentine yelled for me to do so.

The rope broke. The bale crashed on the ground, and hay sprayed everywhere. The tractor and I bolted toward the gravel road.

Right before the tractor reached the gravel road, I got it to stop.

Mr. Workentine could have been angry with me. Instead, he simply came out to the tractor where I still sat. "This is what you do," he said, showing me once more how to shift gears. Then, referring to the incident, he added, "Don't let it happen again."

I didn't.

But I did find a sense of adventure—a feeling that had first budded during my carefree days of playing with the geese in Schneidemühl before the long war years—come alive in me again. Perhaps it started growing with the game we played with the bull. Soon it took other forms, and with other animals on the farm.

Mr. Workentine had two horses on his land. One was brown and the other was large, beautiful and white. He kept the horses in a wire fenced-in area, south of the barn and bordering one of his cornfields.

I loved both creatures, and was especially drawn to the white one. I had admired horses during my days on the acreage in Schneidemühl. They had been such a big part of our lives there, helping with work in the fields and pulling us places in the wagon and sleigh.

Like my spirit of adventure, I found that feeling of wonderment for horses rekindled on the farm in Grafton. Unlike the bull, which evoked power and apprehension, the horses induced a sense of beauty and strength.

One day in fall, just after the harvest of 1953, I visited the horses. They stood, graceful and still. I looked around. No one was in sight. The fields surrounding the barn were bare, and empty of people and machinery.

Seizing the moment, I hopped the wire fence and went up to the white horse. After stroking his mane, I led the creature out of his pen and over to the wooden fence surrounding the bull pen. I climbed the slats of the fence, and then hopped on the horse's back.

The animal did not stand still anymore. Instead, he immediately took off, racing straight toward the cornfield. The corn had recently been shucked, and short dry stalks left from the plants filled the field. The horse's feet pounded through the field, picking up speed as he went. They trampled the stalks. Soon the horse moved so fast that when I peered down, everything below blurred past me.

I grasped at the horse's long mane and tried to stay on. He didn't slow down. Instead, his long legs churned faster. My hands slipped and slid down the mane. I scrambled to regain my hold, reaching up to grab more of the mane.

The horse galloped through the field. The bizarre feeling of freedom as we sailed through the crop stubs, mixed with sheer panic that I could fly off at any moment, swept through me. Soon I was laughing, and then crying— and then laughing and crying at the same time.

My new white ride took a great leap. Together we soared through the air, and then reunited with the Earth. As soon as the horse landed, he sped up, and this time when my hands slipped from the mane, I couldn't regain my hold. Down I tumbled, landing in the shorn corn.

Somehow, quite mercifully, I didn't have any broken bones. Several bumps and bruises appeared on my arms and legs. They were the only consequences of the escapade.

The long farm days of play and work drew to an end, and school started again. This time, it was easier to go to class, do the homework, and take tests.

Shortly after school started we passed our one-year mark in Grafton.

We kept learning English, both at school and church. To help with the process, Mutti insisted we speak English more than German.

There were some exceptions. At times Mutti and Papa conversed between themselves in German, especially when they went grocery shopping together. Also, we spoke German when relatives came.

Mutti's brother, my Uncle Herbert, who had come over to America while we were still living in Harksheide and had written to us about his time in America, had first arrived in Grafton in 1951. Shortly after he settled in the town, he started working for the Baumann family. This was the family that owned a garage specializing in auto parts and also a restaurant in Grafton.

Not long after Uncle Herbert landed in Grafton, he registered for the U.S. army draft. He was sent to a combat engineer unit in France. While in France, he was sworn in as a U.S. citizen.

Uncle Herbert was gone by the time we arrived in Grafton. After some time, however, other relatives came. In 1953, the year the Korean War came to an end, Uncle Arnold and Uncle Reinhold traveled from Germany to Nebraska. Another one of Mutti's brothers, my Uncle Lothar, came over too, with his wife Ruth.

All of them lived in Omaha. Sometimes, they made the 120-mile drive from Omaha to Grafton to see us. When they did, for a few hours no lonely thoughts could be found, and there was no language barrier. In those moments, Mutti's eyes sparkled. She loved being surrounded by her family, making food for them, and spending time together.

Mutti's other brothers—Uncle Gottfriedt, Uncle Hans, and Uncle Kurt—remained in Germany. Her mother, however, my Omi, decided to come and live with the family that had moved to the United States.

Omi first stayed with Uncle Reinhold and Uncle Arnold, who shared an apartment in Omaha. The day after she arrived, the family brought her over to Mr. Workentine's farm to see us. We were excited and had a gathering planned to welcome her.

She gave us all fierce hugs right when she arrived. Mutti was especially thrilled to have her mother with us. We shared a meal, and then listened to the news Omi had brought with her from Germany.

Evening fell, and Omi stepped outside for a bit of fresh air. When she turned to come back in the house, she faced two doors placed next to each other. One of them led from the porch to the interior of the house. The other opened to steps that went down to the basement. The steps were wooden and there was cement at the bottom of them.

Thinking she was going into the main level of the house, Omi pushed one door ajar and stepped in. Unfortunately, the door she chose was the one that went down the stairs. Down she tumbled to the bottom of the basement steps.

We all heard a loud crash, followed by various thuds and a scream. We ran to see what had happened.

There was Omi, at the bottom of the stairs. She had fallen down the entire flight of steps.

Mutti quickly checked her over. Omi had head injuries and lacerations from the fall. Turning to us, Mutti said in German, "We need to take her to the hospital."

"I don't need to go," Omi replied quickly. "I'm alright." Considering she'd had 13 children and lived through two world wars, the fall must have seemed like a minor event to her.

But Mutti insisted, and took her to the hospital. When they returned several hours later, Mutti said Omi's injuries were not critical.

"She has some bruising all over her body," Mutti explained. "But God was with her and kept her from serious injuries." The only thing she needed was rest to recover from the fall. Omi was in her 60s at the time.

Our circle of relatives had expanded with the moves. Having family close to us again, as well as acquaintances in the congregation, was a blessing we felt deeply. Over time, our circles widened and made room for even more special people.

During the fall, we continued to go to mission festivals in nearby congregations as we had during our first year in Grafton. One Sunday, we went to a festival held at a church called First Evangelical Lutheran. It was located in Aurora, Nebraska. The town was a little more than 30 miles northwest of Grafton.

While at the festival, we met a family with the last name of Schmidt.

The family consisted of a husband, wife and four girls. They had come to America from Germany, just like us. Unlike us, however, they first settled in Tennessee. They lived on a farm there, with sponsors who had helped them make the journey.

Unfortunately, upon arrival, the family received terrible treatment. The sponsors acted as if the new immigrants were their slaves. They even beat Mr. Schmidt on occasion. The situation began poorly and grew steadily worse. Eventually, the entire Schmidt family fled from the place.

Traveling far, they arrived in St. Edward, Nebraska, about 55 miles north of Aurora. There they lived on a farm. After settling in, Mr. Schmidt did quite well with farm life.

Mutti was delighted to meet them at the mission festival. Our families were instantly friends.

For our part, Mutti credited Mr. Workentine as one of the biggest reasons behind our happiness in America. He had a quiet demeanor, yet he was compassionate both to us and others in the area. He regularly attended church, and gave bigheartedly in a subtle way.

When it came to everyday matters, Mutti and Papa were proud, and though we had little, they hated to ask others for aid. Had we landed in a large city instead of small Grafton, it might have been more difficult to find such personalized attention and a warm welcoming. In Grafton, instead of being lost in the shuffle, we were integrated with open arms into a community. And I loved it.

CHAPTER THIRTEEN: MOVING ON

"Rock of Ages, cleft for me,
Let me hide myself in thee;
Let the water and the blood,
From thy riven side which flowed,
Be of sin the double cure:
Cleanse me from its guilt and pow'r."
—Augustus Montague Toplady, 1763[149]

During our time in Grafton, the place grew on us. It wasn't merely the wide open spaces, the crops in the fields, and the bright blue summer skies that grabbed our hearts. It was the people, the love they had shown us, the freedom, and the chance to live a life of our own. It was the preaching of the promises of Christ's work for us, of our redemption through him, and the chance to serve in gratitude that replenished our souls.

As the final months of 1953 passed, and the calendar rolled into 1954, I grew absorbed with schoolwork and 4-H lessons. In 4-H, Mrs. Otte was the leader again that school year. Our group's name, reflecting the number of local girls involved, was "The 10 Little Stitchers."

And stitching we did. Once I learned basic sewing skills, Mrs. Otte taught me to make an apron. To start, I cut a pattern out of material that had a black background, and small red flowers with tiny green leaves on it. I sewed the pieces together by hand, added a tie in the back and stitched white rickrack around the edges. It was a half-apron and fit well around my waist. I also made a dress out of cloth with a lovely blue flower pattern.

Besides getting together for lessons, our 4-H group often went on outings. Sometimes we headed to Sutton, where there was a roller rink. I had never been on roller skates before. The first time we went, during the first laps around the rink, I fell repeatedly and got many bruises. But I didn't give up, and eventually, I improved at skating. After that, I loved rolling around at the roller rink.

Soon the girls in my section became more than fellow 4-H'rs; beautiful friendships blossomed. I knew quite a bit of English but still spoke with a distinct accent. Still, nobody seemed to mind.

Throughout the spring and summer that year, our 4-H team went on picnics, and even swimming. There was a pool in Sutton we occasionally visited. On hot days, I loved being in the water, even though I still didn't know how to swim.

One afternoon, while at a swimming party with the other 4-H members in Sutton, I noticed nearly everyone swam to the deep end of the pool. I wanted to be there too, so I made my way across the water in their direction.

My feet inched along the downward slant of the pool's bottom. I could see all the other girls in the deep end, playing and laughing. I didn't want to be left by myself so I continued on. Soon the water reached my shoulders, and then surrounded my neck. A few more steps, and my feet could no longer touch the bottom.

Down I went, my head dipping under water. Frantically, my feet searched for the floor of the pool. When they found it, they pushed up. I surfaced and gulped for air.

But I was in a bad spot. With my head above the water, I couldn't touch the bottom, and went under again. This time, I waved my arms frantically under the water and managed to lift my head up once more for air.

Still I didn't stay above the water. Instead, I went down.

This time, I couldn't get back up.

Panicking, I floundered under the water.

The next thing I knew, someone pulled me up and out of the pool. I was badly shaken, but otherwise, unharmed.

Surprisingly, the incident didn't deter me from going in the water again. I was simply more careful during the next outings about where to step. Even though I had ridden on my Papa's back in the river near our acreage, I never learned to swim.

In fact, going to the waterside became one of my favorite activities. This was especially true when Uncle Lothar and Aunt Ruth, who had moved from Germany to Omaha, Nebraska, came to visit. Then our family and theirs headed over to Linoma Beach.

The beach was located along the Platte River, a main river running through Nebraska. A section of the river's backwater had been used to form an artificial lake. Linoma Beach was situated on this body of water.

The beach, while manmade, had been in existence for more than 25 years when I first stepped foot on it. Its roots dated back further, to 1907, when it was used as a quarry site. That year, the Lyman-Richey Sand Company began extracting sand and gravel from a place along the north bank of the Platte River.

The site was about four miles northeast of Ashland, Nebraska, a city between Lincoln and Omaha. The company excavated there until 1915. Its operations led to a collection of small lakes fed by underground springs.[150]

By 1924, the site had been acquired by another organization. This organization was known as the Inland Development Syndicate. The syndicate soon changed its name to the Linoma Realty Company. It also changed directions for the quarry site, revamping it and opening it up as a resort. The location of the resort was set up at nearly the midpoint between Lincoln and Omaha—about 30 miles from each. As a result, its name reflected the first letters of each city: Lin and Oma.

When it opened, the resort offered guests a beach, café, cabins, and dance pavilion. Hungry visitors could buy a chicken dinner for 25 cents.[151]

In the 1930s, as more automobiles took to the highways, roadside businesses in the state built structures to catch the attention of travelers passing through. This included wigwam-themed buildings in the towns of Hastings and Atlanta, Nebraska. Since Linoma Beach was located near water, the resort opted to put up an attraction with an aquatic theme.[152]

With that in mind, in 1939, a 100-foot lighthouse was constructed beside the highway. The base of the lighthouse served as a filling station. Steps spiraled up the lighthouse, leading guests to lookout points on both the second and tenth floor of the lighthouse. When World War II ended, the lighthouse's beacon flashed the Morse Code V, a dot-dot-dot-dash, for "victory."[153]

When we went to Linoma Beach with our relatives, we always packed a picnic. After driving to the place in the morning, we stayed all afternoon. We talked and laughed in German the whole time.

I loved those carefree times with my family. The days spent with them were some of my happiest, most cheerful days of our new life in Grafton. At the beach our family was surrounded by others who came to soak up the entertainment there as well. A festive atmosphere abounded.

During the summer of 1954, Mrs. Otte explained there was going to be a fair. She said some of the things I had made could be put on display at the event.

Grafton was located in a county called Fillmore County. The area fair, known as the Fillmore County Fair, took place after many of the crops had been harvested but before school started in the fall. It was held in Geneva, 15 miles from Grafton.

With Mrs. Otte's help, I entered the black-and-red apron I had made. I also put in the dress with blue flowers.

The morning of the big event, our whole family piled into Mr. Workentine's car to check out the fair.

At first glance, I was mesmerized. The whole setup had an atmosphere akin to a small carnival. Never before in Germany had I been to such an event. There were people and booths, and games and animals. And the food—it was wonderful. There were hot dogs on a stick, fried funnel cakes that melted in our mouths, brats, and popcorn. Everything smelled delicious and tasted even better.

While we walked along, passing the various stands and taking everything in, we came upon a section where a spelling bee competition was about to start. At that point, I had been in America for nearly two years. I decided to give my English skills a chance.

The spelling competition started and words flashed through the air. I tried my best, and when it was finished, I had a blue ribbon. What a far cry from the trembling girl who stumbled over a reading to a classroom full of fifth to eight grade students!

After the spelling bee, we went over to the section where my 4-H items were on display. There, on a table full of other stitched clothing made by girls my age, we spotted the red-and-black apron, and the lovely blue dress with flowers. The apron had a red ribbon on it for second place. The dress sported a white ribbon for fourth place.

After the fair, I carried on with 4-H lessons. At one session, I discussed the fair results with Mrs. Otte. "You should be satisfied with your ribbons," she told me. "Remember you've only been in America for two years."

She was right, of course. Better yet, by that time, Mrs. Fuerstenau had a sewing machine, and sometimes Mutti and I went to her house to use it. I also learned how to make doilies, cross stitch, and do some basic weaving.

During the fall of 1954, not long after school had started again for the year, one of the members at church, Ms. Baumann, sought me out. Ms.

Baumann was very stylish. She always wore makeup and dressed smart. Her family owned the garage and restaurant in town.

When she approached me, Ms. Baumann had a mission on her mind. "It's time to change your hair," she said.

"What do you mean?" I asked, my hand immediately moving to one of my braids.

I still wore my hair as I had in Germany. It was divided into three sections. Two of these were formed into braids. This resulted in two long plaits of blonde hair on either side of my head. Each braid went halfway down my back. On the top middle of my head, a third section of hair remained. It had been saved from the braids. These upper strands were gathered and rolled in a small comb. This formed a French roll, as it was called, and the comb kept the roll together and in place. In Germany, many other girls had worn their hair the same way. In Nebraska, I was the only one to use the style.

Eager to fit in, but nervous about changing my look, I followed Ms. Baumann's advice and encouragement. One afternoon, she picked me up in her car and took me to a hair salon in Grafton. It was a place she visited regularly to have her own hair done. With me by her side, Ms. Baumann talked to the stylist.

"Let's go shorter," she began.

"Yes, much shorter—and perhaps with some curls," added the beautician.

"What do you think, Elfi?" asked Ms. Baumann, turning to me.

I sat in the chair, looking at Ms. Baumann through her reflection in the mirror. "Umm, okay?" was all I could make out.

Snip, snip. The stylist sheared off each plait, and then proceeded to chop, and chop, and chop some more.

When my hair came down only to my chin, she put away the scissors. As if this change weren't drastic enough, for the next step she got out rollers, bottles full of chemicals, and told me I was going to get a permanent.

By this point, I was mortified. How would my hair end up? Would I have any hair left? And would I never wear braids again?

For all the time I had spent bumping around Germany, living and eating day to day, the fret over a hairstyle was something new. And yet, it was important. I had worn my hair that way for years. It was a big part of who I was, and everything I had been through. In its small, ordinary way, it symbolized a part of my heritage and earlier years in Germany.

The beautician turned me away from the mirror and put curlers in my hair. Then she added some liquid-based substance and had me sit for a while. The process seemed to go on and on.

Finally I felt her hands remove the rollers. My nostrils filled with a strong chemical smell.

"Okay you're done," she said cheerfully.

She turned me back to the mirror, and I studied the hairdo for a minute.

"Whoa," I thought.

It was such a change to go from having really long, straight hair in braids to very short, curly hair.

As I left the salon, the beautician handed me the two braids she had cut off of my head.

When Ms. Baumann brought be back to the farmhouse, Mutti was so taken aback she didn't know what to say. I held up my old braids for her to see.

The farmhouse had one bathroom downstairs and in it, above the sink, there was a mirror. Later that day I looked in the mirror and scrutinized the new style. While distinct, it wasn't necessarily bad.

In fact, once I got used to it, I thought it was pretty cute. My hair now hung in small waves framing my face, reaching just to my ears.

I studied the braids too. Those precious plaits had been with me for years and traveled so far. I tucked them away in a small jewelry box in my room. I wanted to keep the token of my past and former life.

Ms. Baumann, who had overseen the transformation of my hair into a more American look, had a brother close by. This sibling, Don Baumann, was married and had two little girls. After Ms. Baumann helped restyle my hair, her brother occasionally asked me to babysit his daughters. I enjoyed being around the children, and the extra pocket money served as a new source of income for me.

One particular spring day in 1955, Mr. and Mrs. Baumann asked me to watch their girls for a few hours. I didn't have to be to their house until the evening, so I had the afternoon free.

That day, before babysitting, I went out with Wilfried, Rainer, and Jerry, Mrs. Otte's son. The four of us trekked about a quarter of a mile from Mr. Workentine's farm. There we found a ditch with a tree in it.

The tree was tall, and we took turns climbing up and down it. Then I had an idea. When it was my turn, I shimmied up and announced to the others, "I think I can jump down!"

Off I leaped, and flew away from the tree. Slicing through the air was invigorating. When I landed, my left foot hit the ditch at a painful angle.

Moments later, an intense throbbing spread through the top of my foot. I took off my shoe to examine the injury, and soon three other sets of eyes stared at it. We all watched the foot swell. I thought of my arm, and of how I broke it while playing leap frog and endured torment while the doctor set it in a cast.

With those memories on my mind, I quickly shook off the concerned look on the others' faces. "It's not broken; I know it's not broken," I insisted, mostly to put my brothers and Jerry to ease. Hastily I tugged the shoe back on over my foot. Then I walked back the quarter of a mile to get home.

I didn't want to go to the doctor. I had a baby-sitting job lined up, and that meant I would be getting some spending money. I didn't tell anyone—not even Mutti—what had happened to my foot.

By the time we left to go to the Baumann's house, my foot was swelling out of the shoe. Still, I carried on, knocking on the Baumann's door and acting as if nothing was wrong. After short greetings and polite exchanges, Mr. and Mrs. Baumann headed out the door.

I tried my best to ignore the agony. I focused on taking care of the girls, but it was hard to think through the seething pain.

The Baumanns had a staircase in their home leading to the second floor. The girls slept on the upper level, and often played there too. By the end of the night, the discomfort was so intense I couldn't walk up the stairs. Instead, I crawled up and down them. Yet I didn't complain, as I didn't want to go to the doctor and be in misery again. I also didn't want to hear what Mutti and Papa would have to say about me jumping out of the tree, or of their concern over how much it would cost to properly treat the foot.

When Mr. and Mrs. Baumann came home, the pain was even worse. Immediately Mrs. Baumann saw something was seriously wrong.

To the doctor we went. This was a different doctor than Dr. Nuss, but he seemed quite competent. I had broken my foot, he told me. Fortunately, this time the injury didn't require a wooden cast like my broken arm had. Instead, the doctor wrapped the foot in bandages.

Over time, it healed, and eventually, I ran on it again.

I was growing up in America, along with my three brothers. Detlef learned to sit quietly through church. Wilfried and Rainer knew English and had adjusted to both the school and farm situation. Every day seemed to bring a new set of adventures for us all. Each day, as our feet walked over the Nebraska soil, the American life seeped a little further into our beings.

We lived in a prosperous part of the nation, rich in soil and cattle. In 1955, Omaha, Nebraska, had the world's largest livestock market. Furthermore, Nebraska was the leading beef state of the country.[154]

In school, I found niches I enjoyed. One of these was volleyball. Shortly after my eighth grade year began, I learned a volleyball team was forming. I signed up, and soon felt right at home. The team was for the local high school, but since our school was small, I was able to join. I also joined the pep club.

Both activities were fun. I especially enjoyed volleyball, and kept busy with practices and games. I got along well with a girl named Joan, who was my age and on the team.

In volleyball, when it was my turn in the rotation, I was always the setter. I tossed the ball up to Joan, who hit it with such force the other team could never return it.

In March of 1955, I went along with the high school students to a spelling contest in Geneva. I also went to a music contest held in Shickley, Nebraska, about 30 miles from Grafton. With the high school girls, I sang "Water Lilies" and "On a Little Silver Beam."

When I started ninth grade at the local high school, Grafton High School, I was one of four students in the class. There were three girls and one boy. I was the class historian.

That year, I played volleyball again, and our team did well. There were nine of us on the team. We won six out of the nine games we played that season.

Also during my ninth grade year, I was in the pep club once more. There were eight of us in the pep club.

At the end of the school year, we were told Grafton High School was going to close. This was because there were not enough students enrolled in it. I had a choice: I could continue my studies at the high school in Sutton, or at the high school in Geneva. Since we shopped more often in Sutton, I opted for school there.

When the following school year began, I got on a bus every morning, just as I had when attending school in Grafton. This time, the bus didn't take me into the town of Grafton. Instead, it traveled eight miles over to Sutton.

The first day of classes there brought a big surprise. There were 35 kids in my grade alone. This represented more students than I had seen in a classroom with several grades in it during my time in Grafton.

Due to the change, and the adjustments I went through to get accustomed to a different school, the days crawled by. It was a disappointment compared to my time in school at Grafton.

Still, as a whole, our family was doing well—thriving, even, in Grafton. We loved going to church on Sundays, where Pastor Fuerstenau's loud voice carried the message of salvation to the corners of the church building. Mutti loved her little spot on the farm, her garden, and the appointments she arranged over the phone. My brothers and I had grown comfortable with the routines of school and farm life.

There was just one problem: Papa. Since our arrival in Grafton, he had spent his days working on the farm for Mr. Workentine. Before coming to America, the agreement he and Mr. Workentine had arranged required that Papa give part of each paycheck back to Mr. Workentine. This was to repay Mr. Workentine the money he sent to us in Germany, which had been used to cover our travel costs when we came to America.

We had arrived in Grafton in 1952. Four years later in 1956, Papa had still not repaid the debt. That, in and of itself, wasn't cause for alarm. But there was an underlying issue at hand: Papa wasn't happy.

The everyday chores were very different from what he had done as a welder in Germany. And while he was thankful to have a job in America, he didn't feel at home with it. He preferred welding over plowing, and was anxious to get back to his original trade as a blacksmith.

With that goal in mind, after four years in Grafton, Papa and Mutti began to look into other job options. After sorting through the area, they felt the city of Lincoln, located about 70 miles northeast of Grafton, held opportunities.

Going there would mean uprooting the family, relocating to a new place, changing schools, and starting—again—from scratch. Still, Papa was ready to put away the plow, once and for all. And while he didn't have a job lined up in Lincoln, or even any contacts there, both he and Mutti expected he could find something if he looked around.

After coming across the Atlantic and beginning a new life in a foreign country, jumping over to a different town must have seemed like a fairly small task. There were an estimated 120,000 people living in the city of Lincoln in 1956. Surely someone there would offer him work.[155]

The idea of Lincoln holding good fortune was based on anecdotes we had heard from others at church in Grafton. Our family had never set foot in the city itself. But when Mutti and Papa began considering Lincoln as a place to live, they decided to check it out.

One afternoon during the early spring of 1957, our whole family piled into Mr. Workentine's car, with Papa behind the wheel. After more than an hour on the road, we arrived at the outskirts of town. As we approached the edge of Lincoln, we went over a bridge. Descending from the bridge's peak, I caught a glimpse of the city before us. The elegant buildings and well-kept streets contrasted sharply with the leftover war rubble I remembered seeing in Hamburg.

This city, Lincoln, was the capital of Nebraska. I stared, wide-eyed, as we approached the downtown area, where the government headquarters for Lincoln and the state of Nebraska were located. Proud and looming, the nearly white capitol building stood out among the rest. It was a large structure built in the shape of a square, with a tower rising up to meet the sky. A gold-tiled dome perched above the tower. A statue of a person sowing seeds topped the building.

It was magnificent. I couldn't believe this was the city we were going to call home.

And there was a good reason to be impressed with the state capitol building. When the 400-foot tower was constructed during the years 1922 to 1932, it was said to be the nation's first vernacular State Capitol. This meant its design was based on locally available resources and traditions. The building's features represented Nebraska's Native American background and also its pioneer culture.[156]

For Mutti and Papa, after surveying more of the city, they deemed it a good fit. They wanted to live in Lincoln. All that remained was the need to first pay off the debt they still owed to Mr. Workentine in Grafton.

Back on the farm, before Mutti and Papa brought up the discussion of paying off the debt, Mr. Workentine stepped in. As he had four years earlier, when he helped us get visas, make the trip from Germany to America, and find a place to stay, Mr. Workentine offered us another generous deal. He canceled the remainder of the debt Papa still owed him. He also told Papa he was free to find work for himself.

And so it was settled.

The first order of business was to find a home in Lincoln.

After a little looking, Mutti and Papa found a place to rent. It was a small white frame house. The place had three bedrooms, a tiny kitchen, and a living room. It was located on 1010 Harrison St., a central spot near downtown. Many shops and schools were within walking distance from it.

Back in Grafton, we packed up the belongings we had accumulated since our arrival, and bid farewell to our first stop in America. It was painful, in a way, to go. The place and its people represented our first taste of a new life, an introduction to pumpkin pie, new friendships, the chance to learn how to sew, and a church to attend regularly. We would be close enough to visit, but not so near that the trip could be a regular one.

Pastor Fuerstenau told us there was an established congregation in Lincoln that was part of the same church body as Trinity Lutheran in Grafton. The one in Grafton was part of the Wisconsin Evangelical Lutheran Synod (WELS). The church in Lincoln, called Mt. Olive, was founded in 1940 and was also part of the WELS.

In addition, there was a new WELS congregation in Lincoln. Pastor Carl Nommensen, a WELS pastor, had initiated it the year before, in the summer of 1956. Land was purchased in September of the same year, and the first service was held on December 30, 1956. Since no building had yet been constructed for the congregation, those attending worship met in a school close to the property. The school was called Merle Beattie School.

At Trinity in Grafton, Pastor Fuerstenau encouraged us to go to the new church in Lincoln and help build it up.

In March 1957, four and a half years after we stepped foot into the farmhouse on Mr. Workentine's property, we left. We transferred our belongings and furniture to Lincoln, to our next abode on Harrison St.

The day we moved in, our new neighbors came over. They gave us a cake, and explained they were from Germany as well. They chattered away in German with Mutti and Papa for a long time. Their names were Herman and Marie Schulz, and they had a son and a daughter. Mutti and Marie clicked instantly; the Schulz family became our first friends in Lincoln.

As soon as we arrived in Lincoln, Papa looked for a job. He was sure he'd be offered some work in the welding business. He had years and years of experience laboring as a blacksmith in Germany.

Unfortunately, he was 48 years old when he started job hunting in Lincoln. Instead of finding work rapidly, he encountered one dead end after another. Positions in his line of work, especially for people his age, were almost non-existent. After some more searching, he connected with a union for welders, only to meet another road block. He couldn't join, the union members said. They didn't accept workers as old as he was.

Disappointed and at the same time, surprised at the few pickings, Papa grew determined to find a job. After more scouting, he found a Chevrolet auto dealer in Lincoln that was looking for a janitor. The Misles, a Jewish family that had settled in the area, owned the place.

When Papa inquired about the janitor position, the Misles hired him right away. Soon Papa began his duties. Instead of welding parts, however, he spent the days cleaning floors and taking out trash.

Since we moved to Lincoln in March, I hadn't finished the school year back in Sutton. I was in 10th grade at the time. So I enrolled immediately in Lincoln High. It was the city's first high school and had more than 2,000 students enrolled in it. To get there and back, I had to walk a little more than two miles from our place on Harrison St.

For my first day of school, I set out from our house and walked to the school's campus. Once there, with the help of an administrator, I found my new classroom. I felt like I was in a city within its walls. I didn't know a single person at school.

At Lincoln High, there were more than 500 students in 10th grade. This was a far cry from the 35 in my grade level in Sutton, let alone the mere three others in my class in Grafton. The first day passed in a blur, as I searched for my classes amidst the crowd and haze of activity. I tried to hide my tears as I walked through the halls.

The following days, I trekked two miles to school in the mornings, and walked home again in the afternoons. My clothes weren't as fashionable as those the other kids wore, and I sometimes heard laughter and mocking during my trips to and from school. Shirts and skirts that matched were in style, and I didn't have anything to fit in style-wise. Without any friends, I dreaded the excursion every day.

While my language skills had greatly improved by then, I still had an accent. Unlike in Grafton, where my pronunciation was readily accepted, in Lincoln introductions with other students brought comments such as, "You talk different!" or "What is that accent?"

I was quiet in classes. I didn't ever raise my hand and I avoided answering questions. I got little help from the teachers, probably because I was too afraid to ask. On my own, I tried to make sense of homework assignments.

The first Sunday we attended church in Lincoln, we headed to Merle Beattie School. This was the school where the second WELS congregation in Lincoln held services at the time. A small group met there each week.

When the six of us arrived that Sunday morning, we met a pastor at the door. He introduced himself as Pastor Nommensen, and explained that he oversaw the congregation. When we looked past the pastor, we saw several others in the room. There were about five in all. As soon as our family joined them, the group felt bigger.

The congregation was smaller than the one in Grafton. Yet we immediately felt at home with the other members. We were with a family again, a family of Christ where we could see other people, spend time together, and sing each week. Together we studied God's Word.

Mutti was glad Papa found a job, but working as a janitor didn't bring in much income. We were a family with four growing children. With that in mind, Mutti looked for work too.

She found a job as a dish washer at Lincoln General Hospital. The place was about nine blocks east of our small residence on Harrison St. She walked to and from work. Washing dishes meant lifting and scrubbing heavy pots and pans. The work was labor-intense, and Mutti always arrived home with sore arms. Her hands turned red from the hard soap and constant scrubbing.

Even with both Mutti and Papa working, the total pay coming into our home was grim. Money had not been plentiful in Grafton, but it was scarcer now in Lincoln. I was 16 by then. Wilfried and Rainer were growing teenagers, and Detlef was in grade school. There were mouths to feed, school supplies to buy, and all of the other expenses, from clothing to household goods to transportation costs, to take into account. Food and supplies weren't as scarce as they had been during our hard times in Germany, but we all felt the tightening of resources.

While we were getting used to life and work in Lincoln, we still held some ties to Grafton. One of these was with the church there. Wilfried and I were still in confirmation class, which we continued on the weekends with Pastor Fuerstenau. For the lessons, Pastor Fuerstenau came to Lincoln on Saturdays to teach us.

Even though we had moved, we decided to have our confirmation service in Grafton, since that was where the bulk of our studying had taken place. We were on track to be confirmed that spring. Also, Harlan and Mary Ackerman, the brother and sister from the Trinity congregation in Grafton we had studied with, were also ready to be confirmed. Pastor Fuerstenau scheduled a confirmation service for the four of us in the spring of 1957.

For the confirmation, Mutti wanted me to wear a white dress. We looked at the discount stores near our home and didn't find anything. Mutti searched some more, and couldn't locate a single white dress that would work.

One afternoon Mutti and I headed to downtown Lincoln to look for a dress. We wandered from store to store, and still didn't find any good options. Finally, in mere desperation, Mutti walked up to the doors of another place and turned to me. "Let's try here," she said.

This wasn't just any clothing store. Mutti was about to walk into Hovland-Swanson, which was *the* place to buy fashionable styles at the time. The retail shop was set up in a building with an art deco design at 1240 O St. Without even going into the store, I knew we shouldn't be there. The windows touted spring dresses and matching outfits only the elite among my classmates wore to school. It was far too fancy, and too expensive, for an immigrant family trying to get by on a janitor and dish washer income.

Still, when Mutti had her mind made up, there was no stopping her. Engrossed in her hunt for the best white confirmation attire, she marched inside. I followed, a bit embarrassed, at her heels.

As soon as we walked in, the clerks in the store turned to look at us. I glanced at my plain clothes. Only minutes earlier, they had been suitable, but now they seemed drab. We couldn't have looked like we had a dollar to spare. After a quick glance, most of the employees turned away. They must have felt certain our presence would not lead to any new business for them.

The store smelled of new, lovely clothes and a hint of perfume. Mutti began perusing the selection of dresses. I remained still, in place, near the door.

As long, dreadful minutes passed, I stayed in my spot. Mutti kept searching. Surely she wouldn't find a single thing. I knew we couldn't afford to buy a sock at the place, let alone a full dress. I was about to put my hand on the door and signal to Mutti that we should take leave.

Just then, a clerk that I hadn't seen when we entered came over. "Good afternoon," she said and smiled. "Can I help you find anything in particular?"

Her greeting was so warm and kind it took me aback. Startled, I took a step back. Now I was nearly at the door, within reach of slipping out.

Before I could get enough thoughts together to respond, Mutti took over. "We're looking for a dress—a white one for a confirmation for my daughter," she explained.

"Of course, have you tried over here?" And with that, she led Mutti to a section of fine white dresses. I followed behind.

Mutti combed through the dresses, chatting with the salesperson. After some looking, the lady pulled out a dress. Turning to me, she held it up for us to have a look.

Its hem fell to my calves, its stylish sleeves were short, and it had a wide, off-the-neck, collar. Best of all, it was shimmery white, and perfect for my upcoming confirmation. I tried the garment on at the clerk's urging. It fit wonderfully.

There was one catch, of course. It cost $100. Mutti and Papa each made a dollar an hour at their jobs. I knew immediately it was out of our price range.

Mutti had other thoughts. "Do you have a payment plan?" she asked the clerk.

"Of course." The two of them strolled to the counter to arrange a payment plan.

Minutes later, I walked out of the store, carrying a bag with the most beautiful dress I had ever owned.

It all had happened so fast. For a moment, I thought I was dreaming. Then, after walking about a block, I realized what Mutti had just done.

And I felt guilty about it. We were living week to week, and I knew the dress was a big splurge. Turning to Mutti, I started, "You shouldn't have—"

"Don't be silly," she cut me off. "Of course I should have. It's for your confirmation and I want you to wear the best dress we can find."

And I did. The confirmation service was a fine one. Wilfried and I were confirmed with our two friends and classmates, Harlan and Mary, in Grafton. The text Pastor Fuerstenau chose for me that Sunday meant a lot to me: *And we know that in all things, God works for the good of those who love Him, who have been called according to his purpose* (Romans 8:28, NIV).

School ended that year in June, and the summer vacation of 1957 spread out before me. I was grateful to have a break from the intensity of adjusting to such a large school. I was also eager to help out Mutti and Papa.

To do so, I picked up a job working as a waitress at the Johnson Café. The place was a family-owned restaurant, set up along a main highway that entered Lincoln from the south. The café perched on the corner of a busy intersection, and was right across the street from the Nebraska State Penitentiary. The prison was the oldest in Nebraska, having served as a correctional facility since 1869.

The Johnson Café had a menu that included hamburgers, cheeseburgers, hot dogs and French fries for those stopping in for lunch or supper. It also offered salads and cold sandwiches.

In addition to being a place to eat, the business offered a filling station for travelers. The setup consisted of gas pumps and a small auto shop. Those coming in for gas could ask for other simple services, such as air for their tires. The shop was attached to the restaurant. There was a door in the shop which opened into the back area of the restaurant.

I waited on tables at the café, and Mr. Johnson, the owner, usually gave me evening shifts during the week. On Saturdays, I often worked a full day.

After I learned the ropes of waitressing, Mr. Johnson occasionally left me in charge of the entire place. He did this especially during slow periods in the afternoon hours or on weekends. While he was away, I did everything, from taking orders to making the food, serving it, and even running the cash register.

I didn't have to pump gas. The owner's son ran the filling station section of the business. For this, he worked mostly outside. Sometimes he came into the restaurant to get something to eat. He also came in to run transactions through the register, as the till in the restaurant was used both for the diner area and the filling station.

Once in a while, he came to the register to simply grab a little cash for himself.

Mr. Johnson didn't seem to notice his son took from the register. I kept doing my job and didn't mention it to him.

Back at home, even with the money I brought in from waitressing, funds remained tight. Mutti prepared cheap, easy meals that were often reminiscent of Germany. She used basic ingredients she could find at a good price in Lincoln. One of my favorite meals she made during that time was *pellkartoffeln mit quark*, or boiled potatoes with cottage cheese and seasoning. After cooking the potatoes, she peeled them, and then served them with cottage cheese. She often garnished the dish with chives, onions, salt and pepper. It was inexpensive, tasty and filling.

The dish washing job came to be too much for Mutti. The work was exhausting and the hours were long. She went back out on a job hunt, and applied for a position at a candy factory in Lincoln. She got the job and started work right away.

The factory was one of three plants Russell Stover Candies, a candy manufacturer, had in the 1950s. The factory in Lincoln had opened in 1942. The two other factories for Russell Stover Candies were located in Kansas City and Denver.[157]

Mutti rode the bus every day to work. Her job consisted of cutting out candies. She loved working at the candy factory and we loved it too. She was allowed to purchase the seconds, such as ones that didn't swirl together in the right place, for a reasonable price. Mutti always had slightly misshaped chocolate covered cherries, lemon drops, and caramel clusters on the table at home. They tasted sweet and scrumptious.

During our first year in Lincoln, we frequently got together with the Schulz family. Papa especially appreciated them, as we spoke in German at our gatherings. We often had a meal together on Sunday afternoons. Then we ate delicious German food, like sauerkraut and potatoes, or bratwurst and red cabbage.

Mutti was careful with the food budget, and didn't usually buy expensive cuts of meat. On special occasions, she made a mouth-watering roast. To prepare it, she bought a cheaper cut of meat and put it in the oven with potatoes and vegetables. When it was nearly done, she made a rich gravy to serve with it, just as she had done in Grafton. The meat came out tasting as good as a pricier cut. Mutti often made the roast on Sundays after church, when we got together with the Schulz family. At times my uncles and their families came over for Sunday dinner, and occasionally Mr. Workentine joined us as well.

One day, Mutti and her friend Marie Schulz decided to try making American hamburgers. The Schulz family had a grill, so they shaped patties out of ground beef. They placed those on the grill. The end result tasted good. I was familiar with hamburgers from my waitressing job. The creation was different, however, for my German parents.

I continued working at the Johnson Café through the remainder of summer vacation. Before long, it was time to start school again. I dreaded the thought of going back to the walls of Lincoln High School.

The first months of 11th grade at Lincoln High started the same way 10th grade ended— miserably.

Then one day that fall, while sitting in homeroom, I noticed a girl who was quiet, like me. We introduced ourselves. Her name was Ann and she was friendly to me. After spending a few lunches together, we exchanged addresses. In doing so, I learned she lived only a few blocks from my home. We quickly developed a friendship.

Everything about Lincoln High changed when I met Ann. With a friend by my side, suddenly the massive school didn't seem as daunting. We hung out together at school. Outside the classroom, we practically lived at each other's homes. We did homework together and listened to music. I introduced my parents to her mom and dad. Everything she liked, I liked. Everything I was interested in, she was interested in too.

Wilfried and Rainer attended Irving Junior High in Lincoln. The place was close to our home and they made friends through school too.

At the time, I liked Elvis Presley, and kept several pictures and posters of him in my room. Born in Mississippi in 1935, Presley gained popularity and set about uprooting the music industry in the 1950s. His singles sold like crazy: "Hound Dog" sold 2 million copies and "Don't Be Cruel" sold 3 million copies.[158]

As the school year went on, I learned of the Glee Club and the Aeolian choir at Lincoln High School. These were musical groups, and since I loved to sing, I considered joining them. Both of them required trying out.

The Aeolian choir provided a robe for members. Everyone who wanted to participate in the Glee Club, however, had to buy an expensive matching wool outfit. I wasn't sure how I would be able to buy the clothing. I was still working, but I gave most of my earnings to Mutti and Papa, who then used the dollars to pay for our family's daily needs.

I didn't know how to cover the expenses, but I also knew other activities at the school either didn't interest me or didn't seem worthwhile. I had played volleyball in Grafton and enjoyed it. At Lincoln, however, there was so much competition for volleyball that I didn't even try out.

But I did love singing. I tried out, and made both choirs. To help pay for the outfit, I looked for another job. I soon found some cleaning work for a wealthy family that lived by the junior high school Wilfried and Rainer attended. The lady of the house had two children in boarding schools on the East Coast.

The first time I walked into her house, she took me upstairs to show me around. In the children's bedroom, there were two single beds. Everything on the beds, as well as the entire room, matched perfectly. I had never seen such coordination before in my life. I didn't even know it was possible to have so much lavish, uniform furniture all together in one place.

The woman hired me right away, and set about showing me certain things I didn't know how to do, like clean a bathroom the way she wanted it cleaned and make the beds the way she wanted them made. I went to clean at the house once a week after school. When I finished, I returned home to do schoolwork.

With the extra earnings, I was able to buy the matching wool outfit for the Glee Club. We all were required to wear a maroon outfit, and had to purchase it from a particular store. The store wasn't quite the same caliber as Hovland-Swanson, the expensive store where Mutti had purchased my confirmation dress, but it was still quite classy. It was also pricey. We could choose if we wanted a uniform with a straight skirt, or one with a full skirt. I saved up enough cash, and then opted for a straight skirt. I really liked it.

For the singing groups, I attended practices during the week and occasional singing events.

I also learned of the pep club and joined that as well. The pep club participated in all of the pep rallies for football and basketball during the year. Our rallies were almost always held on Friday mornings. The games took place on Friday evenings.

The team and symbol for Lincoln High School was the Links. One of the cheers we always performed at the rallies went like this:

Yeah, red! Yeah, black! Yeah, Lincoln, set 'em back!

And at the games, we often did a cheer about the other team:

Hey there opponent.

Can't you take it, Can't you make it,

Can't you Alabama shake it?

Can't you boogie to the left, can't you boogie to the right

Can't you pull your team together and fight, fight, fight!

I really enjoyed the pep club, and also the Glee Club and Aeolian choir. What's more, I felt proud to be a part of them. These groups gave me a reason to be happy about school that I hadn't felt previously in Lincoln. I even befriended some of the other girls. As for the others, at least they never made fun of me while I was in their presence. And like Mutti often said, "What you don't know won't hurt you."

Unlike when we stayed with Mr. Workentine, in the city we no longer had a steady stream of meat coming in. Potatoes returned to the table more often for meals.

Mutti's relatives in Germany heard about our situation, how we lived with very little, and how Mutti had to work so hard. They wrote letters to Mutti, and scolded her, saying, "Look, now you have to work, and we don't have to work here."

Mutti was hurt by the words, to the point that she sometimes wondered if she had made the right choice. She reflected on the decision to come and worried she shouldn't have pushed so hard to go to America.

But the fact was, Mutti liked living in America. Worshipping regularly was important to her. After ruminating on the what-if's of how our life in Germany would have been if we had stayed, she always concluded, "Here I have my faith and my family, and I get to go to church on Sundays." That was so important to her, and she never forgot it had been hard—and usually impossible—to go to church every week when we lived in Harksheide.

Through our mutual support and encouragement, the bonds of a lasting friendship were forging, both with the Shulzes and at church. It was the kind of kinship that signals true belonging in a place. Our lives in Lincoln had officially begun.

CHAPTER FOURTEEN: LINCOLN BECOMES HOME

"Goodness and mercy all my life
Shall surely follow me,
And in God's house forevermore
My dwelling-place shall be."
— Francis Rous, 1650[159]

The 1950s brought a long list of changes, both in technology and science, to America. Televisions appeared in nearly every single home in the country, air-conditioning came about, and jet planes took to the skies.[160]

The Soviet Union successfully launched the first satellite, the Sputnik, into space with a rocket in 1957. In reaction, the United States launched an ambitious space and missile program.[161]

In our neighborhood in Lincoln, our circles remained small. But they were important to us. Mutti had a way about her that drew people in, and kept them there.

When neighbors, friends from church, or relatives came to visit, Mutti always wished them a good journey as they left. When they headed out the door, with a smile she called after them, saying, "Come safe home." It was her own version of English, and reflected her concern for the visitors' wellbeing.

The tiny white house on Harrison St. served well for our early days in Lincoln. After renting for six months, however, Mutti and Papa started thinking about the possibility of buying a new home. It would be a big step for them, and would help give them a place they could call their own.

It was a good time to buy a house. During the 1950s, Americans across the nation were making the leap toward being homeowners. As 1957 drew to a close, Mutti and Papa joined the thoughts of that demographic and began looking at houses.

Having an idea was one small step; making it a reality would mean taking several other large strides. For starters, Mutti and Papa each earned a dollar an hour at their jobs. Their savings was nonexistent. They didn't know how they could possibly find a house we could afford.

Still, the idea of owning a home appealed to them, and especially to Papa. So Mutti and Papa scouted our neighborhood and nearby areas. And as before, God's guiding ways led them to new opportunities. They soon ran into Lou Sommerhauser, an agent from the Chambers-Dobson agency, an insurance brokerage with a financial services division. Mr. Sommerhauser helped with the hunt.

Before long, Mutti and Papa found a house they liked. It was several blocks away, and a step up from the small place on Harrison St. Its address was 2231 South 15th St.

The new house was a two-story place with a wood frame, wood siding, and large windows. It had an open space downstairs that held a living room, large dining room, and kitchen. There were three bedrooms in it and one bathroom. Overall, it was a larger home than the one we had started in.

The following step was to find a way to gather funds. As a family, we had no collateral. Mutti and Papa wondered how we would make a down payment, and get approved for a home loan.

But Mutti didn't give up. Papa had a life insurance policy at the time. They decided to take some money from it; a total of $200 was needed in earnest money.

The agent, Mr. Sommerhauser, helped make the next arrangements. Even though Mutti and Papa didn't have a credit history, he vouched for them and helped the loan get approved. The balance, when they took out the loan, was $6,246.81. The house payments were to be $65 a month.

I continued working and giving most of my earnings to Mutti and Papa to help pay for expenses. The cleaning job was going well. At the Johnson Café, however, the situation was far from ideal.

In addition to leaving me to run the restaurant on my own once in a while, Mr. Johnson had a blind eye when it came to his son. Often times, his son came into the restaurant and took some change or bills from the cash register. If Mr. Johnson knew about it, he never mentioned it to me. I never spoke of it to him. Still, I saw it happen on a fairly regular basis.

One Saturday afternoon, Mr. Johnson left me in charge for several hours. His son oversaw the pumps outside that day. I ran the inside on my own and waited on customers while Mr. Johnson was away.

Not long after Mr. Johnson left, his son came in to the restaurant. Without acknowledging me or anyone else, he went directly to the till. He opened it up, took out a $5 bill, and went back outside.

I carried on as usual. When Mr. Johnson returned, he greeted me and began tending to customers. About an hour later, my shift ended and I went home.

The following week, I came in to work. Mr. Johnson stood at the cash register, waiting for me.

"There is something wrong here," he began.

"Really, what is it?" I had no idea what he was talking about. As far as I could tell, everything looked the same.

"Money was missing from the cash register last Saturday after you left. A total of $5 was gone."

That was a decent amount of money. And I knew just where it was.

"You should ask your son about that," I replied. "I saw him take the money out on Saturday."

Mr. Johnson bristled. "Surely not."

"It's true, I've seen him take money out other times too."

"That can't be right. I'm reducing your next paycheck by $5," he answered.

"I didn't take anything! It was your son."

Mr. Johnson refused to hear any of it. He insisted it had been me, and subtracted $5 from my next paycheck.

I started looking for a different job.

Soon I found another waitressing opportunity. It was at a place called Cotner Terrace Restaurant. At the time, it was one of the biggest, fanciest places to dine at in Nebraska.

My application was accepted, and I started working at this white linen, white napkin restaurant—a far cry from the café and gas station. The restaurant was on the east edge of town. It was located right off of O Street and Cotner Boulevard in Lincoln, past 48th St. When I started working there, 48th St. marked the end of the main part of Lincoln.

My shifts at Cotner Terrace started in the early evening. On the days I worked there, after getting out of school in the afternoon, I took a bus to the restaurant. I arrived at the elegant eatery at about four o'clock in the afternoon. Once there, I changed into my uniform, which consisted of a black dress with a white apron in front.

Before I began work for the evening, the restaurant provided me with a free meal. The chef made everything from scratch and the food was scrumptious. There were fresh cinnamon rolls to choose from, and a soup of the day, like vegetable beef or mushroom rice. The chef also made an excellent minestrone soup. I always chose that before working if they had it. The restaurant began its dinner hour at 5 p.m. When I finished eating, I helped get everything ready for serving the guests.

Mr. Lutz, the owner of the restaurant, was exceptionally gracious. Each night, I earned $3, plus I got to keep all of my tips. I oversaw six to eight tables at a time, and made sure they were taken care of during the night. On weekends, the restaurant stayed open until midnight, and sometimes I didn't get home until 1 or 2 a.m. I made good money, and I loved the atmosphere. I was also able to help Mutti and Papa with what I earned.

When it was Christmastime, Mr. Lutz allowed guests to use the place for holiday company parties. For large groups, he shut off the restaurant to outsiders. This was always the case for Christmas parties for organizations like Roberts Dairy, a local milk company. All of the employees came for the meal and filled the place. It took many servers to take care of such a large party.

There was a set menu for these gatherings. My job, along with the other servers, consisted of finding out details, such as what type of dressing guests wanted on their salad, and then making sure everything was delivered in the right order and to everyone's contentment.

For small dinner parties, Mr. Lutz would assign one person to take care of the group. Once a man at a table I was serving that night ordered a steak dinner. When I asked how he wanted it done, he replied, "Three minutes on one side and three minutes on the other."

I relayed the message to the chef. When I took out the cut of meat, it was so red I worried it was too rare. As I set it down, the guests studied the steak and noted, "Perfect." I got a good tip from him.

* * *

One of the last days in January 1958, around 2 p.m., I sat in school. Suddenly an announcement came through the intercom system, interrupting our class. The booming voice told us that Charles Starkweather and his girlfriend were running free and could kill anyone. We were told to go home and stay there.

This chaos had been building since December of the previous year. On December 2, 1957, the Lincoln Journal newspaper bore a front-page headline that read, "Lincolnite Slain! Theft Motive Seen!"[162]

Although unknown at the time, the murderer, Charles Starkweather, was from Lincoln. Born in 1938 into a poor, uneducated family, he was the third of seven children. While attending Irving Junior High, he earned a reputation for being one of the meanest, toughest kids in Lincoln, a fame he was proud of. After failing several grades and getting kicked out of Irving Junior High, he transferred to a different school in Lincoln called Everett Junior High.[163]

Starkweather quit school when he was 16 years old. He took a job in 1955 baling paper at the Western Newspaper Union, and got paid 85 cents an hour for it. Later he switched to a job collecting garbage. In 1956, he was introduced to Caril Anne Fugate, who was 13 years old at the time and became his girlfriend.[164]

At the beginning of December 1957, the same month Mutti and Papa purchased our new home, Starkweather got angry at a gas station attendant. To retaliate, Starkweather shot him. This resulted in the alarming front-page headline we saw in the Lincoln Journal that month.

Starkweather was not caught or placed behind bars after the incident. Instead, he roamed free in Lincoln.

Then, on January 21, 1958, Starkweather struck again. This time, he murdered his girlfriend's parents and two-and-a-half year old sister.[165]

Six days later, he murdered a friend and two additional teenagers.

Panic spread throughout Lincoln and the surrounding area as the body count mounted. At this point, the story made front-page headlines not only in Lincoln; it also appeared in newspapers across the country, including the Los Angeles Times.[166]

The morning of January 28, 1958, Starkweather drove his girlfriend to a wealthy part of town. They went to a residence located on the same street as the home I cleaned once a week. There he murdered the couple that owned the house and also their maid.[167]

The Lincoln police discovered the bodies in the early afternoon of January 29, 1958. After the three slayings were found, hysteria took over Lincoln and its outskirts. Local hardware stores quickly sold off all the ammunition stocked on their shelves. Customers wanted anything they could use to shoot. Businesses closed, meetings got canceled, phone lines jammed, and cars driven by terrorized parents in search of their children at school caused serious traffic jams.[168]

Nebraska's Governor Victor E. Anderson called out to the National Guard, who quickly arrived to help hunt down Starkweather. A $1,000 reward was offered for help locating him.[169]

This point in Starkweather's spree coincided with the announcement made at school. I looked around; everyone was in a panic. I sat in front of Starkweather's sister in the class. I turned to look at her.

I was terrified for my own safety, but also concerned for Starkweather's sister. She was short in stature, and had long, dark hair. That day, she hung her head and her hair covered her face. I felt sad for her and her situation. It was hard to know why she had even come to school. Maybe she had nowhere else to go.

Following orders, everyone filed out of the classroom and headed home. I walked by myself. The whole time, I was petrified I might see Starkweather or get caught up in part of the police chase to catch him. As I put one foot in front of the other, Mutti's phrase echoed in my ears: "Come safe home."

I arrived at the door of our house and went inside, my heart pounding. No one was home. Mutti and Papa were working, and my brothers were not around.

I turned on the radio to hear the news. I learned city officials had only told the kids in high school to walk home; the younger children had stayed in the schools they were at to be safe.

Later on that afternoon, my brothers arrived home, as did Mutti and Papa. Wilfried and Rainer said the police came to the school they attended, Irving Junior High, with German Shepherd dogs to patrol the area. The school was situated on the corner of South 21st St. and Van Dorn St. It was close to the home I cleaned and the residence where three of the victims had been murdered.

Detlef was at Saratoga Elementary School at the time, just two blocks from our home on South 15th St. He also stayed inside with other students for a good part of the afternoon, until they were released and allowed to go home.

By then, Starkweather and his girlfriend had fled Lincoln to get away from the police. It took days for law enforcement agents to capture Starkweather. He and his girlfriend made it all the way to Wyoming before police arrested them.

After the Starkweather scare, things quieted down in Lincoln. And while at first I felt jitters when walking to school and cleaning the home so close to three of Starkweather's victims, the nervousness eventually dissipated. I once again felt secure walking to and from school, and walking downtown sometimes to shop.

I was a junior at Lincoln High School at the time. When I went to and from school, I always walked the same route. If I traveled further during the day, I usually took the city bus.

One Thursday after school, when I didn't have to work, I went downtown before going home. I wanted to look at the shops there, which stayed open until nine o'clock only on Thursdays. These stores were located several blocks north and west of Lincoln High School, on O, M, and N Street. The streets running east and west in Lincoln were set up in alphabetical order. O Street was the city's main street.

I had very little money, and didn't buy anything. Instead, I looked in windows and poked around in several stores, dreaming of what I could possibly buy someday.

Normally I would have taken a bus home. But that night, by the time I was finished at the shops, the last bus for the day had already left. It was getting dark, and walking was my only option. I started down 13th street, which was one of the main streets leading from the Lincoln downtown area to our part of the city.

I mentally noted the streets as they ticked by: L to K, and then J, followed by I, then H. In between H and G there was an alley. It was in the middle of the block. There were also trees on the block that caused a darker stretch.

I hesitated. The sidewalk was a good ten feet in from the street. There were large, sprawling homes on both sides of the street. These residences had tall hedges, brick walls or fences that lined their yards, closing them off from the busy street and random passersby.

A chill rippled through the air. It was cold. I wore a full quilted black skirt, a light blue jacket, black and white saddle shoes and bobby socks with lace trim on the edges. It was a nice outfit, and I had worn it to school that day.

Around 9 p.m. I saw a car drive past, turn right onto a side street a little ahead of where I was walking, and stop. The vehicle was on the side I was walking on. It was pretty close, and I could see the tail lights of the car. The engine was still running and there were two people in the car.

Then, seemingly out of nowhere, a man was walking toward me. He must have gotten out of the vehicle. He wore a long coat and kept one hand in his pocket. He had dark hair, white skin and harsh features, and looked much older than I was. I had a sinking feeling in my gut that something wasn't right. I didn't know what to do.

He kept on coming. Instinctively, I knew he would attack me.

Soon he was on me. He punched me in the middle terribly hard. The thrust threw me up into the air. When I landed, I used my hands to brace myself. They hit gravel, and I realized we were in the alleyway. He tried to drag me toward the car he had left on the side street in front of me, but I started screaming and struggling. I knew getting into the car would be bad and I had to avoid it at all costs.

I screamed and screamed. I could see blood on my hands and knees. I yelled as loud as I could.

Then—as quickly as he had come—the man stopped, turned around, and ran back to the car. It sped off moments later.

I bolted toward the street and stood alongside it, screaming and crying in desperation. There was so much traffic I couldn't cross immediately to the other side. When I did get across, I started running back toward downtown.

I could not believe no one stopped to help me. It was not what I had envisioned Americans to be like.

After I sprinted a few blocks, another car slowed down in front of me. A young man inside leaned toward a rolled down window and asked if I needed help. I was scared this driver would try to hurt me too. I yelled, "No!" and kept on running.

As I sprinted further on, I realized he probably did intend to help me, but I was so shaken my reaction was to flee.

I raced all the way to the downtown Continental bus station. There, two men approached me. I screamed again, sure they were going to try to attack me also. But then, both of them opened their coats and showed me their badges.

"We're from the FBI," one of them explained. "I've just been having a cup of coffee with my partner here. How can we help?"

There were other people around, some waiting for a bus and others eating at tables, and the atmosphere helped me settle down.

Once I was calm enough to talk, the two agents listened to my story. Then they said they would take me home. First, however, they asked me to show them the site where the attack had taken place. We got in their car and drove to the alley. No one was there. It was even darker by then, and we didn't spot the men or the car they had been driving.

The agents took me home. Mutti's eyes grew large when she saw me standing between two men, crying. Then she glanced at the blood on me and looked mortified.

My parents and the officers decided to take me to Lincoln General Hospital. The doctors there treated for two sprained wrists and gashes in my hands and knees from the impact with the gravel.

I went home with my hands wrapped in bandages.

The next day was Friday. I didn't go to school that day, and used the weekend to recover from my injuries.

The police suspected the attack may have been instigated by a neighbor or someone who lived near to us. In an effort to track down the individual, they asked me to go downtown and walk to the stores I had visited the night of the attack. They said they would be following me at a distance. I did as they asked, but was scared thinking about the possibility that someone might jump at me again.

The police and I repeated this exercise a number of times. Once, when they were following me, I saw a car with two men in it. I recognized that one of them had been my attacker on that dreadful night. But the car drove away very quickly. I wasn't able to point it out to the officers or catch the license plate of the vehicle.

In the end, I never identified or charged the attacker. While it was frustrating to not track him down, it helped me become more aware of what was going on around me. I was soon able to remember all sorts of details about people, including what they looked like and what they wore.

In spite of the attack, I continued to walk to and from school most days. I also continued working and juggling my jobs and schoolwork.

During the next months in Lincoln, the atmosphere turned calm again. The scare of the Starkweather spree, and the horrible night of the attack, slowly shifted from the front and center of my thoughts. The events were still there, but they managed to move, and then remain, in the back of my mind.

The summer of 1958 filled up between my jobs and our involvement at church. The congregation was growing, and began worshiping in the basement of the pastor's home. Plans were in the works to build a church building and school in the future.

* * *

During much of the 1950s, the fear of polio had gripped the country. And in 1958, it landed in Mutti's family. Her cousin Irma was married to a Lutheran pastor in the city of Augusta, Kansas. That summer, the pastor, William E. Newton, came down with flu-like symptoms. Instead of getting better, he quickly took a turn for the worse. He had polio, and the disease struck him in the lungs. He had five children; the oldest was five years old.

Polio was not a new disease. It had first gained recognition when Franklin Roosevelt was struck with it in 1921. His condition triggered a crusade to conquer polio in the United States. The National Foundation for Infantile Paralysis, with a fundraising campaign known as the "March of Dimes," began in 1938.[170]

A turnaround from polio wasn't immediate. Seasons for the illness came and went, and were always unpredictable. In the summer before we arrived in America, a Washington Post headline had warned: "Polio Cases Set Record So Far in '52." Horror stories abounded, including one that involved a family on a farm in Iowa. Eleven of their 14 children were struck with polio.[171]

After undergoing initial trials, a polio vaccine, created by Jonas Salk, a medical researcher and virologist, was announced to the world in April 1955.[172] In the following years, the vaccine was distributed to a growing number of children in schools throughout the country. The number of new cases dwindled, but the disease still wasn't wiped out completely.

After polio struck Pastor Newton, he remained in the hospital. During his time there, he was placed in an iron lung.

225

While Pastor Newton fought for his life, our day-to-day activities and work carried on in Lincoln. I began my senior year of high school. I stayed active in the Glee Club and Aeolian Choir again, and also participated in the pep club.

* * *

Papa had started working as a janitor at Misle Chevrolet when we arrived in Lincoln. Mr. Abram Misle, who was Papa's boss, ran the car company, and several other businesses, with his two brothers and father.

Not long after he started working at Misle Chevrolet, Papa took on odd jobs at the business that were beyond what his original duties had been. He also carried out extra tasks for the family. He ran errands, including making the occasional drive to Omaha to pick up relatives of the Misles or a rabbi and bring them to Lincoln. He went to dinners with the family too. The Misles even invited him to their bar mitzvah celebrations.

Later on, Mr. Misle grew so much in respect for Papa that he gave Papa keys to the Misle home.

So it was only natural that when the Misles needed a nanny, they asked Papa if he had any recommendations. Mr. Misle and his wife had four children. The oldest, a girl, was 11 years old. The next two in line were also girls, ages 9 and 7. The youngest, a boy, was just six months old.

The family had a problem: every nanny they took on went running off. Their children were just too much for the nannies to care for. When the Misles spoke of the dilemma to Papa, he suggested me.

I went one afternoon to meet Mrs. Misle and the four children. During a short interview, they took to me immediately. I was hired on the spot.

I didn't have any discipline problems with the children. They listened to me, and I enjoyed being with them. Sometimes I watched the four kids in the afternoons after school; other times, I came over on the weekends and babysat for several hours.

Long, low, and sprawling, the Misle house was set up as a ranch style home, and was the most eye-catching piece of real estate I had ever walked into. The home was decorated entirely in sea green. Inside it had sea green toned curtains, carpet, and furniture in the living room and dining room. Everything matched and I found it beautiful. The kitchen and play room had wooden floors.

The play room had pint-sized chairs, tables, and couches. It also had an adjoining, mini-sized bathroom. Every single item in those two rooms was customized for children.

I thought the Misles were the wealthiest family in the world. They certainly lived in a castle compared to the places I was used to living.

Since the family was Jewish, they kept a kosher menu inside their fridge. There were often various prepared meals in casserole dishes stacked on the shelves. I didn't eat this food with them at the table. Instead, I cared for the baby while the rest of the family ate.

Once during dinner, while I held the little boy, one of the daughters asked, "Why doesn't she eat this food like we do?"

"Because she's not Jewish like we are," replied Mrs. Misle. "This isn't something that Elfi eats."

Another time while babysitting, Mrs. Misle pulled me off to the side and talked to me about my faith. "Your mom will want you to marry a Lutheran, just like I want my girls to marry someone who is Jewish," she said. I took her words to heart, and was touched by her concern.

I may not have eaten with the family at the table, but the Misles still offered me plenty of food. In fact, their house stored a large amount of sustenance. One time Mrs. Misle directed me to a cabinet where she said I could grab something to make a sandwich. I opened the door and nearly fell over at the sight.

The cabinet was filled with small round tin cans. Each of them was the same size, and the cans were stacked high. I had never seen a stash that size of food before. All of the cans bore the same marking. I found the label confusing, as it described the contents as "Chicken of the Sea."

"It's tuna," Mrs. Misle explained. I had never had eaten tuna before. I wondered what this ocean-like chicken tasted like. After trying it, I deemed it was good. But even more impressive was the sheer amount of tuna the Misles had.

They also stored Pepsi in large quantities. I tried the soft drink for the first time at their home, and it was simply delicious. I loved it, and best of all, it never ran out; the Misles had cases and cases filled with Pepsi in their garage.

Sometimes after I baby-sat for the Misles, one of their relatives, a 20-year-old man, took me home. I appreciated the lift and enjoyed the company.

Mutti, however, was not happy about the arrangement. She was concerned the family—or the driver—would try to do something to me, since I was a German and Germany had treated Jews so inhumanely during World War II.

I was never once mistreated, though. On the contrary, the Misles were always exceedingly cordial to our whole family, and gracious employers to Papa.

With the onset of the job at Misles, I juggled baby-sitting, house cleaning, waitressing, and homework every week. I still gave nearly everything I earned to Mutti and Papa, keeping only what I needed for my music group outfits and school pocket money. By then, Wilfried and Rainer chipped in too. They each had a paper route, and used the money they brought in to help support the family.

* * *

At Christmastime in 1958, Mutti's cousin, Pastor Newton, went to his home for a visit. He had been in the hospital, in an iron lung, for the past six months. During his time at home with his young family, he remained on breathing tubes. Several days after Christmas, on December 29, 1958, he passed away.

My brothers and I were not touched by polio. Like many children, we had been vaccinated in 1956. For the event, we had gone to Saratoga Elementary School, which was two blocks from our home and where Detlef attended school at the time. We stood in a long line, waiting our turn to get the newly released vaccine. When it was my turn, I received a shot in the arm from a vial filled with cherry-colored liquid. Wilfried, Rainer and Detlef drank their vaccine from a paper cup.

At school, of all the classes I had to take, I loved history and geography the most. I did well in English and algebra too.

Since I had transferred from a different high school, there were some classes I had to take in order to be able to graduate from Lincoln High. One of these was a foreign language. I knew German, and English wasn't available as a foreign language, so I opted for French. Mom loved the sound of the language. I did too. I enjoyed the class and did well in it.

Geometry, however, was a different story. I couldn't understand the word problems that went with the classwork, let alone the homework. At that time, grades were given on a scale of 1 to 7, with 1 being the best and 7 indicating a failure. From my performance, I deserved a 7 or worse.

Fortunately, my geometry teacher took pity on me. Recognizing my struggle, she said, "I'm just going to give you a 5, so you can pass and graduate. I don't think we're going to get through this."

Thanks to her, I earned credit in enough classes, and received high enough grades to be able to graduate. Graduation that year was in June 1959.

As the date drew closer, no plans for a celebration at home were made. I kept working at my jobs. My waitressing position at Cotner Terrace Restaurant continued to produce good wages. Holidays were always hectic: on Mother's Day that year I served so many tables I came home with $60 in tips. That was nearly enough for the $65 monthly mortgage payment.

For the upcoming graduation, Mutti purchased material to make me a special dress. The fabric had a tiny flowered pattern and a horizon blue background.

Mutti spent hours sewing the dress. She stayed up most of the night before the day of the graduation ceremony to finish it. When the dress was done, I tried it on and liked it immediately. It was, by far, the nicest dress I had owned since the fancy white one Mutti had purchased for me for my confirmation.

For the ceremony, Mutt, Papa, and our family walked to school. I received a diploma, and when it was over, we walked home. There was no party lined up at our house, and no celebration held for the event with family.

The lack of festivities for the day struck me as odd. As Germans, we often had gatherings for birthdays and special occasions. Also, I knew all of my friends from high school had parties planned for after the graduation ceremony.

But Mutti and Papa didn't seem familiar with the custom of a graduation party. And if they were, they may not have had the money for it. Whatever the case, they didn't offer to hold any sort of festivity, and I had decided not to ask for one. I didn't want to cause any trouble or stress for them.

The day of the ceremony, however, I couldn't hide my feelings. As we walked home, I stared at the ground and tried to hide my tears. They fell in drops on the sidewalk. The occasion I had so looked forward to had simply passed by. It felt like a letdown.

After graduation, I applied for a job as a long distance operator at the Lincoln Telephone Company. I was hired for the job and started a six-month training session.

The training time was long for a reason. Long distance operators had to speak in exact sentences, in a certain tone, and in a particular manner. I memorized a long list of phrases, including, "That line is busy. May I put you on hold?"

There was a large room for the operators at the Lincoln Telephone Company. The space could fit about 30 operators at one time. Each operator sat at a switchboard surrounded by different cords. When a call came in a light would shine on the switchboard. The operator would plug a cord into the lighted spot and the customer would be connected to the operator. The operator would then help the customer connect to another party.

We couldn't even get on a chair and sit at the board, though, until all of the phrases had been learned. We also had to memorize the names of the businesses in downtown Lincoln and know their numbers by heart. To learn the 7-digit numbers, we glanced at the first three digits and then concentrated on the last four. Our brains would remember the first three digits when it came time to pull up the number, and we'd recall the last four from focusing on them.

While I was in training, I spent time with a German girl who also lived in Lincoln. She was engaged to a man in the service who was stationed nearby, at the U.S. Air Force Base on the west end of Lincoln. The couple regularly went to places, such as Linoma Beach, where my family had frequented, and Louisville Beach, a recreational area about 40 miles northeast of Lincoln. They often invited me along on the outings. When the day was over, they always drove me home and dropped me off. After a few excursions, my friend's fiancé wrote my name and address in a little black book he carried around.

In the spring of 1959, my friend's fiancé learned he was going to be transferred to an air base on the island of Okinawa. Shortly after finding this out, he left Lincoln.

Around that time, I sometimes went with my family and friends to the German American Society, which was based in Omaha. Some of my uncles lived near it, and Mutti and Papa occasionally took us there for events that had a dinner and dance. Sometimes there were also dance contests at the club. I met a German friend who lived in Omaha at the Society, and occasionally participated in these dances with him. I enjoyed dancing with him.

One day when I wasn't at the telephone company, the phone in our home rang. Mutti answered and then said it was for me.

"Hello?" I said, with the receiver to my ear.

The voice on the other end introduced himself as Noel Lee. He said he was in the Air Force and had received my information from my friend's fiancé. The fiancé had come to Okinawa as Noel's replacement. They spent some time together before parting ways. Since the fiancé knew Noel was headed to Lincoln, he gave him a little black book he had with names and contact information for people in Lincoln in it.

Noel then asked if we could meet, and we agreed to go to a movie. He sounded so friendly, and mentioned he was originally from Arkansas. The fact that he knew my friend's fiancé made me feel it would be okay to get together with him.

I thought the date was set for the following Friday, so when that evening arrived, I got ready to go out.

Noel, however, never showed up. While I waited for him, another young man from Omaha called and asked me if I wanted to go dancing with him. He was the same German friend I had met through the German American Society in Omaha, and danced with before. Since I thought my date hadn't shown up, I accepted the offer, and went out that night with the German friend instead.

The next day, Noel showed up; he thought we had agreed to meet on Saturday. We straightened out the confusion and I got ready to go out that night. Noel met Mutti and Papa and visited with them a little. They had a really nice chat and I could tell he made a solid first impression on them. He held the door to the house open for me and also the door of the car. He was very courteous and friendly. He was dressed smart and his manners were impeccable.

During the night out, I learned Noel had been in Okinawa for about a year, and Lincoln was slated to be his last stop for his active service in the Air Force.

During the time Noel spent with my friend's fiancé, he had asked the fiancé if he knew any girls in Lincoln. It was then that his new friend handed him the little black book.

Noel soon left Okinawa, black book packed among his other belongings, to come to Lincoln. To get to Nebraska, he flew to Guam and landed there because his airplane had mechanical problems and had to be repaired. Then he continued his trip to Nebraska, taking small prop jets the whole way. During one stretch, he spent 13 straight hours in the air.

After Noel spent some time settling in to his duties at the Lincoln airbase, he started checking Lincoln out. He also started calling the numbers in the book. He kept striking out, as everyone he called was either married or engaged already. Finally he turned to the last page, where my name appeared. It was the final one in the book.

That night, our first date, took place on June 21, 1959. We went to a western movie at a drive-in theater for the occasion. That night, when the date was over, I felt we were in for a case of love at first sight. I told Mutti, "I think I could marry him someday."

After the first date, I hoped he would call me again. He did. During one of our next dates, he parked his car in the front of the house and we talked for a long time. I asked him if he went to church, and what his faith was. He responded he didn't have a church and wasn't baptized. He had grown up Methodist but no longer went to church.

I also learned his family was living in Memphis, Tennessee. Noel was born in Mytrle, Mississippi, but was raised in Manila, Arkansas. He was one of six children.

The fact that our paths had crossed in such a way seemed more than a coincidence. I knew God had helped me, a German girl, come to Lincoln to make a life. And he had guided a man from Arkansas who had been stationed in Okinawa to Nebraska as well. I felt certain it was not by chance that we had met.

My birthday was coming up, and as September 22, 1959, approached, Noel asked me to a really nice restaurant in Omaha. He wanted to go to it on my birthday. Before the date, I told Mutti and Papa, "I think he's going to ask me to marry him."

When he did, over dinner that night, I said yes.

I also told him I was a Lutheran and if he married me, he'd have to become a Lutheran too. His whole family was Methodist, but Noel started coming to church with me.

Once my family arrived at church on a Sunday and waited for Noel to come too. He showed up a little late for the service. Afterward, he explained he was in such a hurry to get to the service that he was driving pretty fast. He got pulled over and received a speeding ticket on the way.

In addition to attending church, Noel began taking classes with Pastor Nommensen to become a member of the church in Lincoln.

When my six months of training came to an end at the telephone company, I finally got to sit at the board and connect callers. I earned $1.25 an hour, plus more for overtime.

At the telephone job, I worked with long distance calls. For the position, I took calls coming in from faraway places like Grand Island, which was nearly 100 miles west of Lincoln, or even other states. I also placed calls from Lincoln residents trying to connect with others across the country, in cities like San Francisco.

The company hired me for split shifts. This meant I worked for several hours, came home, and then returned to work. Nearly all of the operators, myself included, had to work during busy times, like holidays and Mother's Day.

While the other operators and I sat at our boards, several supervisors walked behind us. If there was ever a problem, the supervisors could plug a cord into an outlet so they could speak to me or hear what the customer was saying. There was specific protocol to follow, even in uncomfortable situations.

On occasion, callers got angry. If they used inappropriate words or swore at us, we told them, "You're not allowed to speak to me this way." If they continued, we responded, "If you're going to speak to me this way I will disconnect you." And if they still continued, we hung up.

Sometimes I was placed on a conference call. For the arrangement, I connected five or six people from across the United States. There was a special spot and chair in the room set up for this type of call. One perk of conference calls was that the operating position to oversee them paid a little more than the regular long distance switchboard work. Whether it involved a conference or just connecting two people, I loved the whole setting and thrived on the phone calls. It was my cup of tea.

Noel and I were engaged for less than a year. Our wedding day was set for Sunday, May 1, 1960.

For the wedding, I wore a beautiful white dress. The service was held at Mt. Olive Lutheran Church in Lincoln, the sister congregation to the one we usually attended. Since Mt. Olive had a building, and our congregation worshipped in the basement of the parsonage at the time, we decided to get married at Mt. Olive.

Mt. Olive was a little white frame church with a tower and a bell. It held about 70 people in all. It was a lovely church to get married in.

Afterward, the ladies of the congregation served a sit down roast beef dinner in the basement of the church for the wedding guests. They also served cake. The Misle family was among those in attendance.

Noel's relatives, who lived in Memphis, Tennessee, weren't able to make the long trip for our wedding. So we decided to use our honeymoon time to visit them. We planned to take a little 1950 Ford Crestliner Noel owned. It was maroon on the bottom and black on top. We packed everything we needed for the trip in the car before the big day.

After the wedding, we went to get into Noel's car. When we went to the driveway where we had left it, however, there was a different vehicle in its place. It was a 1957 Chevy Papa had purchased but hadn't yet driven. Together he and Mutti had transferred all of our luggage into the bigger, roomier car.

Noel and I were completely shocked.

But also very grateful. The trip was long—1,300 miles on mostly two-lane highways. Having a bigger, nicer car made all of the traveling go much more smoothly.

When we returned from the honeymoon, Noel and I moved into a small furnished apartment. While there, Noel continued serving at the Lincoln Air Force base. He also kept taking membership classes. Pastor Nommensen came to our apartment for the lessons. After finishing the last class, Pastor Nommensen baptized Noel right in our apartment.

During the summer of 1960, Noel became a member of the congregation we had been attending. He was taken into membership in front of the congregation during a service. The services were still held in the basement of the parsonage.

When we had first arrived in America, Mutti and Papa had received green cards. After five years of living in Nebraska, they were able to apply for U.S. citizenship. To start the process, they went to the Social Security office in Lincoln. They signed up for citizenship classes, and started attending with other immigrants who were also applying for citizenship. In the class, they learned about the organization of both the local and federal government. They also learned about the president and the Congress and Senate. When it was over, they were ready to take the final test and be sworn in as U.S. citizens.

I didn't take the class, as I had learned about the government in history class at school. But when the day of the test came, in January 1961, I went with my whole family to take it. We had to go to a courtroom for the test. When we arrived, there were several other families and a judge already there.

The judge asked each of us several questions, as a general overview, to make sure we knew the material. We were asked about basic things, such as who the current president was. The test was verbal.

When it was over, we all stood before the judge, raised our right hands, and repeated after him. We were sworn in as U.S citizens.

And in many ways, we had become like Americans. The Chevy Papa had purchased belonged on the list of purely American items, along with homemade pumpkin pie, Pepsi, and grilled hamburgers in the backyard.

Through it all, Mutti had helped us remember that no matter what happened, we would continue on with our life because God was looking after us. It wasn't an accident that we left Germany and came to America. It was because of God. He led us to a place where we could regularly go to church and live our faith. He guided us, protected us, and looked after our needs every step of the way. And in the years to come, He would do the same.

Epilogue

After getting married, Elfi lent her wedding dress to two cousins who were getting married shortly after her. The dress ended up in a total of three weddings.

Elfi and Noel settled in Lincoln and had three children: Monica, Carmen, and Timothy. In 2016, their children, nine grandchildren and six great grandchildren lived in Nebraska and Arizona, while Elfi and Noel remained in Lincoln. Elfi loves to be outside and enjoys gardening, just as her father did. She also likes to read, watch the children in school events, spend time with Noel, and help out at church. She sings in the choir, cleans, helps with monthly altar duties, and sets flowers on the altar for Easter and Christmas.

In her home in Lincoln, Elfi keeps the two braids of long hair that were cut off at the salon in Grafton when Ms. Baumann helped restyle her hair. And, in memory of the fateful slaying of her pet in Harksheide, she doesn't eat lamb.

She still doesn't like thunderstorms, as they remind her of bombs falling.

Elfi's father, Papa, worked for the Misles from 1957 until his death at age 58 in 1968. He led an active life, until his final years, when he became crippled with rheumatoid arthritis. During his time in Lincoln, he served on the building committee to build a church for the St. Mark congregation where the family held membership. He was present at the groundbreaking for the building of the church in 1967. In 1968, his funeral was the first one held in the new church.

Elfi's mother, Mutti, worked at Russell Stover's for 18 years. She was kindhearted and set a Christian example everywhere she went, whether that meant on the bus, at work, among relatives and friends, or at church. Many felt close to her after knowing her for just hours. They often commented on her strong faith and sincerity.

Mutti walked around Lincoln to pay her bills, going from place to place downtown and chatting with the store owners and clerks as they carried out her transactions. For many years, the First Year bank in downtown Lincoln played a Christian song with bells every noon. Mutti loved the song and custom. If she was downtown, she always stopped to listen to the music.

She also cared for people in need. Even though she didn't have much herself, she never let anyone leave her home hungry. She always fed visitors a meal, or offered them something to eat or drink.

Mutti was a true American, and always put her hand over her heart during the playing of the national anthem. Recalling the first sights of the American flag at the embassy in Hamburg, she often talked about its meaning and the impression it had made on her. At that time of transition from Harksheide to America, it symbolized freedom and a new life. Throughout her time in the U.S., the flag held a special place in her heart.

One time when Mutti was watching television with her family, the national anthem came on. She stood up, placed her hand on her heart and remained that way until the song ended.

Mutti believed God allowed her to come to the United States, and she thought it had been the right decision. Even though it was at times hard for her, she felt truly blessed to live in America.

Elfi's brother, Wilfried, met and married a woman who had relatives on the Pine Ridge Indian Reservation in South Dakota. At the time, Wilfried had three children from a previous marriage and the lady he married had children from earlier in life as well. The two of them went to live on the reservation, but the economic situation was difficult and the marriage teetered. In an attempt to get away, Wilfried traveled back to Lincoln. His wife followed him, however, and led him back to the reservation.

It was a tough, dangerous time on the reservation. In January 1976, Elfi received a shocking call. The caller informed her that Wilfried was dead. The family confirmed the death and held a memorial service for him. Finding out the details of his death, however, proved to be impossible. The FBI didn't want to touch the case, due to a fear of losing men on the reservation during the investigative process.

The pastor at the St. Mark congregation in Lincoln at that time, Pastor Bode, helped the family deal with the situation. While the details were never fully revealed, they gathered some information. The family learned Wilfried had been deliberately hit by a car while walking down a highway in the middle of an open stretch of land after his car ran out of gas. He had three young boys at the time.

The family also grew to believe Wilfried's wife had a role in his death. At the funeral, his widow said to Mutti, "For this, I will fry in hell."

The death was particularly hard on Mutti. She kept on working, but mourned Wilfried's death for a long time. It was especially difficult for the whole family to have so many unknowns surrounding his death.

Mutti retired in her 60s, and went on to be a fulltime grandmother. She loved this role perhaps best of all, and spent many hours taking care of grandchildren and great grandchildren. She did this well into her 80s. She went to heaven in 2008, at age 96, after a full life.

When her three children were no longer toddlers, Elfi took a job at Sears. She began her time with the company in August 1971, and worked there until she retired in 2007.

One day, when Elfi came home from work, there was a message on her answering machine. It was from Heidi, the little girl she had spent so many hours playing with in Harksheide. The two were able to connect and eventually visit each other.

Heidi told Elfi she had become a Christian. She mentioned she had watched Elfi's family pray before meals when they were playmates. Heidi hadn't been familiar with the custom at the time, and it had made an impression on her. After getting married, Heidi and her husband regularly traveled the world to help spread the Gospel to other places.

Schneidemühl, the childhood home where Elfi spent her early years, was nearly destroyed after the Russians went through. Today the town is known as Pila, and is part of Poland.

In 2010, Elfi and Noel had the chance to revisit the city. They arrived by train, coming into the exact train station that Elfi and her family had fled from in 1945. At the station, there was still one building that had been damaged from the bombing and not yet repaired.

It was amazing for Elfi to see the modern city of Pila. There were only four buildings that had remained standing after the Russians went through the city. These buildings are now painted green to serve as a memorial. With a guide, Elfi scoured the area for her birthplace. The city, however, had grown greatly in size. The river where Elfi and her father had once swam was no longer outside of the city. In fact, it was almost in the middle of the town.

From the guide, Elfi learned her home had been completely destroyed by the Russians. Some of the material from the home, including bricks, had been used to repave streets in Pila years after the war. Russians took the wood from the home and used it as firewood during the last part of the war

As Elfi walked over those repaved streets, feelings of home flooded back to her. She knew she could have been killed by the Russian army had it not been for Mutti's determination to avoid getting left behind and captured.

Elfi and Noel also toured Schleswig-Holstein, the northern German state that was overseen by the British after the Second World War. It was a landing point for many refugees. Elfi was amazed at the castles and other landmarks that had not been destroyed during or after the war. She saw sights she had never seen as a child, and was impressed with how Germany had rebuilt itself.

The trip Elfi and Noel took was intense, but worthwhile. When it was over, Elfi felt a sense of peace and a coming to terms with that portion of her life.

Elfi's experiences with food in the past continue to direct her actions. "I can't even describe the feeling, but I know my stomach was always hurting," she says. In Lincoln, Elfi prefers to keep her pantry full, to be sure there is always enough to feed her family and visitors.

"Later in my life, when I had all the food I needed, I thought of how good that rationed bread was," she says. "It tasted better than any cake could taste."

Photo Supplement

[Mutti as a toddler with parents during World War I]

[Mutti as a child with her brothers and parents]

[Mutti as a teen singing with the church choir (front row, third from right)]

[Mutt's parents in front of a butcher shop they owned]

[Mutti and Papa on their wedding day, with both sets of parents]

[Papa in front of home and acreage outside of Schneidemühl]

[Elfi as a toddler playing near the forest]

[Elfi with her godmother Kaëthe, playing with the white rabbit Kaëthe gave her]

[Papa (right) taking a break from work outside of Schneidemühl]

[Ruthchen (left), Wilfried and Elfi in Schneidemühl]

[Elfi – first day of school, holding a *schultüte*]

[Six of Mutti's seven brothers, in Harksheide after World War II ended]

[Elfi and family in Harksheide after World War II ended]

[Home (right) built through government program in Harksheide]

[Elfi holding doll she brought to America, with family in Harksheide – 1951]

[Last Sunday in Harksheide, at a family gathering – August 1952]

[*M.S. Italia*, the ship the family took from Germany to America]

[Elfi and family, first Sunday in Grafton]

[Lutheran church in Grafton Elfi and family attended]

[Pastor and Mrs. Fuerstenau (left and center) pictured with Omi]

[Mr. Workentine's farm]

[Elfi and family pictured with Mr. Workentine (right)]

252

[Elfi, Wilfried, Detlef, and Rainer (left to right) by one of Mr. Workentine's cars - 1956]

[Confirmation 1957 – Elfi (front right) and Wilfried (back left)]

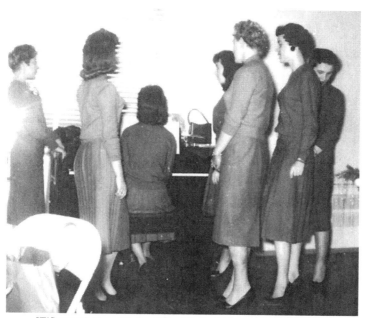

[Elfi practicing with the Glee Club at Lincoln High School]

[Home Mutti and Papa purchased in Lincoln]

[Elfi and Noel on their wedding day – May 1, 1960]

New Hopes, Home . . . and Citizenship

Among the 64 new citizens to be honored by the Women's Division of the Chamber of Commerce Monday is the Walter Gartzke family of 2231 So. 15th.

Mr. and Mrs. Gartzke and their 3 older children lived in eastern Germany until World War II. Their youngest son, Detlef, was born in Hamburg shortly before they migrated to the United States.

In January, 1945, Gartzke was drafted into the German army and was obliged to leave his family in the face of Russian invasion. A month later, Mrs. Gartzke and the children fled to a small community near Hamburg. It was there that Gartzke found them upon his release from the army.

Gartzke was taken prisoner on May 3, 1945, and confined in American and British camps in western Germany. Both Gartzke and Mrs. Gartzke's mother arrived home on the same day, June 4, 1945, amid much rejoicing.

The family continued to live in the suburb of Hamburg and helped to build their own house there under a German government housing plan. As a down payment they had to put in 1500 hours work on the house. They moved into the new house in 1950.

Although physically comfortable, the Gartzkes were so overcome by their war experiences that they wanted to get far away from it all.

Gartzke's father, two brothers and a brother-in-law are still listed as missing. The Gartzkes made many efforts to emigrate; however, the waiting list was long.

When a cousin, a minister in Grafton, Neb., heard that farmer Alton Workentine was anxious to help refugees from Germany, he suggested the Gartzkes. Then the processing really began and soon they were on their way.

The family arrived in Grafton on Sept. 23, 1952, where they lived until 1957 when they moved to

Continued on Page 9C

Chatting with Mrs. Lorena Kay Hoagland (right) are members of the Gartzke family (from left) Mrs. Elfrun Lee, Mrs. Gartzke, Gartzke, Rainier and Detlef.

[article on Elfi's family becoming U.S. citizens]

257

End Notes

[1] Copyright: public domain.

[2] Copyright: public domain.

[3] Yelton, David. "Hitler's Home Guard: Volkssturmman, Western Front, 1944-1945." Osprey Publishing, 2006.

[4] Yelton, David. "Hitler's Home Guard: Volkssturmman, Western Front, 1944-1945." Osprey Publishing, 2006.

[5] Copyright: public domain.

[6] "Chronology and Index of the Second World War, 1938-1945." Greenwood Publishing Group, 1947.

[7] "Chronology and Index of the Second World War, 1938-1945." Greenwood Publishing Group, 1947.

[8] "Hitler plans the invasion of Britain." BBC History. http://www.bbc.co.uk/history/events/hitler_plans_the_invasion_of_britain. Last accessed 27 January 2015.

[9] "Britain bombs Berlin." BBC History. http://www.bbc.co.uk/history/events/britain_bombs_berlin. Last accessed 27 January 2015.

[10] "Britain bombs Berlin." BBC History. http://www.bbc.co.uk/history/events/britain_bombs_berlin. Last accessed 27 January 2015.

[11] "History of WW2: Battle of Britain." History. http://www.history.co.uk/study-topics/history-of-ww2/battle-of-britain. Last accessed 27 January 2015.

[12] Flippo, Hyde. "Remland, Martin et al. "Intercultural Communication: A Peacebuilding Perspective." Waveland Press, 2014.

[13] Anti-Jewish Legislation in Prewar Germany." Holocaust Encyclopedia. http://www.ushmm.org/wlc/en/article.php?ModuleId=10005681 Last accessed 6 March 2015.

[14] "Examples of Anti-Semitic Legislation, 1933-1939." Holocaust Encyclopedia. http://www.ushmm.org/wlc/en/article.php?ModuleId=10007459. Last accessed 6 March 2015.

[15] Johnson, Paul. "A History of the Jews." HarperCollins, 2009.

[16] "Anti-Jewish Legislation in Prewar Germany." Holocaust Encyclopedia. http://www.ushmm.org/wlc/en/article.php?ModuleId=10005681 Last accessed 4 March 2015.

[17] Neillands, Robin. "Bomber War: Arthur Harris and the Allied Bomber Offensive 1939-1945." Endeavour Press, 2014.

[18] Neillands, Robin. "Bomber War: Arthur Harris and the Allied Bomber Offensive 1939-1945." Endeavour Press, 2014.

[19] Copyright: public domain.

[20] Copyright: public domain.

[21] "Seventieth Anniversary of the Liberation of Auschwitz." US Holocaust Memorial Museum. http://www.ushmm.org/information/exhibitions/online-features/special-focus/liberation-of-auschwitz. Last accessed 22 January 2015.

[22] "Seventieth Anniversary of the Liberation of Auschwitz." US Holocaust Memorial Museum. http://www.ushmm.org/information/exhibitions/online-features/special-focus/liberation-of-auschwitz. Last accessed 22 January 2015.

[23] "Seventieth Anniversary of the Liberation of Auschwitz." US Holocaust Memorial Museum. http://www.ushmm.org/information/exhibitions/online-features/special-focus/liberation-of-auschwitz. Last accessed 22 January 2015.

[24] Copyright: public domain.

[25] Abandoned & Little-Known Airfields: Poland. http://www.ronaldv.nl/abandoned/airfields/pl/Wielkopolskie.html. Last accessed 22 February 2015.

[26] Raitz von Frentz, Christian. "A Lesson Forgotten: Minority Protection under the League of Nations – The Case of the German Minority in Poland, 1920-1934." St. Martin Press, 1990.

[27] Copyright: public domain.

[28] Neillands, Robin. "Bomber War: Arthur Harris and the Allied Bomber Offensive 1939-1945." Endeavour Press, 2014.

[29] Neillands, Robin. "Bomber War: Arthur Harris and the Allied Bomber Offensive 1939-1945." Endeavour Press, 2014.

[30] Neillands, Robin. "Bomber War: Arthur Harris and the Allied Bomber Offensive 1939-1945." Endeavour Press, 2014.

[31] "Gomorrah, Operation (July-August 1043). The Daily Chronicles of World War II. http://ww2days.com/gomorrah-operation-july-august-1943.html. Last accessed 22 February 2015.

[32] Read, Anthony. "The Devil's Disciples: Hitler's Inner Circle." W.W. Norton & Company, 2005.

[33] Lowe, Keith. "Inferno: The Fiery Destruction of Hamburg 1943." Scribner, 2007. (Traute Koch, quoted in Middlebrook, *Battle of Hamburg* (London, 1980), p. 274.

[34] "Memories of Hamburg Raid." History Learning Site. http://www.historylearningsite.co.uk/memories_hamburg_bombing.htm. Last accessed 22 February 2015.

[35] "Gomorrah, Operation (July-August 1043). The Daily Chronicles of World War II. http://ww2days.com/gomorrah-operation-july-august-1943.html. Last accessed 22 February 2015.

[36] "Firebombing of Dresden." History.com. http://www.history.com/this-day-in-history/firebombing-of-dresden. Last accessed 22 February 2015.

[37] Lowe, Keith. "Savage Continent: Europe in the Aftermath of World War II." St. Martin's Press, 2012.

[38] Copyright: public domain.

[39] Goeschel, Christian. "Suicide in Nazi Germany." Oxford University Press, 2009.

[40] Goeschel, Christian. "Suicide in Nazi Germany." Oxford University Press, 2009.

[41] Goeschel, Christian. "Suicide in Nazi Germany." Oxford University Press, 2009.

[42] "Nuebrandenburg: History." NetLibrary.net. http://www.netlibrary.net/articles/Neubrandenburg#cite_note-lakotta-4. Last accessed 23 February 2015.

[43] Goeschel, Christian. "Suicide in Nazi Germany." Oxford University Press, 2009.

[44] "Brocken." Peakery. http://peakery.com/brocken-harz/. Last accessed 23 February 2015.

[45] Harz National Park. http://www.nationalpark-harz.de/en. Last accessed 7 May 2014.

[46] "Historical Background." Dora and the V-2. http://www.dora.uah.edu/history.html. Last accessed 23 February 2015.

[47] Kinderlieder. http://www.christliche-gedichte.de/?pg=6103. Last accessed 3 July 2016.

[48] Copyright: public domain.

[49] Glashütte. Norderstedt.de. Last accessed 14 May 2014.

[50] "The Potsdam Conference, 1945." U.S. Department of State Office of the Historian. https://history.state.gov/milestones/1937-1945/potsdam-conf. Last accessed 23 February 2015.

[51] MacDonogh, Giles. "After the Reich: The Brutal History of the Allied Occupation." Publisher Basic Books, 2009.

[52] Fink, Carole K. "Cold War: An International History." Publisher Westview Press; 1 edition, 2013.

[53] Prauser, Steffen and Arfon Rees. "The Expulsion of the 'German' Communities from Eastern Europe at the End of the Second World War." European University Institute, 2004.

[54] Kellmann, Klaus. "Insights into Schleswig-Holstein: Politics – Economy – History." Gestaltung und Satz, May 2012.

[55] Buse, Dieter K. "The Regions of Germany: A Reference Guide to History and Culture." Greenwood Publishing Group, 2005.

[56] Diefendorf, Jeffry M. "In the Wake of War: The Reconstruction of German Cities after World War II." Oxford University Press, 1993.

[57] German History in Documents and Images. http://ghdi.ghi-dc.org/. Last accessed 15 May 2014.

[58] Diefendorf, Jeffry M. "In the Wake of War: The Reconstruction of German Cities after World War II." Oxford University Press, 1993.

[59] Diefendorf, Jeffry M. "In the Wake of War: The Reconstruction of German Cities after World War II." Oxford University Press, 1993.

[60] Deutsche Gesellschaft für Emährung e.V., Bonn. As seen at the Feuerwehr Museum, Norderstedt, Germany. May 2012.

[61] Bombing of Hiroshima and Nagasaki. History.com. Last accessed 8 May 2014.

[62] Smith, Harry Leslie. "Hamburg 1947." Barley Hole LLC, 2012.

[63] Eksteins, Modris. "Walking Since Daybreak: A Story of Eastern Europe, World War II, and the Heart of our Century." First Mariner Books, 1999.

[64] We Children from the Ruetschlehen – the History of a Street and Its Children 1928-1952. http://freepages.genealogy.rootsweb.ancestry.com/. Last accessed 21 May 2014.

[65] As seen at the Hamburg Museum, Hamburg, Germany. May 2012.

[66] Das Gebot der Stunde: Organisieren und Improvisieren. www.aussetellung-angekommen.de. Last accessed 16 May 2014.

[67] As seen at the Feuerwehr Museum, Norderstedt, Germany. May 2012.

[68] Eksteins, Modris. "Walking Since Daybreak: A Story of Eastern Europe, World War II, and the Heart of our Century." First Mariner Books, 1999.

[69] Samuel, Wolfgang W.E. "The War of Our Childhood: Memories of World War II." University Press of Mississippi, 2002.

[70] Smith, Harry Leslie. "Hamburg 1947." Barley Hole LLC, 2012.

[71] Smith, Harry Leslie. "Hamburg 1947." Barley Hole LLC, 2012.

[72] German Christmas Carol.

[73] Copyright: public domain.

[74] An 'Unknown Holocaust' and the Hijacking of History. Address by Mark Weber. Institute for Historical Review. 2009.

[75] Ziemke, Earl F. "The US Army in the Occupation of Germany." University Press of the Pacific, 2005.

[76] Fink, Carole K. "Cold War: An International History." Publisher Westview Press; 1 edition, 2013.

[77] Lowe, Keith. "Savage Continent: Europe in the Aftermath of World War II." St. Martin's Press, 2012.

[78] Smith, Harry Leslie. "Hamburg 1947." Barley Hole LLC, 2012.

[79] Copyright: public domain.

[80] The blockade of Germany. http://www.nationalarchives.gov.uk/pathways/firstworldwar/spotlights/blockade.htm. Last accessed 23 February 2015.

[81] International Military Tribunal at Nürnberg. http://www.ushmm.org/wlc/en/article.php?ModuleId=10007069. Accessed 30 June 2014.

[82] Nürnberg Trials. http://www.history.com/topics/world-war-ii/Nürnberg-trials. Accessed 7 June 2014

[83] International Military Tribunal at Nürnberg. http://www.ushmm.org/wlc/en/article.php?ModuleId=10007069. Accessed 30 June 2014.

[84] The Nürnberg Trials. Author Doug Linder. 2000.

http://law2.umkc.edu/faculty/projects/ftrials/Nürnberg/NürnbergACCOUNT.html. University of Missouri-Kansas City. Accessed 30 June 2014.

[85] Testimony of Marie Claude Vaillant-Couturier. http://law2.umkc.edu/faculty/projects/ftrials/Nürnberg/vaillanttest.html. University of Missouri-Kansas City. Accessed 30 June 2014.

[86] The Nürnberg Trials. Author Doug Linder. 2000. http://law2.umkc.edu/faculty/projects/ftrials/Nürnberg/NürnbergACCOUNT.html. University of Missouri-Kansas City. Accessed 30 June 2014.

[87] The Nürnberg Trials. Author Doug Linder. 2000. http://law2.umkc.edu/faculty/projects/ftrials/Nürnberg/NürnbergACCOUNT.html. University of Missouri-Kansas City. Accessed 30 June 2014.

[88] Nürnberg Trials. http://www.history.com/topics/world-war-ii/Nürnberg-trials. Last accessed 1 July 2014.

[89] Copyright: public domain.

[90] The original CARE Package. http://www.care.org/care-package. Last accessed 23 February 2015.

[91] History of CARE. http://www.care.org/impact/our-stories/care-history. Last accessed 30 May 2014.

[92] History of CARE. http://www.care.org/impact/our-stories/care-history. Last accessed 30 May 2014.

[93] MacDonogh, Giles. "After the Reich: The Brutal History of the Allied Occupation." Publisher Basic Books, 2009.

[94] Smith, Harry Leslie. "Hamburg 1947." Barley Hole LLC, 2012.

[95] Copyright: public domain.

[96] Germany 1946/47. The Hunger Winter. http://www.bellaonline.com/articles/art178861.asp. Accessed 4 July 2014.

[97] Germany 1946/47. The Hunger Winter. http://www.bellaonline.com/articles/art178861.asp. Last accessed 4 July 2014.

[98] Germany 1946/47. The Hunger Winter. http://www.bellaonline.com/articles/art178861.asp. Last accessed 4 July 2014.

[99] Diefendorf, Jeffry M. "In the Wake of War: The Reconstruction of German Cities after World War II." Oxford University Press, 1993.

[100] MacDonogh, Giles. "After the Reich: The Brutal History of the Allied Occupation." Publisher Basic Books, 2009.

[101] Germany 1946/47. The Hunger Winter. http://www.bellaonline.com/articles/art178861.asp. Last accessed 4 July 2014.

[102] Zahnersatz gegen Kochplatte. Von Wolfgang Becker. http://www.spiegel.de/spiegel/spiegelspecial/d-9259176.html. Last accessed 4 July 2014.

[103] Hunter Winter 1946/1947. NDR.de. http://www.ndr.de/kultur/geschichte/Hungerwinter-194647,hungerwinter166.html.

Accessed 4 July 2014.

[104] MacDonogh, Giles. "After the Reich: The Brutal History of the Allied Occupation." Publisher Basic Books, 2009.

[105] Hunter Winter 1946/1947. NDR.de. http://www.ndr.de/kultur/geschichte/Hungerwinter-194647,hungerwinter166.html. Accessed 4 July 2014.

[106] Bundesarchiv Bild 183-B0527-0001-753. Röhnert. 31 March 1947. Last accessed 21 August 2014. German Federal Archives. http://www.bild.bundesarchiv.de/

[107] Smith, Harry Leslie. "Hamburg 1947." Barley Hole LLC, 2012.

[108] Copyright: public domain.

[109] Schmitter Heisler, Barbara. "From German Prisoner of War to American Citizen: A Social History with 35 Interviews." McFarland 2013.

[110] Schmitter Heisler, Barbara. "From German Prisoner of War to American Citizen: A Social History with 35 Interviews." McFarland 2013.

[111] Provan, Dr. John, Kelkheim/Ts. "The Marshall Plan and its consequences." George Marshall Society. http://www.george-marshall-society.org/george-c-marshall/the-marshall-plan-and-its-consequences/. Last accessed 2 September 2014.

[112] Behrman, Greg. "The Most Noble Adventure: The Marshall Plan and the Time When America Helped Save Europe." Free Press, 2007.

[113] Fink, Carole K. "Cold War: An International History." Publisher Westview Press; 1 edition, 2013.

[114] Provan, Dr. John, Kelkheim/Ts. "The Marshall Plan and its consequences." George Marshall Society. http://www.george-marshall-society.org/george-c-marshall/the-marshall-plan-and-its-consequences/.

[115] Henderson, David R. "German Economic Miracle." The Concise Encyclopedia of Economics. http://www.econlib.org/library/Enc/GermanEconomicMiracle.html. Last accessed 1 September 2014.

[116] Henderson, David R. "German Economic Miracle." The Concise Encyclopedia of Economics. http://www.econlib.org/library/Enc/GermanEconomicMiracle.html. Last accessed 1 September 2014.

[117] 20.6.1948: Currency reform in Germany. Today in History. http://www.today-in-history.de/. Last accessed 1 September 2014.

[118] 20.6.1948: Currency reform in Germany. Today in History. http://www.today-in-history.de/. Last accessed 1 September 2014.

[119] 20.6.1948: Currency reform in Germany. Today in History. http://www.today-in-history.de/. Last accessed 1 September 2014.

[120] Samuel, Wolfgang W. E. "Germany Boy: A Refugee's Story." University Press of Mississippi, 2000.

[121] Wallich, Henry C. "Mainsprings of the German Revival." New Haven: Yale University Press, 1955.

[122] Allen, Larry. "The Encyclopedia of Money." ABC-CLIO, 2009.

[123] "Currency reform in Germany." Today in History. http://www.today-in-history.de/index.php?what=thmanu&manu_id=1493&tag=20&monat=6&year=2012&dayisset=1&lang=en. Last accessed 12 February 2015.

[124] Henderson, David R. "German Economic Miracle." The Concise Encyclopedia of Economics. http://www.econlib.org/library/Enc/GermanEconomicMiracle.html. Last accessed 1 September 2014.

[125] Allen, Larry. "The Encyclopedia of Money." ABC-CLIO, 2009.

[126] "Creation of Israel, 1948." U.S. Department of State Office of the Historian. https://history.state.gov/milestones/1945-1952/creation-israel. Last accessed 31 August 2014.

[127] Fink, Carole K. "Cold War: An International History." Publisher Westview Press; 1 edition, 2013

[128] MacDonogh, Giles. "After the Reich: The Brutal History of the Allied Occupation." Publisher Basic Books, 2009.

[129] MacDonogh, Giles. "After the Reich: The Brutal History of the Allied Occupation." Publisher Basic Books, 2009.

[130] Fink, Carole K. "Cold War: An International History." Publisher Westview Press; 1 edition, 2013.

[131] Fink, Carole K. "Cold War: An International History." Publisher Westview Press; 1 edition, 2013.

[132] Fink, Carole K. "Cold War: An International History." Publisher Westview Press; 1 edition, 2013.

[133] Lowe, Keith. "Savage Continent: Europe in the Aftermath of World War II." St. Martin's Press, 2012.

[134] Lowe, Keith. "Savage Continent: Europe in the Aftermath of World War II." St. Martin's Press, 2012.

[135] Lowe, Keith. "Savage Continent: Europe in the Aftermath of World War II." St. Martin's Press, 2012.

[136] Schmitter Heisler, Barbara. "From German Prisoner of War to American Citizen: A Social History with 35 Interviews." McFarland 2013.

[137] Schmitter Heisler, Barbara. "From German Prisoner of War to American Citizen: A Social History with 35 Interviews." McFarland 2013.

[138] Schmitter Heisler, Barbara. "From German Prisoner of War to American Citizen: A Social History with 35 Interviews." McFarland 2013.

[139] Schmitter Heisler, Barbara. "From German Prisoner of War to American Citizen: A Social History with 35 Interviews." McFarland 2013.

[140] Schmitter Heisler, Barbara. "From German Prisoner of War to American Citizen: A Social History with 35 Interviews." McFarland 2013.

[141] History of Turtle Dolls. Schildkröt. Schildkröt Schildkröt. Last accessed 20 November 2014.

[142] Copyright: public domain.

[143] Kungsholm (II) / Italia: 1928-1965.TheGreatOceanLiners.com. http://www.thegreatoceanliners.com/kungsholm2.html. Last accessed 22 September 2014.

[144] Kungsholm (II) / Italia: 1928-1965.TheGreatOceanLiners.com. http://www.thegreatoceanliners.com/kungsholm2.html. Last accessed 22 September 2014.

[145] Kungsholm (II) / Italia: 1928-1965.TheGreatOceanLiners.com. http://www.thegreatoceanliners.com/kungsholm2.html. Last accessed 22 September 2014.

[146] Kungsholm (II) / Italia: 1928-1965.TheGreatOceanLiners.com. http://www.thegreatoceanliners.com/kungsholm2.html. Last accessed 22 September 2014.

[147] Copyright: public domain.

[148] Fink, Carole K. "Cold War: An International History." Publisher Westview Press; 1 edition, 2013.

[149] Copyright: public domain.

[150] "Linoma Beach." Ashland Historical Society. http://www.ashlandhistoricalsociety.org/pages/linomabeach.aspx. Last accessed 21 October 2014.

[151] "Linoma Beach." Ashland Historical Society. http://www.ashlandhistoricalsociety.org/pages/linomabeach.aspx. Last accessed 21 October 2014.

[152] "History." Linoma Lighthouse, LLC. http://www.linomalighthouse.com/history-of-linoma.html. Last accessed 25 November 2014.

[153] "Linoma Beach." Ashland Historical Society. http://www.ashlandhistoricalsociety.org/pages/linomabeach.aspx. Last accessed 21 October 2014.

[154] Weyer Creigh, Dorothy. "Nebraska: A History." W. W. Norton & Company, 2013.

[155] Fifty-third Annual Report of the Auditor of the City of Lincoln, Nebraska. https://www.lincoln.ne.gov/city/police/annual/1956city.pdf. Last accessed 12 March 2015.

[156] "History of Nebraska's Capitols." Nebraska State Capitol. http://capitol.nebraska.gov/index.php/building/history/nebraska-capitols. Last accessed 19 February 2015.

[157] "Our History." Russell Stover. http://www.russellstover.com/jump.jsp?itemType=CATEGORY&itemID=605. Last Accessed 28 November 2014.

[158] Halberstam, David. "The Fifties." Publisher Open Road Media, 2012.

[159] Copyright: public domain.

[160] Halberstam, David. "The Fifties." Publisher Open Road Media, 2012.

[161] Fink, Carole K. "Cold War: An International History." Publisher Westview Press; 1

edition, 2013.

[162] Linda M. Battisti and John Stevens Berry. "The Twelfth Victim: The Innocence of Caril Fugate in the Starkweather Murder Rampage." Addicus Books, 2014.

[163] Linda M. Battisti and John Stevens Berry. "The Twelfth Victim: The Innocence of Caril Fugate in the Starkweather Murder Rampage." Addicus Books, 2014.

[164] Linda M. Battisti and John Stevens Berry. "The Twelfth Victim: The Innocence of Caril Fugate in the Starkweather Murder Rampage." Addicus Books, 2014.

[165] "Charles Starkweather and Caril Fugate." Author Marilyn Bardsley. CrimeLibrary. http://www.crimelibrary.com/notorious_murders/mass/starkweather/index_1.html . Last accessed 28 November 2014.

[166] Linda M. Battisti and John Stevens Berry. "The Twelfth Victim: The Innocence of Caril Fugate in the Starkweather Murder Rampage." Addicus Books, 2014.

[167] "Charles Starkweather and Caril Fugate." Author Marilyn Bardsley. CrimeLibrary. http://www.crimelibrary.com/notorious_murders/mass/starkweather/index_1.html . Last accessed 28 November 2014.

[168] Linda M. Battisti and John Stevens Berry. "The Twelfth Victim: The Innocence of Caril Fugate in the Starkweather Murder Rampage." Addicus Books, 2014.

[169] "Charles Starkweather and Caril Fugate." Author Marilyn Bardsley. CrimeLibrary. http://www.crimelibrary.com/notorious_murders/mass/starkweather/index_1.html . Last accessed 28 November 2014.

[170] Oshinsky, David M. "Polio: An American Story." Oxford University Press, 2005.

[171] Oshinsky, David M. "Polio: An American Story." Oxford University Press, 2005.

[172] Oshinsky, David M. "Polio: An American Story." Oxford University Press, 2005.

CPSIA information can be obtained
at www.ICGtesting.com
Printed in the USA
FFOW05n1434161216